# THEY
# SHOULD
# STAY
# THERE

A BOOK IN THE SERIES LATIN AMERICA IN
TRANSLATION / EN TRADUCCIÓN / EM TRADUÇÃO
This book was sponsored by the Consortium in
Latin American and Caribbean Studies at the University
of North Carolina at Chapel Hill and Duke University.

# THEY SHOULD STAY THERE

THE STORY OF Mexican Migration and Repatriation during the Great Depression

Fernando Saúl Alanís Enciso

TRANSLATED BY Russ Davidson

FOREWORD BY Mark Overmyer-Velázquez

THE UNIVERSITY OF NORTH CAROLINA PRESS CHAPEL HILL

Translation of the books in the series Latin America in Translation / en Traducción / em Tradução, a collaboration between the Consortium in Latin American and Caribbean Studies at the University of North Carolina at Chapel Hill and Duke University and the university presses of the University of North Carolina and Duke, is supported by a grant from the Andrew W. Mellon Foundation.

© 2017 THE UNIVERSITY OF NORTH CAROLINA PRESS

Designed by Sally Fry Scruggs and set in Calluna types by codeMantra. The University of North Carolina Press has been a member of the Green Press Initiative since 2003.

Originally published in Spanish with the title *Que se queden allá: El gobierno de México y la repatriación de mexicanos en Estados Unidos (1934-1940)*, © 2007 El Colegio de la Frontera Norte, Tijuana, Baja California, México; El Colegio de San Luis, San Luis Potosí, S.L.P. México; and Fernando Saúl Alanís Enciso.

Cover illustration: Mexicans picking cantaloupes, Imperial Valley, California, 1937. Dorothea Lange, photographer. Courtesy of the Library of Congress.

LIBRARY OF CONGRESS CATALOGING-IN-PUBLICATION DATA

Names: Alanís Enciso, Fernando Saúl, author. | Davidson, Russ, translator. | Overmyer-Velázquez, Mark, writer of foreword.

Title: They should stay there : the story of Mexican migration and repatriation during the Great Depression / Fernando Saúl Alanís Enciso ; translated by Russ Davidson ; foreword by Mark Overmyer-Velázquez.

Other titles: Que se queden allá. English | Latin America in translation/en traducción/ em tradução.

Description: Chapel Hill : The University of North Carolina Press, [2017] | Series: Latin America in translation/en traducción/em tradução | Translation of: Que se queden allá : el gobierno de México y la repatriación de mexicanos en Estados Unidos (1934-1940). | Includes bibliographical references and index.

Identifiers: LCCN 2017003591 | ISBN 9781469634258 (cloth : alk. paper) | ISBN 9781469634265 (pbk : alk. paper) | ISBN 9781469634272 (ebook)

Subjects: LCSH: Mexican Americans—History—20th century. | Mexican Americans— Employment—History—20th century. | Mexicans—Employment—United States—History— 20th century. | Return migration—Mexico—History—20th century. | Mexico—Emigration and immigration—History—20th century. | Mexico—Emigration and immigration—Government policy—History—20th century. | United States—Emigration and immigration—History— 20th century. | Mexico—Politics and government—1910-1946. | Cárdenas, Lázaro, 1895-1970.

Classification: LCC E184.M5 A65313 2017 | DDC 973/.046872—dc23

LC record available at https://lccn.loc.gov/2017003591

To Manuel García y Griego, FRIEND AND MENTOR

# CONTENTS

# TABLES

# From Repatriation to Deportation Nation
## *A Century of Mexico-U.S. Migration*

Doctrinally grounded in nineteenth-century conceptions of sovereignty, contemporary deportation is a living legacy of historical episodes marked by ideas about race, imperialism, and government power that we have largely rejected in other realms. Implicating much more than border control, deportation is also a fulcrum on which majoritarian power is brought to bear against a discrete, marginalized segment of our society.

—DANIEL KANSTROOM, *DEPORTATION NATION*

The history examined by Mexican historian Fernando Saúl Alanís Enciso in *They Should Stay There* is very much alive today. In 2016, as many Mexican and other immigrants in the United States live vulnerably and in fear of deportation, we would do well to remember the lessons from the 1930s, a period when the U.S. government forced hundreds of thousands of ethnic Mexicans—many U.S. citizens—back across the border in what became the largest "repatriation" movement in U.S. history.[1] Although largely rooted in policies enacted long before his election, the record of approving the deportation of more people than any other president has earned Barack Obama the unsavory moniker "Deporter-in-Chief" from the National Council of La Raza, the nation's largest Latino advocacy organization.

The numbers of "formal removals" have been climbing rapidly since 1996, the year President Bill Clinton signed the Illegal Immigration Reform and Responsibility Act (IIRIRA). Whereas before 1996 immigration courts processed the majority of deportation cases, IIRIRA provided Immigration and Customs Enforcement (ICE) and Border Patrol agents with more authority to conduct nonjudicial deportations. Total deportations increased from 51,000 in 1995 to over 419,000 in 2012, with the majority being nonjudicial.[2] In addition, since September 11, 2001, Congress increased funding to U.S. Customs and Border Protection and ICE by 300 percent, further institutionalizing the militarization of the border and migrant surveillance.[3]

The passing of the 1996 law, however, was only one of the more recent moments in a longer, enduring history of strategic deportation practices by the U.S. government and corresponding actions by their Mexican counterparts. In the United States, this history, for example, has shaped and contributed to the toxic political environment surrounding the 2016 U.S. presidential election. The virulent xenophobia spewed by the unapologetically nativist Donald Trump and his Republican colleagues emerges from a fundamental and entrenched racist, anti-immigrant narrative that always has existed alongside the dominant "land of liberty" national story. Daniel Kanstroom argues against the notion of the development of the United States as a "melting pot, a mosaic, or as a more engaging metaphor puts it, a stir-fry. Rather, it is a history of the assertion, development, and refinement of centralized, well-focused, and often quite harsh government power subject to minimal judicial oversight."[4]

As Alanís Enciso insightfully explains in this important book, Mexico has not been immune to these one-sided, heroic narratives of inclusion and welcoming. While President Lázaro Cárdenas (1934–40) paid ample lip service to championing his compatriots in the United States and aiding their return and reintegration into Mexico's society and economy, much of that rhetoric was meant to offset his attention to assisting Spanish refugees escaping Francisco Franco's overthrow of the Spanish Republic. Cárdenas's critics accused him of ignoring his own countrymen in favor of Spaniards seeking exile.

Before Cárdenas, an anti-immigrant zeal permeated political discourse and action in the years following the Mexican Revolution (1910–20). In 1927, for example, the government officially prohibited the immigration of blacks, Syrians, Lebanese, Armenians, Palestinians, Turks, Arabs, and Chinese in order to "avoid *mestizaje* with them because, in general, they cause the degeneration of the *raza*."[5] The struggles of the Depression caused Mexican elites to further subordinate the relatively small Afro-Mexican population and continue to restrict immigration of foreign blacks to Mexico until 1935.[6] Although antiblack racism played roles in shaping Mexico's modern racialized discourses, an active Sinophobia that had developed starting in the late 1800s was the most forceful example of racist practice in Mexico and epitomized the transborder nature of racialization in the first half of the twentieth century.[7] Taking advantage of Chinese immigrants' constantly shifting legal status, non-Chinese groups often used them as convenient scapegoats for generalized economic and social problems.[8] Scholars have argued that anti-Chinese movements and legislation in Mexico allowed the increasingly muscular Mexican state to flex its centralized power from Mexico City.[9] In 1931, after decades of intimidation and violent repression, the Mexican government under President Plutarco Calles forcibly expelled most of the small but well-established Chinese population.[10]

Given the current and persistent contentiousness surrounding the issues of Mexican migration to the United States, it is vital that we have historical studies that assess the development and impact of migratory trends and practices as they developed in Mexico. Social science researchers have provided us with excellent studies of contemporary migration from Mexico.[11] Likewise, the arrival and adaptation of Mexican citizens to the United States (the only significant destination for Mexican migrants) has received much treatment by scholars of Mexican American/Chicano history. But the field still only has a few historical studies that examine the political contexts of the migrants' departure from Mexico (up to 10 percent of its citizens left, comprising the world's largest sustained movement of migratory workers through the twentieth century).[12]

*They Should Stay There* contributes to that much-needed historical perspective. The book is the first work of history that examines migration and repatriation during the pivotal postrevolutionary years surrounding the presidential administration of Lázaro Cárdenas. Starting in 1929, the Great Depression contributed to the forced migration of hundreds of thousands of ethnic Mexicans. Between 1930 and 1934, unemployment, hunger, deportations, raids, and xenophobia contributed to an unprecedented forced movement of men and women from the United States to Mexico. *They Should Stay There* examines the period following that mass exodus and the shifts in the social and economic situation of the Mexican community in the United States, U.S. immigration policy, and especially the varied and competing policies of state and federal government officials in Mexico toward their own foreign nationals.

Throughout his term, President Cárdenas focused primarily on agrarian reform, the reception of Spanish Civil War refugees, and the nationalization of the oil industry, largely disregarding the resettlement of *repatriados*. With the economic situation stabilized in the United States following the Depression, the U.S. government scaled back its deportation policy and greatly reduced the number of Mexican returnees. This, in turn, was a factor that caused the Mexican government to break from its long-standing policy of repatriation, initiated during the Porfiriato (the reign of President Porfirio Díaz, 1876–1910) and continued with urgency during the presidency of Venustiano Carranza (1917–20).[13]

Yet, this enduring commitment to the support of returning citizens had always been marked with ambivalence by Mexico's governing elite. On the one hand, officials like the influential anthropologist Manuel Gamio espoused a developmentalist argument for the return of migrants as potential engines of modernization who could both civilize society and help grow the economy. On the other, some viewed the migrants' time in the United States as possibly deleterious for Mexico. They argued that instead of becoming civilized, the migrants became contaminated with dangerous foreign political ideas, ideas they would introduce to their native country. Even worse, as Alanís Enciso shows us, officials feared that migrants would betray their allegiance to Mexico and adopt U.S. values of democratic governance and expectations of advanced social services.

In *They Should Stay There*, Alanís Enciso also argues that, despite its ambivalence, "They should stay there" was, and for the most part has been, the Mexican government's response to the emigration of thousands of its citizens to the United States. Officials determined that the economic benefit of continued remittances outweighed the humiliation of so many compatriots in the diaspora. As Alanís Enciso notes, the government's expression of dread and anxiety over the possibility of a massive return of migrants persisted after the 1930s, returning, for example, following the enactment of anti-immigrant laws after the terrorist attacks of September 11, 2001. In general, through the first half of the twentieth century, Mexican federal government policies toward outmigration focused on (ultimately failed) programs to control emigration. The conclusion of the Bracero program (1942–64) and the signing of the 1965 U.S. Immigration Act contributed to the steady flow of inexpensive Mexican workers to the United States. In the early 1970s, the Mexican government—building on long-standing efforts—increasingly shifted to managing and supporting emigrants already north of the border.[14]

The foremost scholar of Mexican emigration history, Fernando Alanís Enciso in *They Should Stay There* and beyond nuances the role of the Mexican government's many and conflicting departments and protagonists, disabusing us of the notion of a single, rationalized stance toward emigration, repatriation, and citizenship more generally.[15] Although federal and diplomatic interaction has shaped the movement and experience of Mexican migrants, most of the impactful and sustained engagement between governments has taken place at the subnational level. In this book, we learn how in the 1930s, the

Ministry of Foreign Relations negotiated directly with authorities in states such as California and Texas to first promote and then later ease repatriation pressures. As David FitzGerald has pointed out, fearing the loss of their labor force, earlier in the century governments in the northern states of Sonora and Chihuahua worked to prohibit the exodus of residents by denying exit permits and preventing the operation of *enganchadores* (labor recruiters from U.S. companies). Similarly, the government of Tamaulipas increased its international bridge fees to dissuade migrants from abandoning employment with local industries.[16]

The history examined in *They Should Stay There* also helps us to ascertain one moment in a global history of irreconcilable relationships between the modern, liberal nation-state and exclusionary immigration laws and practices. As Deirdre Moloney explains, "the marriage of racializing projects and nation-state formation and preservation allows the contemporary state to [secure] the nation through the exploitation of immigrant labor for its economic benefit and yet, at the same time, categorize and place migrant peoples [as others]."[17] Far from matter-of-fact, the U.S. government's strategic, historical construction of the immigrant as an "illegal" subject has placed an entire population in a state of permanent vulnerability and hence exploitability through deportation.[18] Migrant "illegalization" and the related construction of "deportability" is a strategic practice that states employ to reaffirm their sovereignty and control over national citizenship in a global context.[19]

The conditions of illegality and deportability uniquely impact Mexican migrants in the United States. As James Cockcroft has shown, Mexican migrants occupy a special place, providing "U.S. capitalism with the only 'foreign' migrant labor reserve so sufficiently flexible that it can neither be fully replaced nor completely excluded."[20] The immigrant history portrayed in *They Should Stay There* reminds us of the importance of examining the long-standing relationship between Mexican labor and U.S. capital.

That interdependent relationship in the early twenty-first century was critically reexamined in 2008 by sociologist and UN special rapporteur Jorge Bustamante. Bustamante's report on the status of human rights of migrants living in the United States included a scathing critique of the failure of U.S. government policies to adhere to their professed commitment to international laws, human rights norms, and protocols. In particular, he emphasized violations in immigrant deportation and detention actions, violations of migrant worker rights and the rights of women and children, and criticized the recurrence of racial profiling and the absence of habeas corpus and proper judicial review. Highlighting the experience of Mexican migrants, Bustamante's summary of recommendations for the government noted that "the United States lacks a clear, consistent, long-term strategy to improve respect for the human rights of migrants."[21] Unfortunately, since Bustamante's report deportations not only have increased but new legislation enhancing surveillance and further criminalizing undocumented migrants has supported the growth of new for-profit private prisons designed to hold only noncitizens convicted of federal crimes.[22]

## They Should Stay There—Today

We need an understanding of sovereignty, membership, citizenship, and government power that is "supple and flexible" and more functionally reflective of reality as it is experienced by those who have faced this kind of state power. The rights of noncitizens, in sum, should be clearer and grounded more in mainstream constitutional norms, more in their humanity than in their immigration status. —DANIEL KANSTROOM, *DEPORTATION NATION*

The enduring Mexican and U.S. transnational deportation/repatriation regime examined in *They Should Stay There* again has intensified in recent years with the rejection and removal of Central American unaccompanied child migrants. Extending the functional border deep into Mexican territory, the governments of both nations have used the entire country of Mexico as a buffer to stop and return thousands of Central American migrants. With its origins in U.S.-backed dirty wars in the 1970s and 1980s, the violence in Central America has pushed out its most vulnerable populations. Together, the United States and Mexico have deported over 800,000 Salvadorans, Guatemalans, and Hondurans since 2010, including more than 40,000 children. Immigrants' rights activists argue that the children are fleeing extreme violence in the countries of Central America's Northern Triangle and as such should be classified and treated as refugees with Temporary Protected Status and not as rights-limited migrants.[23]

Furthermore, the ongoing historical nature and consistent practice of deportation of large numbers of migrants challenges traditional studies and policy approaches to immigration that focus on paradigms of assimilation and transnationalism. As Tanya Golash-Boza and Pierrette Hondagneu-Sotelo point out, "The deportation crisis also raises a number of new empirical questions for the study of international migration." Although they are focused on the current flood of forced removals, works like *They Should Stay There* challenge us to reconsider how U.S. deportees are "adapting to life in their home countries" and how "deportation affect[s] the dynamics of immigrant incorporation and integration in the United States."[24]

In recent years, Mexican American communities in states such as Michigan and California are working to rescue the history of the period explored in Alanís Enciso's work and demand compensation for the thousands of their family members—many born in the United States—who were deported to Mexico. In 2006, the state of California passed the "Apology Act for the 1930s Mexican Repatriation Program," officially recognizing the "unconstitutional removal and coerced emigration of United States citizens and legal residents of Mexican descent" and apologizing to residents of California "for the fundamental violations of their basic civil liberties and constitutional rights committed during the period of illegal deportation and coerced emigration."[25] The federal government still has not apologized for the repatriations.

A significant work, *They Should Stay There* can now reach a broad English-language audience in the United States and the Anglophone world, including researchers and students of history and Latin American, Chicano/a, Latino/a, American and migration studies as well as political scientists and scholars of global affairs. In addition to advancing a historiography at the nexus of Latin American and U.S. Latina/o history, this book advances our knowledge in four critical areas. It recognizes migration to the United States as a central element in the history of modern Mexico; it links Mexico and the perspective of Mexicans to a scholarly discussion of Mexican American and Chicano/a history; it provides a comparative and transnational study of migration politics and policies relevant in migrant sending and receiving countries around the globe; and, perhaps most important, it examines fundamental aspects of state formation and foreign relations in Mexico and the United States from the ground up through the experiences of individual migrants.

The rich history and transnational context of these individual experiences in Alanís Enciso's *They Should Stay There* helps us understand migrants "more in their humanity than in their immigration status" and argues for more expansive rights for noncitizens abroad and compatriots returning home.

*Mark Overmyer-Velázquez*

# **FOREWORD** TO THE ORIGINAL EDITION

For Mexicans, few subjects produce more ambivalent feelings than migration. Although it concerns a social process that reaches back more than a century, represents an experience shared by millions of Mexican citizens, and touches virtually every Mexican family whatever its socioeconomic level, the idea of "those who set off" continues to be laden with stereotypes. To be sure, a gulf exists between the general perception of migrants that was held during the 1950s and 1960s—when they stood for a person who, upon migrating, ceased to retain the values of the homeland, thereby blurring his or her identity—and today's migrants, who are seen in a less ambiguous light. Mexican migrants now run the gamut from "the remittance heroes," at once lionized and taken for granted by state and federal authorities, to thousands of others whose personal stories fill the television news, whether as survivors of desert crossings, as witnesses to the rhythms and routines of daily life in the United States, or as intruders in a hostile society who voice their grievances in protest marches or as artists, filmmakers, and scientists. All of them achieved success only when they chose to embark upon their own version of the American Dream. Should all these migrants, spanning the full spectrum of age, race, gender, place of origin, and socioeconomic class, who together comprise more than 10 million Mexicans located abroad, decide to return to their native land— what, then, would run through the minds of the authorities? To contemplate that migration might suddenly cease to be the route out of poverty for millions, out of mediocrity for thousands more, or simply the end of a fantasy for a multitude of people, is perhaps the worst nightmare that any Mexican government could entertain. This idea, fundamental to the ambivalence that migration produces, is explored by Fernando Alanís Enciso through his meticulous, detailed account and analysis of the vicissitudes of a specific moment in history when the Lázaro Cárdenas administration (1934–40), sitting squarely on the cusp of its nationalist discourse, undertook a program to repatriate Mexicans.

As the saying goes, the devil is in the details, and it is precisely in the careful, focused handling of details that this book, through its recourse to materials documenting contemporaneous employment programs and to the letters and pronouncements of key figures, manages to weave together a complicated fabric that reveals how the migration policy of that time was constructed. There existed a fervent interest, on the one hand, in "being true to one's country," in this case through the repatriation program, as put forward by President Lázaro Cárdenas; while, on the other hand, financial obstacles militated against both repatriation per se and the successful social and economic reintegration of persons who returned to the country. These obstacles caused those in charge of articulating the program to question whether it was viable for the nation to take a firm stance favoring the return of Mexicans to the homeland. Thus the refrain "They should stay there" signals the simplest course of action, one that avoids further complications. Following this process to the end of the book enables us to say that we have isolated one of the central principles governing the history of Mexican migration policy; or, if speaking of a coherent migration policy seems too extreme or ambitious, we can limit ourselves to noting the positions taken by successive administrations toward the phenomenon; since, without doubt, the doctrine "They should stay there" has been the solution, or the exit strategy, adopted most often by the Mexican government.

One of the most interesting elements of the story concerns the discursive level on which each group articulated its interests with respect to the issue of migration. While members of the elite favored the flow of Mexicans out of the country, the political class was divided between some who believed that, based on what Mexican nationals had learned during their time outside the country, returnees could help "civilize" Mexico; and others who demonstrated a fear, suspicion, or even outright panic in the face of returnees thought to have lost their "Mexican" side. Here we witness the ambivalence mentioned above, the idea—carrying down to the present—that those who emigrate acquire something of the Protestant ethic in the most orthodox sense and therefore "are better," "know something that the rest of us do not know," or "comport themselves differently." To the contrary, however, this book makes evident that just as the programs into which the repatriated population was integrated did not function properly or as intended, so also the "extra" element brought from without either never made it across the border or simply vanished once it had (if indeed it was ever there). Moreover, we should take note of the obverse factor—the element of suspicion, still prevalent, that questions the ties to their country of origin of those who elected to migrate.

Conjure up, if you will, this scene: President Cárdenas openly and publicly calling upon Mexicans to return to their country, while at the same time there exist all of the doubts and contradictions within the political class toward the large-scale return of these same people. For this reason, because it not only reveals opinions and beliefs shared across society but also, in this case, implies policy decisions on migration, we can say that this book offers one of the missing pieces in the jigsaw puzzle history of Mexican migration policy.

In addition, by considering the debate over the repatriation of Mexicans in conjunction with one of the jewels of the Cárdenas *sexenio* (six-year presidential term)—the arrival of Spanish Civil War exiles in our country—Alanís Enciso adds a further measure of interest to his book. This twin turn of events, and maneuverings inside the government related to them, tells us much about what we are as a country: the Cardenista policy of hospitality hand in hand with the incapacity to generate true measures of assistance for Mexicans abroad, so that they could have been able to opt effectively to return to their native country. It is a dualism perhaps best viewed in light of the nationalist Cardenista government's felt need to extend the narrative that "the homeland awaits with open arms its sons who have migrated."

As a work of history, Alanís Enciso's study not only opens up a new window onto the Cardenista sexenio as a defining period in the evolution of Mexican nationalism but also, through the force of its argument, lays bare the inner workings of the political debate that unfolded over migration during those years. Moreover, what stands out is that many of the fears, suspicions, prejudices, and exaggerated predictions voiced by the central figures of that time are not dissimilar to the sensibilities and judgments that characterize the debate today. Clearly, however, the fact that the phenomenon has expanded by an order of magnitude so that it now encompasses the entire country has elevated it to a new level and given it much greater visibility. The ostrich-like posture that for so long symbolized Mexican migration policy, "the policy," as it were, "of no policy," can no longer be sustained. Yet, going beyond the confines of the book, it is not clear to what extent today's political class takes an open position on the issue, finds itself willing to craft new programs and strategies and reframe the terms of the debate. Nor, fundamentally, is it clear to what degree its members continue believing that it is preferable that those who have migrated simply "stay there."

*Leticia Calderón Chelius*

# ACKNOWLEDGMENTS

This work came to fruition because of the assistance I received from various people. First and foremost, I wish to thank Manuel García y Griego, a mentor who has been there for me throughout my professional career and whose teaching, guidance, and support were essential to my completing this book.

Three officials of the Colegio de San Luis, Isabel Monroy, Lydia Torre, and Tomás Calvillo, also deserve a special note of thanks. It was through their support that I found the necessary time, space, and stability to write the text. I am grateful as well to the National Science and Technology Council (Conacyt) for the award of a sponsored teaching post, which proved very beneficial to my research, and to the National Council of Culture and the Arts (Conaculta) and the Veracruz Institute of Culture for bestowing Mexico's 2001 Francisco Paso y Troncoso National History Prize on an earlier version of this book.

My work also benefited from comments and suggestions offered by other friends and colleagues: Luis Aboites, who made a series of important observations based on his careful reading of an early draft; Clara Lida, who similarly raised interesting points through her willingness to read part of the text; Guillermo Palacios and Manuel Ángel Castillo, for the instructive comments they offered after spending considerable time reading the manuscript; Anne Staples, who besides helping me clarify and resolve certain questions and concerns has also been a source of support across my entire professional career; Romana Falcón, for the assistance she extended from the beginning to the end of my research; Hilda Calzada and Lucía de la Cruz, who helped me bring many of the topics in this study into sharper focus by ensuring that I had access to needed materials; and Adriana del Río, for the patience she exhibited in checking and editing the text.

Finally, my mother; Carolina Enciso Alvarado (who inspired my interest in matters related to the U.S.-Mexico border); my daughters, Ipanema, Neretzi, and Nahomi; and my sisters, Lety and Caro, were also instrumental in enabling this project to move forward.

THEY
SHOULD
STAY
THERE

# Introduction

During the six years (1934–40) of Lázaro Cárdenas del Río's presidency, a persistent fear existed inside the government over the possible repercussions of a repatriation[1] of Mexican nationals. A similar expulsion had taken place during the preceding half decade (1929–33), the most critical phase of the Great Depression, when U.S. labor leaders and immigration and public assistance officials expelled more than 350,000 Mexicans, together with their descendants born in the United States.[2] The number of expulsions after 1934 was relatively low, however, due, on the one hand, to the support given to relief and work programs, which reduced the incentive for local governments to pursue expulsions, and, on the other, to the organization of the Mexican community in the United States, as well as the employment and social situation of its members, which allowed them to remain in the country.[3]

Officials in the Cárdenas administration feared that any broad-scale move to return Mexican nationals would harm the country's economy and the various communities to which returnees would be sent. Moreover, they were convinced that Mexicans' return would adversely impact the national labor market, putting the workers who had remained in the country in competition with returnees. What is more, the latter were labeled as disloyal opportunists for having remained outside the country. Their Mexicanness was called into question because, among other things, they now had children of a different nationality. Their return, it was likewise thought, could drive up both unemployment and crime, especially if they resettled in large cities as opposed to going back to their native towns and villages. The government thus tried to gain a more layered understanding of the Mexican population in the United States, so that it could estimate how many people would arrive back in the country and how many would require assistance. Furthermore, it analyzed the conditions in which its compatriots lived in the United States and studied certain regions in the north of Mexico where returnees could be relocated and settled.

Paradoxically, the fear that prevailed in official circles coexisted with an idealized view of the advantages that would accrue to the country from the return of expatriates. The experience migrants had gained from living and working abroad, so the thinking went, would aid the country's development. These individuals would help build the population base, increase agricultural production, and—with the knowledge they had acquired—bring more enlightened, civilized ways to the communities where they put down roots. All the same, when the onrush of returnees failed to materialize, the government promoted an agrarian and labor policy that privileged the Mexican citizen who had remained in his country over the one who had emigrated, and the measures it took to support returnees were characterized by their caution and modesty.

The Cárdenas government acted on different fronts: it supported the return of particular individuals on a case-by-case basis and of small groups that set out to establish new settlements, to whom and for which it allocated minimal funding. In addition, the government sporadically provided rail passage from the border to indigent nationals who had made their way from inside the United States. These approaches showed the range of difficulties the government would encounter in mounting any campaign to organize the reverse movement of a large segment of its population. Furthermore, this diffused way of operating was not new. Mexican governments had responded in similar fashion since the beginning of the twentieth century, when Mexican nationals had been forced to return on a smaller scale. For these administrations, as for the Cárdenas regime, the return of compatriots from the nation to the north did not represent a problem either of national or international importance, for which reason they paid it little attention.

## Historiography of the Cárdenas Government and the Repatriation of Mexicans from the United States

The stance and actions taken by the Cárdenas government in dealing with the repatriation of Mexicans resident in the United States have been little studied by scholars. To date, two books published on this subject have exerted the greatest influence: Abraham Hoffman's *Unwanted Mexican Americans in the Great Depression: Repatriation Pressures, 1929–1939* (1974) and Mercedes Carreras de Velasco's *Los mexicanos que devolvió la crisis, 1929–1932* (1974). Both authors focused on the actions taken by the Mexican and U.S. governments amid the massive return of Mexican nationals sparked by the 1929 market crash and resulting economic depression.

In analyzing U.S. government actions and the expulsion of Mexicans from U.S. soil, Hoffman focuses in particular on events in Los Angeles County. His examination of various initiatives pursued during the Cárdenas administration yields a small store of pertinent data and information. He also studies the policy developed by Los Angeles County authorities in 1937 and 1938 and offers some important perspectives on the process of repatriation. In similar fashion, he analyzes the project launched by President Cárdenas in 1939 to assist the return of Mexican nationals, including the indigent, who wished to resume life in the place they had left. In addition, the Cárdenas project had a more targeted purpose: to select a group of agricultural workers, experienced in the cultivation of cotton from their time living in Texas, who could establish an agricultural colony, named the 18 March, in the northern part of the state of Tamaulipas. Fundamentally, Hoffman views this project as a defensive maneuver, a response to criticism of the government's welcome of refugees from the Spanish Civil War.

Carreras de Velasco analyzes the initiatives taken by the Mexican government on different levels of public administration during the deepest phase of the Great Depression, the years 1929 through 1934, making her contribution to the subject of my study necessarily more limited in scope. She notes that the economic crisis of 1938–39 in the United States was accompanied by a new wave of returnees to Mexico, one that prompted the government to undertake an official program of resettlement of returnees from across the border (the repatriated).[4] In the conclusions to their studies, Hoffman and Carreras de Velasco both underscore that Cárdenas's presidency was characterized by a broad repatriation effort simultaneously linked to its agrarian reform new settlement policies. While both also stress that the Cárdenas government stood out in the level of its support for Mexican migrants returning from the United States, Carreras de Velasco goes further, pointing out that "the settlements that were founded" in this period are the only such communities that have survived. In reality, however, no more than two were founded, one of which ended in failure.

In his dissertation, "Texas Mexican Repatriation during the Great Depression" (1982), Reynolds McKay analyzes the 1930s expulsion from Texas of Mexican immigrants, along with their U.S.-born descendants. Part of his study traces the various routes people traversed on their journey back to Mexico, the destinations they had in mind, and the resettlement projects designed for them.

Although McKay's analysis of the return of Mexicans concentrates mainly on the period 1929–34, he nonetheless contributes useful information on relevant programs of the Cárdenas administration, such as the founding of the 18 March agricultural colony and the efforts carried out in the United States by the Mexican government to help bring about the return of Mexican migrants and their offspring. The conclusion he draws is that the projects undertaken in this period left a record of failure. It should be noted, however, that McKay's study contains certain factual errors, since he conflates the return of migrants who were part of the 18 March colony with three repatriations (from Karnes City, Bridgeport, and Gonzales) that had taken place in 1931. The latter were fundamentally the product of early Depression-era conditions faced by Mexicans residing across the Rio Grande, in southern and northern Texas. In contrast, the establishment of the 18 March agricultural colony reflected a plan devised within government circles at a time, as we will see, when there was great opposition among the population of Mexican origin to leaving the United States.

There are a series of other studies that in a general way treat the subject under consideration. Among them is George Sánchez's *Becoming Mexican American: Ethnicity, Culture, and Identity in Chicano Los Angeles, 1900–1945* (1993), which examines repatriation as it took place in Los Angeles as one factor that helped shape Mexican Americans' cultural and ethnic identity. For its part, Camille Guerín-Gonzáles's book *Mexican Workers and American Dreams: Immigration, Repatriation, and California Farm Labor, 1900–1945* (1994) explores how the American Dream—latched onto, in keeping with its traditional role, as a beacon of opportunity—was turned around and used as justification for the exploitation and repatriation of Mexicans in California. Both studies analyze the meaning and repercussions of repatriation for the Mexican population in the United States.

One of Moisés González Navarro's books, *Los extranjeros en México y los mexicanos en el extranjero, 1821–1970* (1994), contains a general description of the settlement projects carried out during the Cárdenas administration, among them the 18 March agricultural colony. According to González Navarro, the colony was founded to offset the arrival in Mexico of Spanish Civil War refugees, and its installation proved to be a failure.

In their *Decade of Betrayal: Mexican Repatriation in the 1930s* (1995), a work grounded in social history, Francisco E. Balderrama and Raymond Rodríguez reconstruct the repatriation movement as implemented during the 1930s, relating in some detail the treatment accorded to the Mexican community by U.S. and Mexican authorities, respectively. Although the authors state that their study encompasses the entire decade, it has little to say about the six years of the Cárdenas administration. Its review of this period is limited to analyzing the work of Ramón Beteta, Mexico's undersecretary of foreign relations, who headed up the administration's repatriation movement from the U.S. side, and to examining a series of colonization projects in the north of Mexico to resettle people who had returned to the country voluntarily, while also treating the problems they experienced in their efforts to reassimilate. With respect to the Cardenista repatriation project as a whole, Balderrama and Rodríguez come to the same conclusion as Hoffman: that it happened "on the rebound," springing to life as an answer to the pressures exerted on the president after he opened Mexico's doors to Spanish Civil War refugees.

Let us return for a moment to the work of Carreras de Velasco and Hoffman. Both authors deal with the repatriations that occurred at the height of the Great Depression and with the measures taken on this front by the government, which they describe as energetic and wide ranging. Similarly, they believe the Cárdenas government's actions generally to have been outstanding, especially its agrarian reform and new settlement initiatives. Both authors, however, infer things about the government's repatriation policy without supporting these inferences with documentation. On the one hand, they largely base their findings about repatriation policy on information pertaining to the project aimed at bringing back Mexicans that Cárdenas promoted during the first months of 1939. On the other hand, the works by McKay and Balderrama and Rodríguez, which together with Hoffman's provide the most in-depth treatment of the subject, suggest that the Cardenista policy of repatriation was ultimately a failure as well as a response to the fait accompli of the arrival in Mexico of refugees from the Spanish Civil War. They leave this last theme undeveloped. In his more abbreviated analysis, González Navarro reached the same conclusion as these three authors. Their common findings notwithstanding, in their research none avail themselves of a wider range of primary source material to analyze the factors that led Cárdenas to promote the return of Mexicans from the United States, nor did they interpret the results of the project.

What is more, the works mentioned do not place the analysis within a wider context. Thus, they exclude any examination of measures taken prior to or after the repatriation project of 1939. So far as the movement on behalf of returning Mexicans to their country was concerned, they likewise fail to study collectively the initiatives undertaken by the regime from Cárdenas's ascent to the presidency until he left office. They focus solely on a project that lasted a mere three months (April to June 1939). Until now, the interpretation of the Cardenista policy of repatriation has therefore been based on the examination—by no means incomplete—of an isolated action taken by the executive authority at the end of the 1934–40 *sexenio* (six-year presidential term). In addition, the reasons behind the failure of the Cardenista project have yet to be explained, nor has there been any explanation either of the government's objectives in pushing the repatriation campaign or of its final results, not to speak of an attempt to sort out its meaning for and within the larger history of Mexican migration. Little wonder, then, that a study cutting wider and deeper is at odds with prior opinions regarding the success of the project.

## Contributions and Proposals

This study is centered on the policy of the Mexican government during the presidency of Lázaro Cárdenas (1934–40) as it pertained to the repatriation of Mexican nationals from the United States. It employs a preeminently political slant, based on the study of the government's initiatives when faced with the return of Mexicans who had emigrated with the hope of bettering their economic situation. This slant is also based on the information I obtained from primary sources, which related principally to two events that began to overlap in 1934: first, a change in how the movement of migrants between Mexico and the United States was handled, as reflected by a decrease in the previously massive numbers of people returned, and second, the installation of a new government in Mexico at the end of 1934.

My central argument here is that, on the matter of repatriation, the Cárdenas government adopted measures that were only partially fulfilled, with the result that the government accomplished less than what previous studies have found. The error of earlier historians derives from a simple mistake: the projection of initiatives undertaken between 1929 and 1933 onto a later period and the mistaken supposition that the energy the government expended on a repatriation project in early 1939 fed its repatriation policy as a whole. In parallel fashion, these historians have also inferred that the emphasis Cárdenas put on agrarian reform and the founding of new settlements extended to his government's actions on the repatriation of migrant workers. My study asserts that, in applying its policy on repatriation, the Cárdenas administration in fact followed a much less rigorous course because its national and international priorities lay elsewhere and, above all, because during the second half of the 1930s the numbers of migrants coming back across the border neither warranted that the issue be accorded high importance nor dictated that the government take measures to support those returning to the homeland.

In contrast to other studies, my work places the Cardenista repatriation policy in a wider context and, partly for this reason, reaches different conclusions. I start with a basic fact—the initiatives taken by the Cárdenas regime were inspired by the belief, entertained and subscribed to in official circles since the beginning of the twentieth century, that returnees would increase the country's population and contribute to its uplift and development through knowledge and practices they had acquired while living abroad. To this way of thinking, Mexican migrants in the United States, farmworkers in particular, were foreseen as the beneficiaries of Cárdenas's agrarian and demographic policies. In practice, however, the government's actions on such policy pronouncements were few and far between, since Cárdenas never gave priority to establishing new settlements with Mexicans returning from the United States, nor did he incorporate them into his agricultural policies. In short, the repatriation policy was marked by a wide gulf between what the administration proposed, on the one hand, and what it actually did, in the public sphere, on the other.

Whether through their own means or with assistance from the government, Mexican nationals who returned from the United States to reap the benefits of Cardenista population policies and agrarian reforms were decidedly few. Although the government, from the time Cárdenas assumed the presidency, had actively investigated the possibility of establishing new colonies in various parts of Mexico, Baja California in particular, its plans never took concrete shape. Among other reasons, there was considerable fear within official circles that such efforts could cause social and economic problems in their locales. The government was also convinced that it needed to deal first with the demands for work and land expressed by Mexicans who had not left the country. They were the priority. And conversely, according to Cárdenas, the conditions that would justify converting the returning migrants into the settlers of new communities had not come about. That is, there were no mass movements of returning nationals that might spur the president to immediately find a place to resettle them. On the agenda of national problems, the return of Mexican workers from the United States was a matter of secondary importance for Lázaro Cárdenas.

This study also demonstrates that the Cárdenas administration's repatriation initiatives did not break new ground. As a rule, the government under Cárdenas acted largely as had other administrations that had not had to confront the return of massive numbers of their compatriots: by arranging rail passage back to Mexico for a limited number of indigent migrants, by endeavoring in certain instances to see that Mexicans living in the United States remained in that country, and by studying the possible establishment of colonies in which to resettle agricultural workers, though at times doing so indifferently and inattentively and, more pointedly, with a consuming fear of the negative effects of the return of thousands of people. In short, the Cardenista policy on repatriation was similar to and a continuation of the government's policy promoted since the start of the twentieth century.

This work also provides a more detailed and nuanced explanation than previous studies of the reasons that led Cárdenas to launch a repatriation project at the beginning of 1939. I do not reject the argument that Cárdenas's promotion of the project was influenced, up to a point, by his decision to admit Spaniards seeking refuge from their country's civil war. That the promotion of the repatriation project in the waning months of the Cárdenas presidency softened and deflected criticism of the regime's willingness to give sanctuary to the refugees is demonstrably true; but two factors, both ignored by earlier studies, have still greater importance: First, in the final months of 1937, the government declared its support for a plan of repatriation, which it proceeded to develop over the course of 1938. The plan, then, began to be elaborated *prior* to the arrival in June 1939 of large numbers of Spanish refugees, and showed the executive's direct interest in implementing a pilot plan to guide the return of Mexican nationals. Second, as of 10 November 1938, the Mexican government had already negotiated an agreement with the authorities of Los Angeles County to implement a repatriation plan. In large measure this agreement came about because of pressure exerted by the county authorities, who wanted more Mexicans deported (Hoffman 1974, 162–63). For its part, the Cárdenas government was openly disposed to sign the agreement, which, in a certain way, aligned with some of the basic premises of Cardenista migration policy. Mexican governors, with the help of local and national labor unions, would scan their states for places where people who returned could be resettled. The government's other commitments included allocating large tracts of land and impeding the future outflow of migrants. Moreover, the administration needed to implement the project both to fulfill the terms of an agreement reached between itself and a foreign governmental entity and to secure certain internal benefits: above all, the public and expeditious display of its policy to aid returning migrants, as well as the softening of attacks to which Cárdenas was subjected at the end of his presidency by different elements in Mexican society that were opposed to his regime.

Thus my study, in contrast to others, does not extol the Cardenista achievements with respect to the repatriation of Mexicans from the United States but, instead, offers a critical appraisal of the results obtained in this sphere. In equal measure, it elucidates certain subtle features of the Mexican government's migration policy toward its nationals residing in the United

States, features that have been little studied by migration scholars, such as the disposition at times to prefer that migrants remain in that country ("They should stay there") and—above all—the horror expressed in official circles at the prospect of any mass return. Both inclinations trace back to the early twentieth century and even now persist in attitudes displayed by the Mexican political class, two examples of which were the reaction provoked by the U.S. Congress's passage in 1986 of the Simpson-Rodino Law (Immigration Reform and Control Act), whose two principle objectives were to reduce the population of undocumented people in the United States and to respond to criticisms directed at the United States on the subject of migration; and the reaction to the hardening of U.S. migration policy following the terrorist attacks of 11 September 2001 on New York City and Washington, D.C. In both cases, there was palpable alarm among Mexican officialdom, on both state and federal levels, that these events could lead to the return of massive numbers of their compatriots. While this did not occur, as during Cárdenas's presidency, neither of the two administrations holding power squarely faced and actively prepared for the possibility of a mass repatriation.

Another dimension of the topic on which I place special emphasis is the situation faced by the Mexican community north of the Rio Grande during the second half of the 1930s. Until now, works that have analyzed this period have taken the view that the Mexican community was betrayed, subjected to harassment, and compelled—in great numbers—to leave the United States. I do not downplay the reality of the Mexican diaspora in that country. In the very process of emigrating north, in the work and living conditions they encountered, and in seeking social acceptance within the larger society, these emigrants were forced to contend with one set of challenges after another. At the same time, however, a combination of factors (among others, the support received from various welfare and public assistance agencies as the result of the national recovery program, the organized strength of political and labor groups within the Mexican community, and the struggle to secure the rights of children born to Mexicans in the United States) permitted this community to establish a solid base on which to affirm and consolidate its presence as part of U.S. society and, above all, to oppose its wholesale return to Mexico. What is more, its position in this regard was bolstered by initiatives that the U.S. government promoted during these years.

The present study reflects wide-ranging research carried out over several years in public and private archives in both Mexico and the United States, complemented by a systematic combing of contemporaneous newspapers and periodicals. My main lines of argument were likewise finalized only after years of reflection and enriched through readings, corrections, discussions, and informal conversations with colleagues. Ultimately, they were assembled into a narrative that covers a stage in the history of Mexican emigration to the United States that researchers interested in the subject have yet to study in depth.

## CHAPTER ONE

# Migratory Movements between Mexico and the United States, 1880–1934

## Emigration to the United States: First Stage, 1880–1917

Two interlocking factors fueled the wave of workers who began to migrate from Mexico to the United States beginning in the late nineteenth century and early twentieth: first, the expansion of the U.S. economy and the integration into it of southwestern states via the development of the railroads, agriculture (cotton, beetroots, fruits, vegetables, and citrus products), and mining, which created a demand for cheap, abundant, low-skilled labor (Cardoso 1980, 18–37; Katz 1986, 13–14; Reisler 1976, 3–17); and, second, the difficult economic and social conditions in Mexico, fed by such developments as the expropriation of village communal lands and a decrease in wages on rural estates between 1876 and 1910.

The influence of the railroads was exceptionally important, since the railway companies provided transportation at various points along the tracks. Moreover, the railway lines were the principal means by which Mexican workers were imported on a large scale into the U.S. Southwest (Clark 1908, 469–73; Martínez 1950, 3–5, 11). Since 1880, Mexican labor had been heavily used in the construction of the Southern Pacific and Santa Fe lines and, to a lesser extent, was also employed in the agricultural and mining sectors. From 1890, Mexicans had trudged on foot toward the cotton-producing areas of Texas to find work at harvest time (McWilliams 1972, 199–200), and the first years of the twentieth century saw an uptick in the demand for Mexican labor to harvest cotton, beets, fruits, and vegetables in California, Colorado, and Michigan (Montejano 1987, 96–159; García 1981, 7–10; Cardoso 1980, 18–19).

Greater possibilities for work opened up for Mexicans with the 1902 Newlands Reclamation Act, which sanctioned the use of federal funds for large irrigation systems and development projects. As a result of this legislation, extensive tracts of desert areas were made usable for the cultivation of vegetables, cotton, and citrus products. In the areas that benefited from irrigation, the existing production of fruits and vegetables increased. In line with the great increase in rail traffic and the sharp expansion of the mining sector, numerous groups of Mexicans were added to the workforce laboring in the copper, coal, gold, and silver mines of New Mexico, California, and Oklahoma. Through their participation in these key sectors in the economic development of the U.S. Southwest, Mexican workers helped build the U.S. economic empire (García 1981, 1–8; McWilliams 1972, 193; Reisler 1976, 4–13).

As noted above, conditions in Mexico also spurred emigration. During the Porfiriato (1876–1910), the country experienced change and development that upset the existing social and economic equilibrium. Although the national economy grew, and in certain sectors such as mining, agriculture, and commerce reached unprecedented heights, its leap forward was accompanied by serious social problems that sparked the departure of hundreds of people to the United States (Buve 1990, 27–29; Coatsworth 1976, 45–62; Cosío Villegas 1989, 37–81; Guerra 1993, 324–38; Haber 1992, 27–62). Foreign investment in Mexico fostered urban development and the creation of centers of commercial activity, leading to the internal migration of hundreds of workers. Linkages to markets in the United States also opened avenues for work and increased the volume of exports, but also left the country exposed to the vagaries of U.S. business cycles. The pattern was repeated in the north of Mexico, where the mining boom brought with it high wages and the founding of new cities, while at the same time upending the economic life of entire communities and creating populations that were transient, unstable, and prone to rebelliousness. The labor policies of U.S. employers and business leaders, based as they were on discrimination toward Mexicans, provoked intense nationalistic fervor (Katz 1990, 177, 213; Knight 1987, 21–29.)

If, on the one hand, the railways shortened distances, brought down freight charges and the cost of shipping goods, and tied markets together, on the other, they drove up the price of lands lying idle, which in turn hollowed out and left isolated both traditional centers of commerce and production not served by the rail lines and the oligarchic interests that benefited from them (Coatsworth 1976, 2:41–76). The introduction of modern farming and agronomic techniques was also transformative. While it led to the consolidation of a remarkably dynamic sector, it also contributed to the destruction of the traditional peasant economy and to the usurpation of the time-honored rights of villages and rural communities, forcing their inhabitants into a wage economy and, with it, hunger, debt peonage, and emigration. In this way, over the course of the Porfiriato, life for the majority of Mexicans was marked by inflation, lower wages, detrimental work conditions, far-reaching change in the countryside, loss of means of subsistence, and reduced access to land.

From 1880 to 1910, migration was on the rise. At the end of the nineteenth century, a multitude of people from the states of Sinaloa, Sonora, and Baja California emigrated to California, while many Sonoran families also departed for Texas and Arizona. The flow of emigrants was increased in the beginning of the twentieth century by individuals and families leaving the cities of Zacatecas and Guadalajara. In 1906 alone, 22,000 *tapatíos* (people from Guadalajara) left for the United States. The migratory current also grew in the area of the U.S.-Mexico border. For example, during 1907 more than 1,000 *braceros* per month passed through Ciudad Juárez, Ciudad Porfirio Díaz, and Matamoros. In 1908, approximately 16,000 Mexicans were hired on contract in El Paso to work on the railway lines. Victor S. Clark, an official in the U.S. Department of Labor, calculated that more than 100,000 workers came into the United States annually from Mexico. In 1910, the Mexican minister of development, colonization, and industry put the figure at above 50,000 (Clark 1908, 466; González Navarro 1954, 263, 271; McWilliams 1972, 199–200). In short, between 1900 and 1910 migration from Mexico to the United States nearly doubled.

Later, the military phase of the Mexican Revolution (1910–20) brought devastation, chaos, danger, and economic upheaval that prompted massive migration from various localities. Some 25,000 Mexicans trekked across the border annually; as immigrants (both legal and illegal), as seasonal laborers, and as refugees—rich and poor alike—fleeing violence and persecution. It is generally agreed that approximately 1 million Mexicans crossed into the United States between 1900 and 1930 (Hall 1982, 23; Gullet 1995, 82).

## The Second Stage of Emigration, 1917–1928

During the decade 1917–28, Mexican emigration to the United States continued to set new records, although the deportation of thousands of Mexican nationals during the postwar economic downturn of 1920–23 briefly checked its progress. The rising number of emigrants was caused by two principal factors: a surging demand for labor in the United States both during the country's participation in the First World War (February 1917 to November 1918) and across the 1920s; and the social and economic conditions prevailing within Mexico itself. During the nearly two years in which the United States fought in the Great War, records show that its government sponsored the admission of some 72,000 workers, who found employment in industries considered critical to the war effort (Alanís Enciso 1999, 10–20; Reisler 1976, 24–30). Starting in

1923, as the national economy began to recover from the postwar economic depression, Mexican emigration to the United States reached new heights.

Meanwhile, political and religious violence continued to wrack certain regions of Mexico even after 1920. The armed movement attracting the greatest attention and notoriety during this period was the Cristero Rebellion, which took place in 1926–29 and embroiled primarily the center of the country— the states of Jalisco, Michoacán, Durango, Guerrero, Colima, Nayarit, and Zacatecas (Cardoso 1980, 85–87; Meyer 1994, vols. 1 and 2). As the result of this conflict, peasants, peons, and those fleeing political persecution once again found themselves obliged to emigrate.

The number of Mexicans who crossed illegally into the United States every year during the 1920s has been calculated at 100,000, to which of course should be added those whose entry was legal and officially recorded by the immigration authorities (Cardoso 1980, 85–87; Gamio 1930a, 10–20; Gamio 1930b, 22). Mexico's national statistical agency recorded the departure of 331,602 Mexicans between 1925 and 1934, including 81,396 in 1927 and 13,686 in 1929. Of these people, 26 percent had agriculture as their principal occupation, 23 percent were the wives of emigrants, 19 percent were the children of emigrants or minors without any occupation, and the remaining 22 percent "were distributed, in small groupings, among further categories of work." In general terms, the agency calculated that peasant farmers and other rural workers and their family members represented slightly more than 50 percent of the total number of emigrants.[1]

In the United States, the wave of Mexican migration became an important element in the country's consideration of immigration in general; and while no restrictive laws were passed to target Mexicans alone, short-term law enforcement measures were invoked to guard the border and proposals were advanced to curtail land-based migration (including the establishment of the Border Patrol in 1924) and to put in place new measures and a bureaucratic apparatus aimed at restricting the flow of migrants over and across the border. Some members of the U.S. Congress introduced proposals to set strict limits on the entry of foreign nationals into the country, efforts that culminated in the Immigration Act passed on 26 May 1924. Subsequently, during the second half of the decade, the attitude toward Mexicans became polarized. While the business community clamored for more workers and favored flexible migration laws, another current of opinion, led by Congressman John C. Box (D-Tex.) and the American Federation of Labor, argued that the influx of foreigners needed to be more tightly controlled (Divine 1957, 7; Levenstein 1968, 206–7; Reisler 1976, 203–15).

## The Great Depression and Massive Repatriation, 1929–1934

The next stage in the history of Mexican migration to the United States, 1929–34, was defined by the contraction of the U.S. economy and rising unemployment, the effects of which were to depress the demand for labor and increase the pressure on and hostility directed toward Mexican workers, leading to the call for them to leave the country. To further restrict the inflow of foreign laborers, immigration laws were made harsher and, as the issue became inflamed, the deportation of such workers was promoted. Consequently, some 423,026 Mexican nationals, in a mass movement that lacked any advance planning or control, made their way back to Mexico (see table 1.1), crossing over at all the accessible points along the border (Carreras de Velasco 1974, 58–59, 138; Hoffman 1974).

The deportation policies and initiatives were applied throughout the country against any and all groups of foreigners with the twin purposes of reducing unemployment and giving preference to U.S. nationals in filling jobs. The deportation plan implemented by Los Angeles County was one of the most successful nationwide. Ruthlessly efficient, it was carried out by federal as well as local officials, who staged roundups in public squares and parks, apprehending hundreds of Mexicans without regard for whether they had entered the country legally or illegally or enjoyed U.S. citizenship as the U.S.-born children of Mexican parents.

Between 1931 and 1935, the Los Angeles County Charities and Public Welfare Department routinely expelled thousands of Mexicans, paying for their trip to the border since this proved less costly than paying benefits to hundreds of unemployed people. U.S. immigration agents, led by the secretary of labor, William N. Doak, intensified their command and control efforts in the country's largest metropolises as well as in such states as Texas, Illinois, Michigan, and Arizona. The nature and success of their tactics and operations may have varied from place to place, but the objective was always the same: to round up and expel migrant workers (Hoffman 1974, 41–42, 83, 85–107, 115, 175; McKay 1982, 36; Romo 1983, 164; Betten and Mohl 1973; Simon 1974; Humphrey 1941; Bogardus 1934, 90).

## The Mexican Government and Emigration

Since the late nineteenth century, the emigration of its people to the United States had not only focused the interest of the Mexican government but also led it to articulate a policy designed to stem the process, because it was considered to equate with an important loss of labor and man hours for the country. Accordingly, during the long years of General Porfirio Díaz's rule (1877–1911), the emigration of Mexicans to the United States began especially

TABLE 1.1  Repatriation of Mexicans, 1929–1934

| YEAR | NO. REPATRIATED |
|---|---|
| 1929 | 79,419 |
| 1930 | 70,127 |
| 1931 | 138,519 |
| 1932 | 77,453 |
| 1933 | 33,574 |
| 1934 | 23,934 |
| TOTAL | 423,026 |

SOURCE: Hoffman 1974, 175, based on U.S. National Archive, Record Group 59, 811.111, Mexico Reports / 59, 80, 99, 122, 141, 142. Data gathered by the Mexican Migration Service.

to concern the governors of the country's central and northern states, who expressed opposition to the movement. Through the press, posters, and placards, they denounced the dismal work conditions that those who emigrated had to endure, the manner in which their labor was contracted, and the abuses to which they were subjected. They exhorted workers not to leave the country, insisting that the absence of their services left a void in Mexico. The newspaper *El Imparcial*, a government mouthpiece, supported this campaign, discouraging workers disposed to migrate by making emotional appeals to their patriotism (González Navarro 1954, 278–79).

The governors of the border states similarly lined up in favor of keeping their workforce within the country. To dissuade workers from leaving, they informed them of the undesirable conditions that migrants encountered in El Paso and Los Angeles. The executive requested of Mexican authorities that they make a note of the abuses committed against workers and asked officials in Jalisco, Guanajuato, and Zacatecas to warn those they governed of the risks they ran in crossing the border and the dangers to which they exposed themselves in contracting with *enganchadores* (in this context, a person who gets someone into his clutches)—an irresponsible lot who rarely delivered on their offers of work.[2] To discourage emigration, the government stressed the precarious situation that braceros faced in Ciudad Juárez, a tactic to which the political chief of the district of Bravos, in the state of Chihuahua, also adhered. In the main, Mexican governing authorities were unified in branding emigration as a via crucis, and the federal government continued trying to halt it.[3]

During the Revolution, a nationalist sentiment took hold as a counterpoint to emigration, and the calls to avoid and shun the latter increased. In the presidential campaign of 1910, Francisco I. Madero expressed sorrow over the humiliations to which those who emigrated were subjected and declared his opposition to his compatriots' leaving Mexico for the United States (Cardoso 1980, 31). The government of Venustiano Carranza (1917–20) first launched a campaign, through the national press, to condemn the difficulties experienced by braceros in the United States and the awful conditions in which they worked. Later, it tried to suspend the issuance of passports both on the border and in the country proper, again to impede people from leaving. Ultimately, it applied contingency measures, with limited practical benefit, such as imposing high migration quotas, spreading word about the availability of work inside the country, and placing *contratistas* (the middlemen, or work contractors) under detention.[4] The Carranza government also mandated that all emigrants be under formal contract. To this end, it promoted a model work contract set down in Section 26 of Article 123 of the Mexican constitution of February 1917, specifying that every agreement concluded between a Mexican and a foreign businessman had to be legalized by the municipal authority competent in the matter and also endorsed and certified by the Mexican consular official in the locale where the migrant worker would be going. A clause in the pertinent section also clearly specified that the costs of repatriation were to be borne by either the employer or the contracting party (Alanís Enciso 2001a:1–20; Rouaix 1992, 91–93, 102).

This official government concern to contain emigration persisted into the 1920s, when the Ministry of the Interior (Secretaría de Gobernación, or SEGOB) proposed that notice be given in the national press of abuses that Mexican workers suffered at the hands of the contratistas. In the middle of the decade, the idea of crafting a national plan to control emigration was bruited, and the Foreign Relations and Interior Ministries widely publicized the difficulties experienced by Mexicans who had crossed into the United States (Carreras de Velasco 1974, 47, 52). Thus, from the end of the nineteenth century into the postrevolutionary period, the policy of the Mexican government toward emigration was framed by an effort to impede it that had little chance of practical success.

## The Mexican Government and Repatriation

The emigration of Mexican workers to the United States was accompanied, year in and year out, by a reverse flow of this population back to Mexico. In some instances, the reverse stream was purely a matter of routine, groups of people voluntarily returning to their home villages and towns after working for a time on the other side of the border. On other occasions, however, it involved large numbers of people forcibly returned en masse to Mexico, in deportations organized and carried out by U.S. labor leaders and immigration authorities. These mass deportations occurred by and large during periods of economic recession, when the labor market was adjusted and foreign workers were displaced so that preference could be given to U.S. citizens. For their part, the Mexican authorities chose to ignore the reasons that underlay these mass returns and, in the majority of cases, classified those sent back in this manner as people who repatriated, that is, willingly returned to the homeland.

Since the middle of the nineteenth century, when Mexico lost the territories of Texas, Arizona, New Mexico, Upper California, and other regions to the north of these lands, the government of Mexico had taken the position that it was duty-bound, morally and as a nation, to repatriate its citizens who had remained in the annexed territories (Zorrilla 1965; Miller Puckett 1950, 269–95; González Navarro 1994, 10–21). At the end of that century and during the twentieth, as the level of workers emigrating climbed higher, the government continued regularly to call for the return of those who had left for the United States in search of a better life but, once there, found themselves poverty stricken, facing racism, segregation, and mistreatment, exploited and made to work in miserable conditions. As part of its declarations, the government asserted that it sought to facilitate their return and, at the same time, to channel and capitalize on the work experience they had supposedly acquired in the United States to propel Mexico's own development. Yet, for all the government's frequent statements in favor of a return of its nationals, it did little to further this goal. Doing so was not a high priority in its national migration policy. Moreover, apart from a minority who perhaps thought otherwise, government officials recognized that the country could not do much either to finance a return movement or to grant land to those who came back.

## 1880–1918

Since the return of its workers and their families from the United States was not a subject that held much interest for the Porfirian government, it turned its attention to the matter only sporadically. The 1883 *Ley de colonización* (a law regulating the disposition and settlement of vacant or public land) said nothing about repatriation in any of its sections. Nevertheless, the record suggests that the government did grant some deeds of ownership, free of charge, to Mexicans who returned from the United States. One such case occurred in the Baja California community of Tecate, where the government "established poor, repatriated settlers." Reference was also made to opening settlements on lands along the Río Yaqui with Mexicans who returned from California and Arizona. Similarly, a group of mining families from Texas were repatriated with the purpose of founding settlements in the municipalities of La Sauteña and Zacapu, in the states of Tamaulipas and Michoacán, respectively.[5]

Official intervention to support the return of Mexicans was triggered when the contraction of the U.S. economy led immigration authorities and labor leaders there to advocate and carry out mass deportations. Accordingly, the 1907–8 depression resulted in the expulsion of hundreds of Mexican workers, who were relieved of their jobs in factories and mines around the country. U.S. immigration officials on the border denied more than 250 workers entrance into the country. In mid-1908, Ciudad Juárez counted among its population 1,000 braceros who had not managed to secure work and found themselves stranded in the city. Notified of the situation, the federal government sent funds for their relief and to help them return to their villages and communities. In turn, the governor of Chihuahua, Enrique Creel, offered them work in the state's mines and helped to repatriate 100 to 150 braceros daily, at a cost of more than 8,000 pesos (González Navarro 1954, 263–64, 278; Martínez 1950, 11).

During the period of the Revolution, calls went out designed to promote the return of Mexican nationals. In 1910, the Ministry of Foreign Relations (Secretaría de Relaciones Exteriores, SRE) sent a circular to Mexican consuls in the United States spelling out that they should offer assistance in repatriation only to Mexican nationals who were indigent, for which purpose a small sum of money was allocated. Toward this same end, and to take advantage of their renewed presence in Mexico, Francisco I. Madero submitted a bill to promote the return of Mexican workers who were in the United States (Carreras de Velasco 1974, 44; González Navarro 1954, 263–64).

Later, in 1913, the Ministry of Development sent a circular to the Mexican consulates in the United States explaining that they needed to repatriate Mexican nationals working in that country so the latter could help develop Mexico. According to the ministry, repatriation needed to be undertaken as soon as possible, though the urgency applied only to those migrants with skills that would be advantageous to the nation. Nothing would be gained by hastening the return of workers who lacked such skills. For this reason, preference should be given to those who had accumulated some capital, gained work experience, and possessed intelligence—qualities and conditions Mexico needed for its development—and who also had the will and desire to become small landowners. The ministry proposed to offer them land at low cost, to be financed on easy payment terms, located in "healthy climes," and near railway lines or close to populated areas with buying power. Nonetheless, the government recognized it was not yet in a position to carry out such an undertaking (Carreras de Velasco 1974, 45).

The government presided over by Venustiano Carranza (1917–20) promised very little with regard to repatriating its citizens and tried to get the employers who had brought them to the United States to take responsibility for their return to Mexico. Thus was it set down in Section 26 of Article 123 of the Constitution, not on the basis of action taken by the Carrancista government but as the result of the uneasiness, which had been building since the start of the century, over the question of how migrant workers might be better protected. These worries were expressed by the individuals charged with writing this section of the document, among them José Inocente Lugo, head of the Development Ministry's Labor Department, and Pastor Rouaix, a constituent member of the Congress of Querétero and former minister of development under Carranza (Rouaix 1992, 91, 93, 102; Alanís Enciso 2001a). When the United States decided to intervene in the First World War, the increase in the number of Mexicans who left to find work there was matched by a large number of their compatriots who set off in the opposite direction, departing the United States by crossing the Texas-Tamaulipas border, because they feared they would be drafted into the U.S. Army. The Mexican government arranged their repatriation and, to facilitate their return, opened an immigration office in Ciudad Juárez. The Ministry of Agriculture and Development was also brought into this operation and requested that those returning under this plan be allowed to bring in their personal effects duty free. It also promised to make a study of colonization projects so that the migrants who returned might come back as settlers.[6]

## 1919–1928

The end of the First World War (November 1918), and the return of the U.S. economy to peacetime conditions, led to an economic depression whose results began to be felt in early 1919 and worsened in 1921 and 1922. A campaign to deport Mexican workers soon got under way, with the government of General Álvaro Obregón forced to contend with the return of some 100,000 compatriots. Obregón's administration assisted in the repatriation of more than 50,000 people. It underwrote the expenses incurred by the repatriated in traveling from the border to the place where they lived in Mexico. It deployed special commissions, one of the most notable directed by Eduardo Ruiz, Mexico's consul in Los Angeles and the person charged with overseeing repatriation and evaluating the situation of Mexican nationals in the United States. The government also allocated significant sums to the various aspects of the repatriation project. In addition, it established a Repatriation Department within the SRE.[7] With Obregón's intervention, the government had moved aggressively to provide assistance so that thousands of Mexicans could return to their country. Such support, however, dried up after the urgency of the situation had passed.

Once conditions in the U.S. economy improved and the deportations subsided, the Mexican government's disinclination to take firmer measures to assist the return of its nationals reasserted itself. Indeed, it declared that its hands were tied, that official government action to sponsor and carry out repatriation was impossible, since in its judgment all those who had left the country had done so as free agents, under their own authority, and were therefore responsible for the consequences of that choice. Furthermore, the Ministry of the Interior stated that for economic reasons it was unable to institute any kind of permanent repatriation service. Additionally, rules issued on 20 April 1921 by the Obregón government, pertaining to the colonization law, did not contain any variations on what, in essence, that 1883 law and its regulatory apparatus had established. The migration law still in force in Mexico was that of 1908, and none of its sections said anything about repatriation.[8] In 1923–24, the Ministry of Agriculture and Development received a request from some Mexican nationals who wished to repatriate so they could dedicate themselves to farming. The ministry replied that the country did not as yet have any land set aside and prepared for such settlement (Durón González 1925, 95–149).

In 1926, laws were promulgated that covered colonization and migration, respectively. The migration law did not touch on repatriation, whereas the colonization law did take into account agricultural workers who expressed the desire to repatriate with the intention of taking up farming. Some years later, the 1930 *Ley de migración* contained the general stipulation that "Mexicans abroad will be protected," and, in addition, that their repatriation would be given preference over the immigration of foreigners into the country. To facilitate repatriation, a new government office was established—the Migration Advisory Board.[9] A year later, in 1931, following a request from the Mexican consul in Los Angeles about land that might be available for settlement, the Agriculture and Development Ministry explored the possibility of founding several settlements. All the same, however, it still held that the time was not ripe for mounting an intensive effort in the United States to repatriate Mexicans working there, because there were no suitable lands on which to resettle them.[10]

The section within the Ministry of Foreign Relations that oversaw the provision of protective services and, since mid-1927, interfaced with Mexicans abroad, also included repatriation as part of its remit (SRE 1928b, 27). The ministry proposed to extend special opportunities to those who requested them and sent instructions to customs officials to admit returning migrants back into the country without their having to pay duty on either their personal effects or household items. Nonetheless, only in exceptional cases and on proof of urgent need did the government authorize repatriation on these terms. In all other cases, repatriations organized and managed by the Mexican consuls involved no cost to the country. Rather, they were financed by U.S. welfare groups and organizations, or took place as and when returnees could obtain passage on military vessels or on ships carrying oil that docked in Mexican ports (SRE 1926, 835–36; SRE 1927, 157).

During 1927–28, the SRE's response to requests made to it by various Mexicans who sought repatriation was that its budget did not include funds to pay these costs. At the same time, it announced that it was studying plans for colonization projects and would release information about them in due course. This gesture notwithstanding, an organization called the Cooperative Land Settlement Corporation was formed in Los Angeles in 1927. The SRE entrusted it with establishing settlements in different parts of the country for Mexican migrants residing in the United States. The following year, the corporation revealed that, after scouting out suitable parcels of land in Baja California, it had acquired 404 hectares in a northern district of the state and divided these up into separate lots of 19 hectares each. Little is known, however, about what came out of this scheme or how many people actually returned to take advantage of it (Carreras de Velasco 1974, 53).

Further moves were made on this front in 1928, when the SRE sent a circular to Mexican consuls in the United States informing them of an agreement concerning the repatriation of Mexicans who wished to dedicate themselves to farming (SRE 1928b, 855). The plan was to promote the return of people the consulates believed would be best prepared to farm successfully, but no practical steps were taken on the Mexican side to implement the plan. To those who continued to submit repatriation requests, the ministry responded—as it had before—that it lacked funds to pay the costs of transportation and could not identify any suitable parcels of land. It was also constrained by the absence of specific regulations to facilitate the return of Mexicans from the United States, though by now it had examined ways to do so, in keeping with options available and acceptable to the government (Carreras de Velasco 1974, 54).

During the 1920s, various functionaries and emigration authorities espoused the advisability of realizing a repatriation operation that targeted "the better Mexican elements" resident in the United States, a notion that had been advocated since the start of the century. Anthropologist Manuel Gamio, one of the leading experts on Mexican emigration to the United States in this decade, best distilled the image that persisted in certain circles of Mexican society with respect both to people who emigrated and to their repatriation. He praised the qualities of the migrants and pronounced himself in favor of their return because, in his view, they would be of great service in the development of the country. He believed that they would help educate the Mexican people and would leave their imprint on Mexican culture. In his judgment, the time that migrants spent in the United States had given them useful experience in agriculture and industry. They had learned to use machinery and modern tools and had acquired discipline and good work habits. In addition, Gamio believed, they had made more subtle character strides, rising to a higher level of culture and learning to modulate their temperament and save money. For Gamio, in short, the return of these people boded well for Mexico (Gamio 1930a, 236).

The anthropologist argued that people possessed of such characteristics and practices could help lift the country, bringing it a more abundant life and more productive work, with people coming to one another's aid, as they had done in the United States, through *núcleos progresistas* (centers of progressivism, or of progressive action). Gamio further thought that through a campaign on behalf of the migrants' return, the government, and the Ministry of Public Education (Secretaría de Educación Pública, SEP) in particular, would have the opportunity, at little cost, to diffuse among millions of uneducated Mexicans the kind of all-embracing education that the returned migrants had "stored up." He suggested that a repatriation effort ought to be carried out at low cost, on a small scale, and confined to a selective group of agricultural workers. Gamio's proposals highlighted a viewpoint that had prevailed since the beginning of the century, one that various leaders, such as Francisco Madero, had expressed; namely, that when a repatriation took place, it should be composed of the better element of Mexicans (Gamio 1930a, 236–41; Gamio 1935, 54–73). For all that, however, the government had done precious little to translate rhetoric into reality.

Alfonso Fabila, a militant ethnologist affiliated with the World Workers' House, who at the instigation of Manuel Gamio authored a work on the braceros, *El problema de la emigración de obreros y campesinos*, held a similar opinion—that the government should promote the return of laborers, able mechanics, and agricultural workers, "the better elements" who had developed expertise in fields and industries then unknown in Mexico. He too believed that they would elevate the country's fortunes. Also sharing these views was Gustavo Durón González, a representative of the Ministry of Agriculture and Development (Fabila 1929, 39–43; Durón González 1925, 95–149).

Mexican leaders also worried that repatriation could have negative consequences. Gamio, for example, thought that people who repatriated (Mexican nationals who at some point might elect to return from the United States) could become criminals, bandits, rebellious types, as well as competitors for jobs with Mexican workers who had remained in the country. Moreover, he expressed the opinion that many of the repatriated, having failed to reintegrate successfully, made their way back to the United States and never returned to Mexico. Once reestablished across the border, they proceeded to criticize the repatriation-colonization projects, spreading word about their own experience, which turned other migrants away from returning to the homeland (Gamio 1930a, 238). The Mexican consul in Denver, Quijano Aguilar, maintained that the government's expenditures on repatriation were wasted, since the majority of those repatriated came back to the United States. Furthermore, during their time back in Mexico, they constituted a problem, because they took on work for lower wages, which brought them into conflict with the local population, especially in the states of Sonora and Coahuila (Carreras de Velasco 1974, 48–49). Another critic was Enrique Santibáñez, the Mexican consul in San Antonio. In his opinion, repatriation contributed nothing to the marketplace or to the improvement of national production because his compatriots failed to learn any type of skill that could be useful to Mexico. To the consul's way of thinking, repatriation should move forward only when the country had reached a highly advanced level of organization (Santibáñez 1930, 123–25).


## 1929–1934

As we have seen, during the depths of the Great Depression—from 1929 to 1934—with millions of U.S. citizens thrown out of work, Mexican migrants living in the United States felt its sting in the form of mass deportation. The phenomenon of Mexicans returning to the homeland ceased to be sporadic or simply the object of study and analysis. Instead, the government faced a genuine need to take action and support the repatriation of its nationals. From 1929 until 1933, the sheer number of requests and the conditions underlying and propelling them made it impossible to sift through and select those who returned. The government found itself obliged to render assistance to its citizens at various points on their route of return—starting in the United States, then along the border, then within Mexico itself—by deploying a range of government agencies: the SRE, the consular service, the Ministries of the Interior and of Finance and Public Credit (SHCP), as well as the national railways. Government aid focused on providing transportation and, if possible, locating jobs for those who returned, as well as the formation of committees and the design of projects for establishing settlements (Carreras de Velasco 1974, 66).

Mexican consulates helped facilitate the repatriation of their citizens living in Texas, California, Illinois, Michigan, and other states. They organized the mechanics of the return, supplied needed funds, helped secure free transportation to the border, and, in some cases, furnished information about work prospects in Mexico. From July 1930 to June 1931, the Mexican government, together with committees set up by the consulates and individual Mexicans acting on their own, underwrote the cost of repatriation for 60,207 men and 31,765 women, or 91,972 Mexican nationals in total, the majority of them from Texas and California (Carreras de Velasco 1974, 68–69; McKay 1982, 272–73, 303–4). The corresponding total of people repatriated in the following year—July 1931 to June 1932—was 124,894, or more than one-third higher. In this latter period, the government's outlay for food relief alone was 73,404 pesos.

In response to the crisis, the railway lines established a special fee structure on the border, collected donations, and provided some passages free of charge. To ease the burdens of travel, the Customs Administration, a unit of the SHCP, exempted returnees from paying duty on personal belongings brought into the country. On the border, public officials as well local relief and welfare organizations set up facilities for feeding and housing the flocks of people returning to Mexico. They also took up collections on their behalf and engaged in other activities to lend assistance to hundreds of Mexican nationals who arrived at the border in a pitiful state.[11]

The government likewise developed plans to render aid within the country itself. With the Interior Ministry, the National Repatriation Committee supervised and supported returnees' readaptation into Mexican society. The ministry drew up a program for establishing agricultural colonies, first in the south of the country, then later in the north, the effect of which was that repatriation came to be seen as a form of self-settlement. There was discussion about establishing colonies in the states of Guerrero, Sonora, Sinaloa, Chihuahua, Baja California, Coahuila, Veracruz, and Oaxaca. At the end of 1932, the settlement plans began to take shape when two colonies were organized (Carreras de Velasco 1974, 121; Hoffman 1974, 139–43).

The first colony, designated Number 1, was established in El Coloso, located near Acapulco, and had a modest beginning. At the start of December 1932, a group of around twenty Mexicans arrived from Detroit to settle in it. Little is known about the particulars, but the record indicates that the majority of this small group soon abandoned the colony. Land in the area of the municipality of Pinotepa Nacional, in Oaxaca, was also selected by the government as a site on which to resettle Mexican nationals coming back from the United States. Accordingly, in April 1933, the move of 362 people to this settlement, designated colony Number 2, got off the ground. Initially, the situation seemed very promising, since the colony received financing and agricultural machinery from the Ministry of Agriculture and managed to install water pumps for irrigation during drought. However, the hostile environment, a coastal climate to which they were not accustomed, sicknesses, and bad planning all conspired to force the colonists to leave. By February 1934, only eight remained (Hoffman 1974, 140–41).

Those who returned to establish settlements in places suggested by the government or purely on their own initiative had no more luck than the people who settled in El Coloso and Pinotepa Nacional. In 1933 a large group established settlements on lands in Juárez Municipality (in the state of Coahuila) and Lampazos (in Nuevo León), where the Don Martín dam and reservoir are located. The latter colony was given the name Ciudad Anáhuac. The success that it enjoyed in the first year convinced some observers at the time that, while colonization in the tropical zone (Pinotepa) had failed, it would succeed in desert areas when accompanied by irrigation systems. Subsequently, however, Ciudad Anáhuac became impoverished and little by little was abandoned. During Lázaro Cárdenas's administration those who remained in the settlement were moved to Matamoros, Tamaulipas, to join forces and work with other repatriated nationals (Carreras de Velasco 1974, 123–24; McKay 1982, 282–84).

Prior to 1934, colonization projects populated by Mexican nationals returning from the United States failed for a variety of reasons, including bad planning and poor organization, hastily arranged returns, the quality and conditions of the land, and the settlers' limited experience in agriculture. The Pinotepa colony was emblematic of these unsuccessful projects, failing for all of the above reasons. Furthermore, from a comparative perspective, these colonies attracted a small number of people. According to a study conducted in 1934, only 5 percent of those who returned to Mexico joined these projects; 80 percent returned to the communities in which their relatives and friends lived, and 15 percent made their way to a city. In general, returnees adjusted quite rapidly to life in their communities, although for some things went badly. The impact of a strange environment—something that above all affected the children born in the United States to Mexican parents—and the difficulties and setbacks that returnees faced in Mexico (insecurity, violence, unemployment, meager resources, etc.) impelled some of them to return to the United States (Gilbert 1934, 140; Hoffman 1974, 80, 91, 148–51; Carreras de Velasco 1974, 141; McKay 1982, 133–36, 145).

From 1929 to 1934 the governments of generals Pascual Ortiz Rubio (1929–32) and Abelardo Rodríguez (1932–34) had to extend help to hundreds of Mexican nationals so they could make their way back to Mexico. This return flow of migrants focused the government's attention on repatriation and spurred it to consider repatriation as integral to migration policy. The *Plan sexenal* (six-year plan)—or political platform that in 1933 the *jefe máximo* (supreme leader) Plutarco Elías Calles ordered President Rodríguez to draw up to solve the country's problems—highlighted that a repatriation policy had been put into effect "so that the reincorporation of our emigrants is carried out under favorable and workable conditions" (PNR 1934, 73). The plan devoted a section to proposals having to do with the population of the country, including repatriation.

Andrés Landa y Piña, chief of the Interior Ministry's Migration Department, authored a tract titled *La política demográfica estatuida en el Plan sexenal* (Demographic Policy as Established in the Six-Year Plan), in which he laid down the policy lines that the government intended to put into practice over the following six years as concerned population issues in general and repatriation in particular (Landa y Piña 1935, 6; Landa y Piña 1930). Like Gilberto Loyo, a preeminent demographer who helped craft population policies during the 1930s (Loyo 1931, 27; Loyo 1935, xiv, 29–30, 369–70, 375–76, 385, 439, 446–47, 456), Landa y Piña thought that Mexico required a population sufficient and adequate to the task of creating a state of well-being for the nation as a whole. To this end, he called for the return of its "absent sons" to confront problems and reinforce productive activities.

The Migration Department chief, in a clear allusion to the problem created by migrant workers, proposed two specific remedies: halting the departure of braceros and promoting their repatriation. With respect to the latter, he believed that action needed to be taken on five fronts: (1) organizing a special repatriation service that, in combination with the consular service, could encourage and facilitate the return of compatriots and, at the same time, take charge of their distribution across and readaptation to the country; (2) tackling and solving the ensuing unemployment problem by sending the repatriated to agriculturally productive areas of the countryside or to centers of population where they could find work; (3) establishing agricultural colonies in suitable areas, taking into account the geographic situation, the fertility of the soil, and the nature of the climate, with preference given to areas as yet not heavily settled but close to centers of population, to help in the reincorporation of the recently arrived and in the assimilation of their knowledge and skills by native, local inhabitants; (4) formulating a technical plan to prepare land that could be granted to repatriated people; and (5) setting up a special fund devoted to the promotion and development of agricultural colonies for the repatriated (PNR 1934, 57–58).

Simply put, Landa y Piña espoused the idea that repatriation could be carried out by placing people, according to a systematic, accommodative plan, in agricultural or industrial colonies. Moreover, he believed that return to Mexico should be promoted only in cases that warranted it and that it should apply to special groups, those with farming experience in particular. In other words, the return of Mexican nationals needed, first and foremost, to be selective (Landa y Piña 1935, 14). As with other elements of the Six-Year Plan, the guidelines set forth as measures to deal with the return of migrants were general in nature, with few specific mandates, and they lacked any reference to precisely how the proposed objectives were to be achieved. The thinking behind the plan and its approach also revived the bias that had existed since the beginning of the twentieth century to favor a repatriation that would be small in scale, tightly organized, and targeted to agricultural workers. For the proponents of the plan, the purpose of repatriation was, ideally, to support the country's development, raise the level of production, and help drive up the population base.

During the first three decades of the twentieth century, the flow of migrants back to Mexico that went hand in hand with their emigration attracted the attention of the country's political leaders. In turn, leaders regularly displayed interest in the matter and committed themselves to support the return of those who had left to work in the United States. Their commitment was motivated by the idea that these migrants, or a certain class of these migrants, had absorbed knowledge, a level of technical expertise, and disciplined work habits abroad that could be used to advantage in Mexico, or— put more optimistically—could be exploited and become a fount of progress for the country. Yet, during times when the flow of migrants coming back slowed, few measures were actually taken to support a more systematic return. During this three-decade period, the legislation enacted on colonization and demographic matters did not set any firm, clear line. If it is true that on some occasions a policy on repatriation was thought about and deliberated in conjunction with a policy on colonization, it is also true that no uniform policy was ever clearly defined, and that no established ruling ever undergirded the repatriations that were carried out.

The measures taken by government authorities centered on promoting studies of and schemes for colonization. The objectives behind this effort were several: to analyze the conditions of different sites on which agricultural settlements could be founded in a gradual, organized way and to finance, in exceptional cases, the return of indigent migrants by paying their railway passage from the border so they could make their way back to their home communities, while permitting them as well to bring personal effects back in duty free. What prevailed above all, however, was the idea of instituting the organized repatriation of small groups of agricultural workers and farmhands who would contribute to the country's development. Nonetheless, little was actually done to bring this ambitious idea to fruition. No budget was allocated for it, nor were areas of land prepared for these would-be settlements of farmers. What was set forth on paper did not take concrete form.

Political leaders after the Revolution also opposed promoting a repatriation movement out of fear of the social and economic effects it could have on the country, especially in towns and communities located near the U.S.-Mexico border. As reasons for not supporting repatriation, they specifically cited the economic conditions prevailing in the country and the state of the national treasury. In addition, an organized, large-scale return of migrants was viewed as a threat to workers who had not left the country. It would create competition for existing jobs, which in turn would spark tension and social conflict. Moreover, since those who had left the country had done so at their own risk, it was only logical that they should bear the consequences of their decision.

Ultimately, the most decisive and pronounced official actions with respect to repatriation came about when U.S. immigration authorities and labor leaders carried out mass deportations of Mexicans as a result of the recessions that battered the world economy (1908–9, 1920–23, and 1929–32). In these instances, Mexico's political leaders did react, finding themselves forced to take measures with no time for advance planning. As events unfolded, they helped their compatriots return. It was only in these times of crisis that official government action was so pointed; the situation that obtained in the second half of the 1930s was fundamentally different, since the conditions surrounding the Mexican community in the United States had changed from those that had prevailed during the depths of the Great Depression (1929–34).

## CHAPTER TWO

# The Mexican Community in the United States, 1933–1939

After 1933, the worst years of the Great Depression were over, and the social and economic conditions that impelled the departure of thousands of Mexicans from the United States, together with the children born to them there, began slowly to change. This altered situation was due, on the one hand, to the assistance the Mexican migrant population received from work programs and from relief and charitable organizations, which lessened the incentive for local governments to drive them out of the country; on the other, it resulted from the social solidarity, labor situation, and growing organizational strength of the Mexican community, which opened up for its members the possibility of remaining in the United States and lessened their interest in leaving it.

## The United States, 1933–1939

Beginning in 1933, in an effort to overcome the economic depression, President Franklin D. Roosevelt (1933–45) launched the set of reforms known as the New Deal. The objective of this reform program, which enjoyed partial success, was to provide employment to thousands of individuals and extend relief and assistance to the indigent. In all, the New Deal led to the enactment of fifteen key laws bearing on currency and financial matters; agriculture, industry, and work; and transport and social welfare. It also resulted in the creation of numerous civil agencies and offices to oversee and guide crucial aspects of the national economy (Brinkley 1991, 10–50). In 1934, only a year after Roosevelt took office, business activity had gone up by 20 percent and the unemployment rate had gone down by the same percentage. In turn, the precarious situation and hard circumstances of many were at least temporarily alleviated. The National Recovery Administration enlisted and obtained the cooperation of more than 600 companies, through which some 2 million jobs were created.

Support for Roosevelt's New Deal, however, was hardly universal, and as the second half of the 1930s began, the president was concerned over growing opposition to his reforms from the business community. The U.S. Supreme Court appeared poised to dismantle Roosevelt's reform program. Moreover, the National Industrial Recovery Act (NIRA, 1933), which authorized the president to regulate industry, had not yielded its expected results, and many companies and businesses steadfastly resisted its application. It had not managed to stop a rise in prices, which then reinforced a downward trend in consumption and, correspondingly, in levels of both work and production (Hawley 1966, 19–146; Nevins and Steele Commager 1994, 416).

The demand for labor derived less from a renewed flourishing of business and commerce than from a reduction in piecework and day labor and a prohibition against child labor. In addition, since they established and administrated work codes, it was businessmen and company executives who controlled the space for production or augmented and broadened the power they already wielded. In 1934, not only did the NIRA enter a death spiral, disappearing the following year, but so did the Public Works Administration (PWA), which the Roosevelt administration had created to boost the number of jobs through a broad program of investment in public works that would lift both industrial production and consumer purchasing power (Brinkley 1996, 558–59; Hawley 1966, 100–146).

Further court decisions in the last months of 1934 put an end to the federal government's remaining projects with respect to business and industry. By the beginning of the following year, Roosevelt's reforms seemed to have exhausted their possibilities. Industrial production had declined; income from agricultural activity was half of what it had been in 1929, and more than 10 million people still found themselves out of work. Anxious to find a new opening, the president launched the Second New Deal, with the ambitious goal of providing employment to millions of Americans and improving their living standards. To this end, a major new agency was created, the Civil Works Administration (CWA), which carried out an emergency program and employed 4 million people in the construction and maintenance of roads, water works, airports, schools, parks, and recreational facilities and sports fields. Within a short span of time, the CWA helped to create 191,000 jobs in Texas alone and, by January 1935, had employed—across the country—239,264 people in the delivery of social relief and assistance (Brinkley 1991, 152–53; Morison et al. 1993, 739–40; McKay 1982, 233–38).

In April 1935, Congress passed the Emergency Relief Appropriation Act, which authorized the president to undertake massive public works programs.

Another agency created at this time—a successor, in effect, to the PWA—was the Works Progress Administration (WPA), which in the years following became the primary administrative vehicle for channeling federal aid. Between 1936 and 1943, 8.5 million unemployed people were placed on the federal payroll, working on a total of 1.4 million projects. Among other things, this new workforce constructed and repaired thousands of miles of highways, roads, streets, and bridges as well as a multitude of public buildings, schools, hospitals, parks, and some airports. In addition, other offices were established to aid destitute and needy families from rural areas, to deploy people to work in conserving and protecting wilderness areas and federal lands, and in giving employment to youth and younger workers (Suárez and Parra 1991, 197–98).

Roosevelt's energetic reforms won public support. Nonetheless, during his second term (1936–40), the Second New Deal suffered its most severe economic blow. A recession that struck the economy from 1937 to 1939 exacted a high political price. As he began his second term, Roosevelt was worried about the growing national debt, fearful that the disaster of 1929 might be repeated, and convinced that the problems wrought by the Depression had been overcome. He thus drastically cut the budget for a series of federal programs, including the one administered by the WPA. Between January and August 1937, this office reduced the number of workers on its payroll from 3 million to 1.5 million. The president also ordered the country's Federal Reserve System to increase the capital on deposit that member banks were required to maintain (May 1981, 95; Morison et al. 1993, 739). The recession was an outgrowth of these actions.

Among the recession's effects was a contraction of credit, a fall in the stock market, a drop in industrial production, and a radical increase in the number of unemployed, from 7.7 million in 1936 to 10.4 million in 1937. In a matter of several months, consumers' purchasing power also shrank. It was the abrupt end of four years of partial recovery. In reaction to this reversal, Roosevelt tilted back toward large-scale public expenditures and systematic debt financing. Congress, meanwhile, passed the final reforms of the New Deal. It created the Farm Security Administration, which extended small loans to tenant farmers and sharecroppers who had been forced off their land, so they could acquire or improve their property. This agency also regulated conditions affecting work and workers' housing and set up a special fund to provide relief to small-scale farmers who found themselves in emergency situations (Brinkley 1991, 167; Brinkley 1996, 566). These initiatives were complemented by two important laws, both enacted in 1938: the Agricultural Adjustment Act and the Fair Labor Standards Act.

Although the recovery program that Roosevelt had promoted since 1933 encountered strong opposition, it nevertheless helped attenuate the problems and poverty that resulted from the Depression. In this context of partial recovery, the Mexican community in the United States faced two situations. Some within this community managed to secure benefits that allowed them to sustain themselves. Yet policies on work and social assistance that privileged the native-born over the foreign population brought high levels of unemployment and indigence in the Mexican community, whose members were routinely subject to deportation and strict enforcement of the migration laws then in force.

## U.S. Work and Welfare Policy toward Mexicans

After 1933, state governments as well as the federal government promoted a wide-ranging campaign to restrict the hiring of foreigners. Relief and charitable organizations targeted their assistance to U.S. citizens and worked aggressively to exclude foreign residents from any help. At the same time, this policy made it possible for some of the children born in the United States to Mexican parents, or those who had become naturalized citizens, to obtain work and assistance from relief organizations so they could sustain themselves and remain in the country.

## Labor Policy

From 1933 to 1940, the PWA, CWA, and WPA all pursued a policy of employing U.S. citizens and of not employing foreign residents. In 1935 and 1936, the same policy was followed by Lawrence Westbrook, CWA director in Texas; by officials of the Farm Labor Bureau; by authorities in California, Louisiana, New Mexico, Texas, and Arizona; and by industrial firms. In Texas, the state government denied employment to hundreds of Mexicans in road construction and maintenance as well as other public works projects. Likewise, in the majority of Texas's communities, similar strategies were used to exclude Mexicans from participating in any federal employment projects.[1]

The call to intensify restrictions on foreign residents' employment so that only U.S. nationals could obtain work gained force in 1937. In that year, a detailed review of the WPA's employment records led to the reduction in the number of its foreign workers to 72,000. The agency sent a notice to foreign workers to inform them that they would lose their jobs if they did not submit papers for naturalization. To obtain such status, they were required to produce either a birth certificate or documents verifying their citizenship.

Faced with this demand, various Mexicans living in Los Angeles declared their intention to become U.S. citizens and, more than likely in expedited fashion, submitted papers requesting their naturalization. In this way, they not only secured permanent residence in the United States but also gained assurance that they would qualify for federal work programs.[2]

In 1938, having survived the economic reversal, 800 Los Angeles seamstresses of Mexican origin were promptly relieved of their jobs by the local WPA office. Similarly, after a prolonged strike, nut producers in Texas indicated that they were ready to have work start again, but only with white workers, not Mexicans. The big beetroot companies, the nut growers, the packing businesses, and the rope factories, all of whom depended in large measure on cheap Mexican labor, also lined up behind a policy of excluding foreign workers and hiring only U.S. nationals.[3]

As a general rule, labor policy in the United States excluded the hiring of foreigners but at the same time allowed various noncitizens to receive help in preparing and submitting naturalization papers, and children born in the United States to foreigners were of course not among the excluded. In 1935, many in the latter category were employed in repairing streets and roads in California. In addition, the California Relief Administration and the WPA employed some 75,000 people in agricultural fields and processing plants.[4]

In 1936, according to a study by Jesús M. González, a Mexican residing in the United States, around 100,000 of his compatriots, among them various U.S. citizens of Mexican descent, lived at the expense of WPA programs. They comprised less than 10 percent of the total number of people who received assistance in the United States. They earned thirty dollars a month. In 1937, an additional number obtained employment through the Central Labor Councils established in such places as Los Angeles and Stockton, California. The following year, the WPA provided work for some 350 people in the construction of pavements and sidewalks. Although the CWA and later the WPA gave preference to U.S. citizens, the two agencies still had a positive effect on the Mexican community, since they eased the burden carried by social assistance and charitable organizations and helped avert the continued promotion of mass deportations.[5]

## Public Relief and Assistance

Relief and assistance organizations put forward plans and issued constant calls to deny public aid to those who did not hold U.S. citizenship. For example, in 1934 and 1936, Los Angeles County authorities announced the withdrawal of assistance to Mexican families who lived in their jurisdiction and were unemployed. Similarly, Marvin T. Brandford, administrator of the public assistance program in San Antonio, Texas, sought not only to have aid to such families withheld but also to have them deported. The Relief and Rehabilitation Committee of Bexar County, which includes the city of San Antonio, identified illegal foreign residents in its jurisdiction with the twin purpose of removing them from relief rolls and expelling them from the country.[6]

In California, Michigan, Illinois, and elsewhere in Texas as well as in other places, relief and social assistance officials strove to deny such aid to foreign residents living in their midst. Such exertions notwithstanding, in Los Angeles, no fewer than 15 percent of the city's Mexican residents, including children born to them there, or nearly 4,000 families, were receiving aid from the municipal government. According to the study by Jesús González, the federal government spent approximately $100,000 a day on relief to unemployed Mexicans—clearly an inflated amount, because the figure itself is simply too high and assisting this group was not a priority for Washington—exclusive of additional outlays for hospitals, clinics, and other aid to the sick. In San Antonio, Brandford—despite his move to deny assistance to the city's population of Mexican nationals—did in fact provide aid to various people in this community who were unemployed. The lists of people of Mexican origin in the San Antonio area who received relief include the names of 42,514 individuals.[7] There the U.S. government came to the aid of the unemployed by providing some cash assistance. This support was complemented by the work of charitable organizations that distributed clothing, food, and medicine to those in need. A great many Mexicans depended for their subsistence on aid supplied by county-level charitable and social assistance organizations.[8]

At the beginning of 1937, the number of unemployed heads of household in California rose to 35,000. Although many in this group were of Mexican origin, relief organizations nonetheless agreed to come to their aid. Still others who were unemployed received provisions as well as money to pay their rent and utilities. In 1938, many of the seamstresses in Los Angeles who had been dismissed from their jobs by the WPA received provisions from the county while they looked for new work. The following year, Gordon L. McDonough, a Los Angeles County supervisor, announced that, of the general unemployed population, 2,065 people had benefited from county assistance.[9]

During the second half of the 1930s, social assistance organizations in various states, among them California, Texas, and Illinois, helped hundreds of people who were either born in the United States to Mexican parents or who, after living in the country for a period of years, had put down strong roots in their respective communities. Moreover, the Mexican community in the

United States experienced a major transformation during the 1930s, going from being composed primarily of people born in Mexico to a majority born in the United States. The rootedness of Mexican families in this country, the cessation of emigration by Mexican workers to the United States as a result of the Great Depression, and the return of thousands of migrants to the home country meant that over the 1930s and 1940s most people of Mexican descent in the United States came to be second-generation. In Los Angeles, for example, the number of Mexican residents born in Mexico declined from 56,304 in 1930 to 38,040 in 1940, whereas the figure for people born in the United States to Mexican migrants rose dramatically, from 45 to 65 percent of the total during the same period (Sánchez 1993, 228).

Simultaneously, the effort by U.S. authorities to remove people of Mexican origin from the country became less coercive. Since thousands had already been deported during the first half of the 1930s—in Arizona, California, and Texas the population of Mexican origin shrank by almost 50 percent from 1930 to 1940 (see table 2.1)—and because others had obtained work through official programs or in some other way, the number of people requesting assistance had declined correspondingly. For these reasons, the pressures to expel elements of the Mexican population lessened greatly, and local charitable organizations received fewer appeals for help.

Not only had the number of indigent Mexican nationals who needed assistance declined, but local charitable groups and relief organizations were in a better position to extend aid because of the support they received through the government's various recovery programs. In addition, the burden they bore to provide assistance to unemployed and indigent U.S. citizens had also been lightened.

As noted earlier, while various official agencies such as the CWA and, later, the WPA gave preference to U.S. citizens, their activities nonetheless affected the Mexican community positively. The support they received from presidential initiatives lessened the burden on relief and social assistance organizations. Furthermore, their work acted as a check on the massive deportations promoted so enthusiastically during the early 1930s and which, until then, U.S. authorities had relied on to remove hundreds of foreigners from the country. Consequently, many people of Mexican origin were able to avoid being deported to Mexico.

## Deportations and Expulsions

During the second half of the 1930s, U.S. immigration, labor, and relief and social assistance authorities kept up a constant drumbeat of threats to continue mass deportations of people seen as a public burden or of foreigners who

TABLE 2.1 Mexican-origin population in the United States, 1930–1940

| STATE | 1930 | 1940 |
| --- | --- | --- |
| Arizona | 47,855 | 24,902 |
| California | 191,346 | 134,312 |
| New Mexico | 15,983 | 8,875 |
| Texas | 262,672 | 159,266 |

SOURCE: Lorey 1993, 40.

lacked documents making them legal residents (Hoffman 1974, 52–53; 107). In general, however, the deportations promoted and carried out at the beginning of the decade were significantly down-scaled.

The reports on deportations taking place in 1935 are quite limited, though it is known that Los Angeles authorities deported 3,317 people. In Texas, at the same time that the Bexar County Relief and Rehabilitation Committee—working with the U.S. Immigration and Naturalization Service (INS)—identified foreign illegals in order to dismiss them from their jobs, it also took measures to have them expelled from the country.[10] Among the civil authorities who made constant threats to pursue deportation against noncitizens were Marvin Brandford, the chief of public assistance in San Antonio, and Rex Thomson, a member of the Los Angeles County Board of Supervisors.[11]

Further action was taken on this front in 1936, when a large group of families was expelled. These families made their way back into Mexico principally through Nuevo Laredo and Ciudad Juárez, the two border cities that received the largest flow of migrants returning from the Pacific Coast and southwestern states of California, Arizona, New Mexico, Colorado, Texas, and Oregon. After reentering the country, the aim of these families was to return to their home communities and states or, in some cases, to make their way to Mexico City. In July 1936, 1,129 people returned to Mexico; the corresponding figure for the following month was 782. In the next year, between August and September, 97 deportees arrived in Nuevo Laredo.[12]

At the beginning of 1937, under an agreement drafted by Grover C. Wilmoth, a district director of the INS in Texas, 550 Mexicans were deported through El Paso. Spokesmen for the Ciudad Juárez Chamber of Commerce asserted that throngs of deportees had become a permanent presence in the city. From the early months of the year to 24 August, 1,700 people had arrived in Ciudad Juárez, with more following all the time. Based on the statistics it gathered, the Ministry of the Interior reported that from September 1936 to August 1937, 1,920 Mexicans were deported from different parts of the world, the majority of them from the United States.[13]

By mid-November 1937, the effects of the economic downturn had begun to be felt. One hundred Mexicans were deported from California and Kansas through Ciudad Juárez. The group included a large number of Mexicans who were U.S. citizens—the children of Mexican parents living in the United States. At the end of December, an additional 250 people who had been living in Texas, Arizona, New Mexico, California, and Colorado were deported. During all of 1937, U.S. authorities deported a total of 8,829 people, of whom more than half, or 4,928, were Mexicans, with the remainder being either Canadians or Europeans.[14]

The highest number of deportations in the second half of the decade was registered in 1938, as the problems afflicting the U.S. economy worsened. A stream of convoys carrying the expelled kept flowing to the border. In May, a number of deportees arrived in Ciudad Juárez from Arizona, New Mexico, Texas, and California, followed at the start of the next month by a group of 100 people.[15]

This trend continued, as the number of returnees increased during the second half of the year. In July, 200 people reached Ciudad Juárez, but this was only a trickle compared to the approximately 3,000 who were deported in October through El Paso and the 4,000 who arrived at the border during that month and in November, after being expelled from Los Angeles County.[16] Although the number of people deported had shot up in 1938, it did not reach the levels attained before 1933. Moreover, a countermessage was sometimes also heard. At the start of 1939, for example, Gordon McDonough, a Los Angeles County supervisor, stated that Mexicans would not be obliged to return to their country. In general, the return flow to Mexico caused by the deportations enforced by U.S. authorities lessened significantly after Roosevelt assumed the presidency. At the same time, however, many in the United States wanted to continue the deportations and place tight controls on the influx of foreigners.

## U.S. Immigration Laws and Mexican Nationals

During the second half of the 1930s, U.S. immigration authorities adopted new policies and developed new programs designed to contain both the legal and the clandestine entrance of foreign nationals into the United States. In addition, the existing immigration laws were strictly enforced, above all along the border, to prevent people from entering the country without the necessary papers and expel those who had managed to enter.

At the beginning of 1936, the *Los Angeles Law Journal* published a ruling issued by the U.S. Federal Court in Buffalo, ordering that "immigrant Mexican Indians" no longer be permitted to enter California. The intention behind the court's decision was to curb the entrance of foreigners into the country, in particular people of certain ethnicities and, at the same time, to restrict immigration in general by making it more selective. For its part, the INS approved a regulation stipulating that every foreigner who had entered the country before June 1921 and who did not have documents certifying legal residence could obtain them, but also ordering that those who had entered the country after that date, without legal permission, would be sentenced to a year and a half of forced labor and subsequently deported. In a court in Brownsville, Texas, a Mexican, José Flores, became the first foreign resident found guilty of having violated this regulation, for which he spent the requisite time in a federal prison in Texas. A year later, in 1937, U.S. immigration authorities ratified the new regulation. In Washington, meanwhile, legislation was promoted that would prohibit Mexican workers from crossing into the United States. The U.S. House of Representatives sent a companion initiative to the Senate that prohibited all Mexicans and Canadians from entering the United States to work if they lived in one of the border states or provinces.[17]

During this same period, U.S. authorities in both El Paso and Brownsville chose to apply the immigration laws with particular care. Federal immigration agents were particularly severe with people who had crossed into the country in violation of the relevant laws. At the end of 1937, the federal prison at La Tuna, near El Paso, was filled with Mexicans serving sentences of two to six months for having violated the immigration laws or for having committed crimes of "little moment." The commissioner of the INS, Mary Ward, headed up this aggressive enforcement effort. Ward traveled to El Paso to examine both the problem posed by Mexicans who crossed the border illegally and that surrounding the contraband trade in "heroic drugs." Accompanied by INS border patrolmen, she made several visits to the line separating the two countries, "except that instead of carrying a powder compact with a mirror and rouge, she wore two six-shooters around her waist and hefted a 30–30 rifle."[18] Sometime later, the chairman of the Committee on Immigration in the U.S. House of Representatives, Samuel Dickstein, advocated reinforcing the patrols that were carried out along the border with Mexico.[19]

U.S. immigration authorities also acted to stop the smugglers of migrants. Two such people, Salvador Rojas and Ernesto Muñoz, had opened a job placement agency in El Paso without securing the necessary license from local authorities. They were rounding up some of their compatriots and sending them

TABLE 2.2 Legal immigration of Mexicans to the
United States, 1935–1940

| YEAR | NO. OF IMMIGRANTS |
| --- | --- |
| 1935 | 1,560 |
| 1936 | 1,716 |
| 1937 | 2,347 |
| 1938 | 2,502 |
| 1939 | 2,640 |
| 1940 | 2,313 |

SOURCE: Lorey 1993, 104.

to Michigan to work in the beet fields. The two were identified and taken into
custody. They were accused and convicted of having violated the country's immigration laws and, under the terms of the Federal Penal Code of the United
States, were sentenced to a minimum of three years in prison.[20] The authorities
also took a hard line toward those who had come into the United States legally,
closely scrutinizing their documents to ensure that all requirements for admission and residency had been fully met. The U.S. consul in Matamoros adhered
carefully to the criteria. He received numerous requests for visas from people
who wished to return to the United States but refused to grant them (or a great
many of them) because these applicants did not satisfy the literacy requirements stipulated under the law and because, in his view—and this matter concerned him more—they stood a good chance of winding up on the public dole.[21]

In mid-1937, Frances Perkins, the U.S. secretary of labor, reported that Mexican
immigration had been "totally" blocked and, as such, no longer constituted a
problem for the country. In reality, it had diminished in volume for several reasons, among them the intense campaign against the influx of immigrants and
the restrictive measures applied to allowing in workers of all nationalities, coupled with the severe enforcement of current immigration laws. Furthermore,
the low demand for cheap labor had caused the market for smuggling workers
largely to dry up. By and large, Mexican immigration to the United States slowed
considerably during the second half of the 1930s (see table 2.2).

## The Work and Social Situation of People of
## Mexican Origin in the United States

After 1933, the work and social situation of many Mexicans in the United
States, as well as the children born to them there, helped many of them

remain in the country. Their work conditions varied. While some were unemployed, others found casual employment and odd jobs. A small number gained a better position as employees in one industry or another, thereby reaping the benefits of a stable wage and a certain degree of job security.

## The Labor and Employment Situation

In mid-1930s, Francisco Urbina, general secretary of the North American Federation of Mexican Workers, reported that a number of his compatriots in the United States found themselves unemployed and without any way to earn a living. They struggled desperately, walking the streets and making the rounds of markets and hotels, poking in garbage bins for scraps of food to eat. Antonio Nava, a member of the Mexican federal legislature, traveled through the southern United States to examine the conditions in which his compatriots were living. In Los Angeles, he noted that many Mexicans were unemployed and that in the more marginal neighborhoods people lived in extreme poverty. In the communities of Big Spring and El Monte, some were entirely indigent.[22] Others, in contrast, were living a very comfortable life.

There were various industries in the United States in which Mexicans born in the United States, to migrant parents, could find work. The majority of these employers, however, offered only temporary jobs. These descendants of Mexican migrants were hired in California to work in the textile, furniture, construction, carpentry, and canning industries, though again on a temporary basis only and for very low wages (Castillo and Ríos Bustamante 1990, 220–24). Many within this same population found work in identical sectors in Texas, Indiana, and Michigan, where low wages, seasonal employment, and few work incentives, such as bonuses, were again the order of the day. The packing plants were a source of stable but unpleasant jobs. At the same time, requests for Mexican workers were constantly forthcoming, with many who responded then hired, by large-scale agricultural interests as well as by businessmen in the Lower Rio Grande Valley, Brownsville, and Harlingen, Texas; or through the chambers of commerce in Arizona and Louisiana; or by different railroad companies in Salt Lake City and Montana.[23]

Thus various places in the United States generated a demand for cheap foreign labor, labor that was exploited and directed to the least appealing work in agriculture and other sectors. It was thanks to this type of employment, however, that some people managed, if only sporadically, to locate jobs. The wages may have been low, but they were the lifeline that enabled these people to survive (McKay 1982, 225–26).

According to estimates by the Department of Statistics of the Los Angeles municipal government and by the U.S. Bureau of Statistics, the work situation for the descendants of Mexican migrants followed a different course in that city.[24] While many of them were poor, a small group raised their standard of living upon securing a job, or profession, or business that afforded them financial security. Still others lived in comfortable homes, with gardens, located in districts that supplied a full range of services. Moreover, as happened in Texas, many owned small truck farms or had a certain amount of money to invest. During the 1930s, it was not unusual for people of Mexican origin in Los Angeles to acquire property. Indeed, according to a census in 1933, the amount of total property in the hands of this subcommunity in Los Angeles reached 18 percent.[25]

In the mid-1930s, some Los Angeles families of Mexican ancestry were able to live on a stable income, while others had to subsist the entire year on wages earned over a few months. Rope factories employed some 15,890 workers continually. Of this workforce, 75 percent was composed of women of Mexican origin. Some found their way into the furniture industry, where, in general, the companies were small and managed to carry on with a workforce of around twenty-five employees (Castillo and Ríos Bustamante 1990, 227–28).

## The Social Situation

The roots that families of Mexican origin had put down in the United States, their connections with the community in which they lived and their familiarity with the dominant culture, along with the struggle they had mounted so that their rights as U.S. citizens were recognized, were, collectively, determining factors enabling a good part of this community to remain in the country.

The large-scale departure of thousands of people of Mexican origin that had taken place at the beginning of the 1930s left its mark on the Mexican community in the United States, not least in the form of deep changes in its social fabric. During the second half of the decade, the earlier expulsion of a third of its population brought about an important demographic transition witnessed in various places. In Los Angeles, the descendants of Mexican migrants—primarily second-generation children and adolescents who had been born in the country and held U.S. citizenship—grew in number relative to other segments of the community's population (Sánchez 1993, 224–25).

In the city of Houston, many Mexicans had been resident for more than fifteen years, a pattern repeated in other parts of Texas. Some in this population worked in the agricultural sector and enjoyed a satisfactory standard of living. In addition, they had developed a variety of interests within their respective communities and, outside the circle of their own family ties, had built up friendships and business relationships. Although many of them, in the older generation especially, had not been naturalized, they had nonetheless—in their own ways, through family and community influences and simply by absorbing what was around them—adapted to their environment. Their personal experience formed part of the history of the Mexican American collectivity. Many followed the example of Zeferino Ramírez, leader of the Mexican community in Los Angeles, and elected not to give up their Mexican citizenship to become U.S. citizens. Although he journeyed back to Mexico at the end of the 1930s, Ramírez came to the conclusion that he would never return permanently to his native country. Instead, he wanted to remain in the United States for the remainder of his life, content to see his children, who had been born on U.S. soil, grow to maturity, furnishing them as best he could with the resources that would enable them to prosper (Sánchez 1993, 274). Zeferino's case illustrates two essential, interconnected things: that some Mexicans decided to settle definitively in the United States and, above all, the critical role that their children born in the United States played in this process.

Children under the age of twenty who fell into this category attended school, spoke English, and were opposed to going back to Mexico, among other reasons because to them it was a foreign country where they believed they would face an even more difficult situation.[26] While the Great Depression forced many people to reconsider their residence in the United States, for members of this Mexican American generation, it also created a unique context that affected the construction of their identity and their struggle to obtain a space within U.S. society.

In their quest to forge an identity, these second-generation youth encountered an environment that denied them opportunities, coupled with the oppressive hand of government authorities who promoted their expulsion from the country without consideration for their nationality, treating them as if they were foreigners. For those Mexican Americans who managed to remain in the United States, this period signified a break with the past and left them feeling anxious about the fragility of their position within the larger society. At the same time, the children who had been born to immigrants and grown up and come of age in the United States found that they were capable of exercising their citizenship and their rights, so they fought to be recognized as Americans. One of the advocacy groups that assisted them in this process was the Mexican American Movement (Sánchez 1993, 12–14, 255–56, 274; Romo 1983, 142–48).

Reflecting this sharpened awareness, many younger Mexican Americans started to become more actively involved in organizations and unions. Inspired by the ideas and work of different labor leaders who fought for equal rights and for a share of the space and spoils under the umbrella of New Deal programs and reforms, they took up the fight for recognition of their own civil rights. This assertion allowed them, as constituent members of the working class, to adapt culturally without at the same time having to gain much upward economic mobility (Balderrama and Rodríguez 1995, 28–45; Sánchez 1993, 12).

## Mexican Americans and Their Organizing Activities

The 1920s and 1930s were very fruitful for the unions that formed, especially in the agricultural sector, to advance the cause of Mexican Americans. These unions emerged from conditions produced by the nation's economic depression, the waves of deportations, the drastic reduction in short-term and daywork, and the oversupply of labor. The community of second-generation Mexicans organized collectively to secure economic benefits (Arroyo 1975, 255). As a result, its members gained job security, learned to adapt to prevailing conditions, and fought for their rights.

During the 1920s, efforts to organize Mexican Americans began to boom. In this period, the urban centers in the United States that held large contingents of the Mexican American population, among them Chicago, Los Angeles, San Antonio, and Laredo, grew both in size and in the organization of their social and cultural life. In areas where agricultural production predominated, such as California's Imperial Valley, Mexican Americans also began to build up this stability, which in turn fed and strengthened the solidarity that led to the founding and organization of mutual aid societies. Two pioneering groups of this type were the Benito Juárez Mutual Aid Society, formed in the community of El Centro in 1919, and the Hidalgo Mutual Aid Society, started in the neighboring town of Brawley in 1921. These two societies spearheaded the formation, in 1928, of the Imperial Valley Workers Union (Unión de Trabajadores del Valle Imperial). Two other Mexican American organizations that formed in this period were the umbrella Federation of Unions of Mexican Farmers and Workers (Confederación de Uniones de Campesinos y Obreros Mexicanos) and the Order of Sons of America (La Orden de Hijos de América). The latter, founded in San Antonio in 1921, was the predecessor organization to the League of United Latin American Citizens (LULAC), established in 1928 in Harlingen, Texas (Tirado 1970, 56–57; Nelson Cisneros 1975, 453–61; Nelson Cisneros 1978, 71–74; Gómez-Quiñones and Maciel 1991, 176, 181–91).

In urban areas, like Los Angeles, people of Mexican origin also played an important role in helping organize the unions that joined the Committee (later Congress) of Industrial Organizations (CIO), and they went on to participate in many of its activities. They were also instrumental in helping build two other unions within the CIO, the International Longshoremen's and Warehousemen's Union and the Furniture Workers Union (Arroyo 1975, 277–78).

At the beginning of the 1930s, the American Communist Party became active in the arena, promoting councils for the unemployed and intervening in the growing efforts to organize agricultural and industrial workers. The Party was a catalyst within many union organizations serving working-class members of minority groups. An important result was the organization of Mexican American workers, which took concrete shape in the activities of unions affiliated with an umbrella group, the Trade Union Unity League. Among these were the Cannery and Agricultural Workers Industrial Union; the Workers Alliance; and the International Mining, Engineering, and Foundry Workers, the third group being the successor to the Western Federation of Miners. In the hierarchy of these unions and organizations, U.S.-born descendants of Mexican migrants occupied both low- and high-level positions. Elsewhere, in Texas, workers from both the agricultural sector and service industries organized and joined together. In Laredo, they created the Asociación de Jornaleros, or Journeyman's Association (also referred to as the Agricultural Workers Union). In San Antonio, Mexican Americans who shelled and milled nuts formed two unions: El Nogal (The Pecan Tree) and the Pecan Shellers Union (Trabajadores de la Nuez)—the latter being a company union. Another group, the League of Spanish-Speaking Workers (Liga Obrera de Habla Española), was formed to organize mineworkers in the New Mexico towns of Gallup, Madrid, and Santa Fe (Weber 1972, 319–26; López 1970, 101–2; García 1979, 44–51; Nelson Cisneros 1975, 247–330).

On occasion, Mexican Americans took public stands and demonstrated through the groups and unions that they themselves had organized (the Federation of Unions of Mexican Farmers and Workers, the Order of Sons of America, and LULAC) or through their involvement in national labor groups with a broad multiethnic, multiracial membership, such as the American Federation of Labor (AFL), the CIO, and the United Committee of Agricultural, Packing, and Allied Workers of America (UCAPAWA) (Nelson Cisneros 1978, 71–74).

The participation of the descendants of Mexican migrants in U.S. unions and other organizations founded by the unions created the context in which migrants could forge a new identity and, at the same time, opened a path for them to enter fully into the political arena. This activity and self-assertion gave birth to a new and important organization, the Congress of Spanish-Speaking People of the United States (Congreso de Personas de Habla Hispana de Estados Unidos), whose mission and purpose was to advance the cultural, social, and economic interests of the Mexican American population and to battle and overcome discrimination against it. A local organization also formed in this period, the Los Angeles Federation of Spanish-Speaking Voters (Federación de Votantes de Habla Hispana), perhaps the first group organized by members of a Mexican American community in the United States that was exclusively political in its focus and purpose (Acuña 1976, 236–37; Castillo and Ríos Bustamante 1990, 229–30, 232; Sánchez 1993, 12, 250).

The 1930s were marked by the rise of various unions founded by Mexican Americans to organize collectively to fight for their social well-being and their rights and benefits as workers. These included the Mexican Federation of Laborers and Farmworkers (Mercedes, Texas), the North American Federation of Mexican Workers, the California Federation of Mexican Laborers and Farmworkers Unions, the Mexican Sugarbeet Workers Union (Michigan), the Federation of Mexican Societies (Los Angeles), and the Mexican Community Association. Mexican associations and societies also appeared in the midwestern cities of Chicago, Detroit, Kansas City, and Gary, Indiana. Two other important advocacy and support groups, the Sociedades Mutualistas Mexicanas (Mexican Mutual Aid Societies) and the Congreso de Pueblos de Habla Española (Congress of Spanish-Speaking People, founded in 1938) also rose to the fore at this time. In sum, U.S.-born descendants of Mexican migrants made strenuous efforts to secure their rights both by organizing and participating in labor unions and by claiming a share of the promise offered by New Deal policies and programs (Sánchez 1993, 12; McKay 1982, 275–78).

## Participation in Strikes

Between 1936 and 1938, hundreds of Mexican Americans took part in a great many strikes and, in doing so, gave clear evidence of the strides they had made in organizing themselves and in fighting to improve their position in the labor market and in society more generally. Finding themselves without rights in a hostile environment, they went on strike a number of times, either independently or with the backing of the AFL and the CIO, over the low wages they earned and the work routines imposed by growers who—with the government—violated their human rights and civil liberties, subjecting them to arbitrary deportations and repressive measures (Arroyo 1975, 255).

In 1936 some 10,000 people of Mexican origin who picked and harvested fruit in the orange and lemon groves of Los Angeles and Orange Counties went on strike. Still another 12,000 employed by beet growers declared a general strike in California for an increase in their daily wage. Similarly, 7,000 Mexican American seamstresses in the Los Angeles and Long Beach garment industry began a work stoppage.[27]

The wave of strikes grew during 1937. Among the most important were those carried out by the workers who harvested the lemon groves in Fillmore County, California; by the seamstresses who worked in a total of forty factories and sweatshops in that state; and by workers who picked cotton in the fields of Texas. In that year, approximately 28,000 descendants of Mexican migrants took part in work stoppages. The strikes continued during 1938, including one at the National Packing Company in the port of San Diego, another among that same port's longshoremen, and a third in the fruit groves of Orange County.[28]

One of the key strikes in this period occurred at the beginning of 1939 in the pecan shelling industry in San Antonio, fanning out to other parts of Texas.[29] Led by activist Emma Tenayuca Brooks and supported by the CIO and the UCAPAWA, around 15,000 people took part in this work action. The strike had its origins in the refusal of the Southern Pecan Shelling Company to increase wages. The company took harsh repressive measures against the striking pecan shellers. The labor-management struggle assumed national importance, since nut production in Texas formed one of that state's most important agricultural industries. Ultimately, rather than increase wages, the plant owners opted to use machines for shelling, throwing thousands of people out of work.[30]

Taken together, the strikes—in which the descendants of Mexican migrants predominated—demonstrated the degree of collective effort these people had mustered in demanding improved pay and work conditions, while also giving evidence of their desire and disposition to engage in the struggle to overcome obstacles and better their lives generally. Moreover, the support they received from major national unions and labor organizations bore out how far they had come toward incorporating themselves into the U.S. organized labor movement. In some cases, they won wage increases, while in others they were thwarted, their efforts put down severely, and in still others, they were punished by being deported. This action was taken, for example, against Jesús Pallares because of his labor sympathies and the work he did to organize Mexican Americans born in the United States (Acuña 1976, 243–45). One of the outcomes of such participation, however, was that it helped this group gain a certain degree of job stability, which in turn helped its members remain in the United States and consolidate their position in the country's working class. Despite adverse work conditions and their difficult position vis-à-vis U.S. society as a whole, few Mexican Americans or their Mexican parents showed much interest in emigrating or returning to Mexico and abandoning the United States, because—whatever the obstacles—they had forged a sense of identity that rooted them here.

## People of Mexican Heritage Who Requested Repatriation

In general, relatively few descendants of Mexican nationals in the United States submitted a request to the Mexican government to approve their emigration to Mexico. In the majority of such cases, it emerged that the person making the request would "return" only if the government guaranteed assistance and official support. Among the migrant population, only those who were unemployed or who faced a truly wretched situation wanted to reverse their status and return to Mexico.

Working through an aid agency or simply on their own, various people requested an allocation of land and a source of credit to go with it, so they might return and form agricultural colonies. Two instances of this involved a group of 400 unemployed Mexican agricultural workers and their U.S.-born children living on the outskirts of Houston, as well as a number of individuals in both Texas and Illinois.[31] The leaders of various organizations in California also requested government assistance to repatriate Mexican nationals who either languished unemployed or lived in extremely difficult conditions. These leaders included Estanislao Ortiz, representative of the Club General Lázaro Cárdenas, a workers organization in Los Angeles, and representatives of six other organizations: the Convention of Chambers of Mexican Workers in North America (Convención de las Cámaras de Trabajadores Mexicanos en Norteamérica); the Latin American Chamber of Commerce of the Americas (Cámara de Comercio Latina-Americana de las Américas) in Los Angeles; the Confederation of Chambers of Mexican Workers of North America (Confederación de Cámaras de Trabajadores Mexicanos de Norteamérica); the Confederation of Chambers of Mexican Workers in the United States of the North (Confederación de Cámaras de Trabajadores Mexicanos en Estados Unidos del Norte); the United Chamber of Labor (Cámara Unitaria del Trabajo) of Ciudad Juárez; and the Confederation of Mexican Societies (Confederación de Sociedades Mexicanas) of Los Angeles.

In similar fashion, various people unaffiliated with any organization of this type submitted requests to the Mexican government—either on their own or through a spokesman—for tools, credit, land, and other items they would need so they could return and set up agricultural colonies.[32] They also asked the government to spell out and implement specific measures to bring them back.[33] One such individual was José de Landozequi, a Mexican residing in Los Angeles. He explained, in his request for repatriation, that he was unable to leave the "Estamos Undidos" because he lacked the means to do so. He thus requested the sum of 100 U.S. dollars to cover certain commitments as well as the expenses of his trip, which he promised to repay once he began to work. In addition, he also asked the government to furnish him with a rail pass that would take him from Nogales to Mexico City.[34] Such requests that reached Mexican government ministries from indigents who, pleading urgency, wanted to return and escape a critical situation, were relatively few.

U.S. authorities' less categorical attitude in carrying out mass deportations of Mexicans, and the work situation and social position of the Mexican community in the United States, were such that many who had not left during the depths of the Great Depression remained in the country, and returns to Mexico declined proportionately.

## Official Figures for the Flow of Returnees, 1934–1949

Official figures recorded by Mexican Migration Service authorities reveal a sharp drop in the flow of returnees beginning in 1933. During the previous year, 77,453 people returned to Mexico; a year later, this number had decreased almost by half, to 33,574 (see table 2.3). In 1934, the downward trend continued, and in the following year the government's statistical agency announced that the number of Mexicans returning from the United States was lower than it had been during the first years of the decade, a trend that persisted through 1937.[35]

This trend, reinforced by the significant decline in the number of returnees in 1937, shows that the return flow no longer took the form of a massive displacement of people back to Mexico. That problem had greatly diminished in scope. Nonetheless, the figure rose in 1938 because of the economic downturn, which prompted a revival of deportations. In 1939, there was a further, though slight, uptick due in large measure to a program promoted by the Mexican government that assisted more than 6,000 people to return. In the following year, however, the downward trend reestablished itself. In general, except for the deportations that were carried out during the second half of 1938, the flow of returnees proceeded at a moderate pace between 1933 and 1940.

Furthermore, the thousands who returned to Mexico over this eight-year period were anything but a monolith. On the contrary, their reasons for returning varied considerably. In some cases, individuals or entire families were given no choice. Immigration authorities or welfare agency officials forced them to leave (forced or involuntary repatriation) because they were unemployed and

TABLE 2.3  Mexicans repatriated from the
United States, 1933–1940

| YEAR | NO. REPATRIATED |
| --- | --- |
| 1933 | 33,574 |
| 1934 | 23,934 |
| 1935 | 5,368 |
| 1936 | 11,599 |
| 1937 | 8,037 |
| 1938 | 12,024 |
| 1939 | 15,925 |
| 1940 | 12,536 |
| TOTAL | 132,997 |

SOURCE: Hoffman 1974, 175; Mexico 1940, 23; Secretaría de
Economía Nacional 1941, 20.

viewed as a burden on society and the public purse. In other cases their deportation resulted from a legal hearing, though at times it was purely arbitrary
and occurred without any formal proceeding. On still other occasions people
returned with the help of county governments, with the backing of public
assistance agencies or through private support. Some returned voluntarily
(assisted by the federal government upon being dismissed from their jobs),
and some returned in a planned, organized way thanks to the intercession
of Mexican consular officials and the support extended by a community in
Mexico.

The figures shown in table 2.3 are not broken down into these different
categories nor do they (or can they) denote the various reasons for which
people returned. The action of the federal government is blended in, as is the
will of those who returned independently, on their own. The great majority
of returns were in fact registered as falling under the general rubric of repatriation, that is, as purposeful journeys back to the homeland.[36]

During the second half of the 1930s, the Mexican community in the United
States encountered rigid policies in matters affecting employment, assistance,
and migration. Nevertheless, various economic and social factors internal to
this community helped it solidify its presence and carve out a space in the
United States. Generally speaking, as the decade wore on, the number of people of Mexican origin who evidenced an interest in returning to the country of
their ancestors grew smaller, a turn of affairs that coincided with the advent
of a new government in Mexico.

## CHAPTER THREE

# The Mexican Government and Repatriation, November 1934–June 1936

On 30 November 1934, General Lázaro Cárdenas del Río (1895–1970) assumed the presidency of Mexico. His elevation to the office took place when the country's political life was still strongly influenced by another general, Plutarco Elías Calles, the "supreme leader of the Revolution," as he was then known, and the person who in reality controlled Mexico. The *Callistas* dominated the national legislature, and the majority of the country's governors and top military officers remained faithful followers of the Calles camp. Faced with this situation, Cárdenas devoted the first year of his government to laying the foundation that would sustain and solidify its operations. At the same time, however, he took different measures to break with the previous regime and impose a government free of its grip.[1]

Although the executive branch was forced to devote most of its attention to negotiating and steering through a confrontational political climate, it nonetheless made time to inform itself about the situation of the Mexican community in the United States. The subject was not new to Cárdenas; he was already aware of the difficulties faced by his compatriots who had migrated in search of work. He had acquired that understanding during the four-year period, 1928–32, when he served intermittently as governor of Michoacán—one of the states, along with Jalisco and Guanajuato, with the highest levels of migration—and also during the unrest that still afflicted the country during the 1920s, when the number of Mexicans leaving for the United States increased notably. In addition, the mass return of his compatriots that occurred in the early 1930s, and the problems they confronted once they had arrived back in Mexico, did not escape his notice. Indeed, during his campaign for the presidency in 1933, Cárdenas called attention to the case of the repatriated who had settled in Pinotepa, Oaxaca, and to whom he extended help (Hoffman 1974, 141).

The expectation that the border between Mexico and the United States would continue to see migrants, in considerable numbers, flowing back and forth across it was never far from his mind. At the same time, however, it was well known that the return of Mexican nationals stoked fear within official circles and that concern was growing over what actions the government should take if a mass repatriation occurred and what preparations it should make. For the time being, the government did nothing either in the legislative arena or in the wider public administration context to focus on or promote the return of its compatriots. It confined itself to giving support in urgent cases only and to studying and analyzing conditions in Baja California with the objective of using that state as a place to locate and settle Mexican nationals coming back from the United States.

## The Threat of Expulsions and the Ensuing Reaction

At the end of 1934, as Cárdenas was being inducted into office, the Mexican government faced the threat of a massive return movement when public assistance officials in Los Angeles County appeared to be on the verge of deporting between 15,000 and 25,000 families of Mexican origin. Francisco J. Múgica, the incoming administration's minister of industry and commerce, believed that the country might have to welcome back at least 50,000 people, a development he believed would pose a "truly urgent, complex" problem of "transcendent importance." It could only be addressed if the government devised a plan to confront it, one that detailed just how these thousands of individuals would be accommodated.[2] Múgica thus set about pondering the different aspects of the problem.

One of these intertwined with the issue of migration, since it involved the arrival of a large assemblage of people who would, supposedly, affect the country's demographic balance. Another aspect dealt with juggling finances, since it was vital that support for these people's subsistence not upset the country's overall economy. A third aspect pertained to the labor market, since the majority of those who returned would be rural or industrial workers for whom Mexico had no jobs available. In addition, Múgica had to interface with the Ministries of Agriculture and Foreign Relations to arrange the reentrance of these people into the country and to get them established afterward. In this regard, care needed to be taken to avoid a precipitous mobilization that harmed the effort. Above all, it would be essential to bring about "a methodical and calm move." Múgica also believed that only from time to time should returns to the country be allowed, and then only on the condition that all necessary arrangements had been made with the corresponding authorities. The position he took on this issue reflected the fear that the prospect of a wholesale return of migrant nationals elicited among some within the country's political class.[3]

Múgica's emphasis on assuring "a methodical and calm" move was fundamental in shaping the way the Cardenista government confronted the return flow of migrants, from the beginning of the sexenio to its conclusion. He made clear from the very start that the government proposed to act in a manner that was orderly, systematic, and unharried. It would take no hasty measures, nor would it publicly enunciate any policy, direct or indirect, to promote a return because, according to Múgica, the country's economic conditions would prohibit it from taking in large groups of people in the immediate future. Moreover, the government would not be disposed toward investing large sums to deal with this matter.

Clearly, the return of a sizeable number of migrants would carry important implications for Mexico demographically as well as across its financial sector and labor market and in its relations with the United States. Yet so far nothing had been done on a practical level, maintained Múgica, to prepare for the arrival and resettlement of thousands of the country's citizens who were poised to return, even though "there had been a great deal of speculation around the issue" ever since the crisis in the world economy had initiated a return flow.[4] Múgica realized that something had to be done, "if only to uphold the dignity of the government and the nation."

As the first step in the process, Múgica thought it indispensable to gather personal data regarding all those who might be returned, classifying and documenting them according to their marital status and trade or line of work as well as their likely economic prospects. To accomplish this task, he proposed that Mexican consular officials carry out a census inside the United States or at the border and, using this information as a base, determine the number of people who, for lack of their own resources or imperfect knowledge of the country, would need to depend on government support to get reestablished in Mexico. The industry and commerce minister further advised that three specific actions be taken to deal with and manage the return flow: that a strict selection be made, whether on U.S. soil or at the border, focusing on returnees who satisfied his criteria; that facilities be established to permit a swift border crossing, and that the repatriated (or the majority of them) be set up and housed in agricultural colonies.[5]

It was Múgica's opinion that the appropriate way to absorb and incorporate these people was through the creation of such colonies or settlements.

To prevent a repetition of earlier failures, such as occurred with the Pinotepa and El Coloso colonization schemes, he advocated that the government carefully select farmhands and agricultural workers who expressed an interest in belonging to one of these communities. At the same time, the process of getting any such group established would have to be closely overseen and the place where its members were to be settled vetted with equal care, since the colony would be reliant on the government, and the government alone, for whatever help it needed.[6]

Múgica also argued that the government's preparations to incorporate and reintroduce people who returned be based on a range of measures and legal orders. The first task was to compile an official list of every category of company and factory operating in Mexico, with the purpose of verifying how many workers each employed, their nationality, and the kind of work they carried out. Also, legal concessions should be granted to foreign interests so they would sink capital into business ventures that promised practical benefits for the country, on the condition that a certain number of positions were set aside for Mexicans. Similarly, some defined number of jobs on government public works projects would be reserved for the heads of repatriated families.[7]

For their part, the different Mexican states should accept responsibility for the tasks that properly fell to them—specifically, providing short-term shelter for natives of their territory and to offering assistance to women and children—while the federal government figured out the longer-term solution for their accommodation and settlement. Múgica's final suggestion was that the president call on business leaders who ran companies in Mexico to commit to hiring, for a year or for at least six months, one or two heads of household out of the total group expected to return to the country. This plan was targeted solely at the heads of household because the problem of men who were single, "[when] detached from the social problem as a whole," was less severe.[8] Múgica likewise proposed that greater assistance be given at the border, since "experience has clearly shown" that, absent such help, many had to incur expenses they could ill afford and divest themselves of valuable items, leading them to arrive at their destination as indigents "when, though poor, they could have managed it with a sense of dignity." In some cases, it would be necessary for the government to bear the cost of a move all the way to its end point.[9]

Múgica thought that if the requisite data about his compatriots in the United States was gathered ahead of time, if their passage across the border was monitored and well managed, if the Mexican states stopped simply "standing on the sidelines" and prepared to assist returnees in some way, "be it ever so modest," and, finally, if some provision were made with respect to housing and settling them, the problem could be resolved satisfactorily. In conclusion, he proposed the adoption of an integrated plan in which each of the ministries and departments that dealt with the public business would participate, to ensure that expenses were shared equally among them and that the presence of the repatriated would not create a difficult situation for unemployed workers already in the country.[10]

In the end, Los Angeles County officials did not carry through on their threat to deport thousands of Mexicans, so—to its relief—the Cárdenas administration did not have to cope with a mass return of its citizens. Still, with respect to the potential for such an occurrence, Múgica's observations had, for the most part, conveyed a core belief that ran through the official discourse during all six years of Cárdenas's presidency: the preferred course was a selective repatriation of a manageable (that is, small) number of people experienced in farmwork who would be deployed to agricultural colonies. The different measures that were proposed to deal with the arrival in Mexico of his compatriots, and the distribution of responsibilities among various state departments and ministries—both of which implied the existence of a corresponding administrative structure—met with the approval of President Cárdenas. The interest he took in understanding the situation of Mexican nationals in the United States was also evident.

## Cárdenas and the Repatriation of Mexicans

Cárdenas's chief concern was to comprehend the conditions under which Mexicans lived and worked in California, from which, at the beginning of the 1930s, members of this community had been expelled and deported. The focus on California was partly driven by numbers, since this state had the second-largest population of Mexicans in the United States, after Texas. Cárdenas put Julián Velarde, president of the Latin American Chamber of Commerce of the Americas, in charge of establishing and working out the budget for a new commission, known as the Commission Responsible for the Organization, Enumeration, Repatriation, and Settlement of Mexicans in the American Union. The organization that Velarde represented had gone to considerable effort to defend and help Mexican nationals when and where it could. It therefore was thoroughly up to date on the problems faced by its compatriots, especially in California. Velarde's commission functioned independently of Mexico's consular offices. Its reports, compiled weekly, were sent directly to the office of the president, informing him of the work that had been carried out and that work's results. This active line of communication demonstrated Cárdenas's interest in staying abreast of the matter.[11]

On 6 February 1935, Velarde delivered a plan and set of recommendations to Cárdenas that addressed a series of points. His first recommendation was that Mexico engage U.S. authorities to secure the release of thousands of Mexican nationals held in U.S. prisons and organize their return to the homeland. As Velarde saw it, resolving this situation ought to be high on the list of the president's priorities. Although no exact figures are available, the number of Mexicans jailed at that time certainly ran into the hundreds, as they either awaited expulsion or served the long sentences imposed on them following their arrest by police or immigration officials as part of the organized campaign to frighten foreign residents into leaving the country. During the first half of the 1930s and even beyond, thousands of Mexicans were apprehended by immigration agents on city streets, on roads and highways, and in town squares and other public places. Although most were expelled after spending a short time in local jails or federal prisons, others remained incarcerated for longer periods (Hoffman. 1974, 39, 59–63; McKay 1982, 106, 132; Guerín-Gonzáles 1985, 249).

Another of Velarde's recommendations was that the government determine suitable sites within the country where the repatriated could be located and accommodated, that it employ them in the construction of highways and dams, and that it send them, or some portion of them, to found settlements in the states of Tamaulipas, Nuevo León, Coahuila, Chihuahua, and Baja California. Velarde also proposed that once they had been identified and organized, the "thousands of Mexicans" who were unemployed and poverty stricken should be welcomed at the border. The government should then proceed, according to a plan as yet not worked out, to locate them in places designated by the president.[12]

Despite the fact that Velarde had undertaken his study on the express wish of the Mexican executive, its suggestions and recommendations were not followed or incorporated into government policy. No concrete action came out of the commission's work, nor were any related initiatives pursued. This lack of movement was due to a simple fact: the Mexican government saw no mass return of its nationals looming on the horizon. Consequently, it felt no pressure, immediate or otherwise, to intervene. Moreover, as Velarde realized, so far as the issue of placing returnees was concerned, the government simply had not formulated any plan.

## Interest in the Size and Reach of the Mexican Population in the United States

Nonetheless, its fear of a mass return of its citizens led the Mexican government to continually seek to understand the magnitude of the Mexican population residing in the United States. Cárdenas and other government leaders were anxious to know what a return flow would look like. In mid-July 1935, amid a full-blown political crisis over the Calles-Cárdenas power struggle, Juan de Dios Bojórquez, then interior minister, ordered that a survey be conducted of Mexicans residing in the United States so that the government could estimate the scope of future return flows and the number of its citizens it would have to assist at any given time. The results of Bojórquez's venture are unknown.[13] Given the political maneuvering and disruptions, however, it seems highly unlikely that he would have had time to finish it. In the struggle for supremacy between the Cárdenas and Calles factions, Calles came out the loser. In an ensuing cabinet reshuffle, Bojórquez was replaced by Silvano Barba González, who later ordered a resumption of work on the survey and report.

The country's national statistical agency was also interested in calculating the size of the Mexican population in the United States. Neither the data it gathered nor its estimates were made public, however. Manuel Gamio, one of the leading experts on Mexican migration to the United States, also made counts of the Mexican community north of the border and studied its migratory movements to locate both those who aspired to return to Mexico and those who *had* returned definitively. According to Gamio's calculations, Mexico faced the "imminent" return of more than half a million of its nationals then living in the United States. Jesús M. González, who at the request of Gustavo L. Talamantes, a senator from the state of Chihuahua, analyzed the economic situation of Mexican workers in the United States along with the issues of repatriation and resettlement, shared this belief.[14] As for the question of where—that is, in which U.S. cities—Mexicans interested in returning home were to be found, Gamio believed no answer was possible. Although locations were known for 300 or 400 people in California and Texas who had requested government assistance so they could reestablish themselves in Mexico, locations for thousands of others could not be ascertained (Gamio 1935, 65).

Gamio's estimate of the number of people who could and likely would return to Mexico was contradicted by the reduced flow of returnees. Nonetheless, his observations were central to a viewpoint widely held during those years and to the fear generated by any hint of a new wave of deportations from the United States. The various calculations made were based on the effects of the mass returns that occurred during the early 1930s as well on studies carried out at the beginning of the decade.

Some of Mexico's consular officials also displayed an interest in determining the size of the Mexican community in the United States. A case in point was the consul in San Antonio, who announced that he had undertaken a study for this purpose. During the year 1936, the Mexican government insisted that it needed "exact knowledge of the names and addresses of all Mexicans residing in the United States." It wanted to learn how many were living there illegally, to enable it to take measures on their behalf and give them the protection they needed to remain in that country.[15] Although the fear of a new wave of deportations, arising from the events of the first years of the decade, was ever present in different circles of Mexican society and led the government to propose a count of all Mexicans living in the United States, none of this prevented the government from disseminating exaggerated figures about another mass return, which—as we will see—did not occur.

## Studies Undertaken about the Situation of Mexicans in the United States and Proposals Made for Their Return

The possibility of a massive return concerned not only some government ministers and the president but also legislators and labor leaders who analyzed the situation of their compatriots in the United States and sent the government proposals on how to manage such a return. In general, they advocated modest levels of official support. At the end of 1935, Antonio Nava, a federal deputy from the state of Michoacán, traveled through the southern part of the United States to examine firsthand how his compatriots were faring. On the basis of his visit, Nava proposed that the government appropriate enough money to cover the expenses of a repatriation campaign and to provide assistance to Mexicans residing in the United States.[16]

In Los Angeles, Nava met many Mexicans living a marginal existence in poverty-stricken neighborhoods. In the community of Big Spring, California (east of Los Angeles), conditions seemed even worse. His compatriots there were desperate, languishing in a state of indigence that neither the government nor public charity could remedy. The picture in El Monte, California, was equally dismal, with much of the Mexican migrant population living in deplorable conditions in the makeshift neighborhood known as Hicks Camp. Nava suggested that a budget line be set aside and increased every year to repatriate and give employment to Mexicans who "in great numbers want to return to their country." However, lack of funds kept the government from being able to repatriate anything approaching the number who wished to return. Nava therefore argued that the government should export certain services to them. He requested that the executive branch create schools attached to Mexican migrant communities in the United States as well as mobile libraries with Spanish-language texts and instructional materials.[17]

Nava's remarks and the suggestions he offered in the wake of his U.S. tour reflected the willingness of many people in Mexico to funnel assistance to Mexican migrants residing north of the border. The proposal to establish schools in the United States arose from this impulse to express solidarity, but the plan was hardly realistic given how difficult the government found it to build schools and educational facilities within its own territory. Similarly, while arguing for an official repatriation campaign to be financed by a federal budget line, Nava recognized that the government should not earmark large amounts of money.[18]

Jesús González, also proposed a solution to the problem. He thought it urgent that the government prepare "to confront the unusual situation that awaits us." His first suggestion was that Mexican workers in the United States be grouped into agricultural cooperatives as a way of better organizing their return. Subsequently, these cooperatives would be in communication with a new federal entity also called for in González's proposal, the National Repatriation Commission, composed of people with expertise in various aspects of the problem. This commission, operating under the aegis of the president's office, would maintain a link with the Mexican consulates, which in turn would create departments of repatriation to maintain registries of migrants and migrant families in their jurisdictions. Sunday radio broadcasts, sponsored by the government through the Ministry of Public Education, would disseminate information about the repatriation project.[19]

In addition, González's proposed commission would help people return to the country "in an orderly and fiscally manageable way," and be assured of work upon their return. As for where they were to be placed, he proposed the north of the country, especially the states of Sonora, Chihuahua, and Baja California, since he believed the returnees would adapt more easily to the way of life in the border region. The quality of the soil and ability to irrigate it, the weather and climate conditions, and the available transportation and communication links all had to be taken into account. Gauging these factors was essential, since the failure to do so had led to the collapse of the earlier colonization projects in Pinotepa Nacional (Oaxaca) and El Coloso (Guerrero).[20]

When González urged that repatriation be carried out in a way that kept down costs and maintained order, he was demonstrating the recognition—widespread among politicians—that few resources could be directed to such a venture. A year before, Múgica had made a similar suggestion, and President Cárdenas neither proposed an ambitious repatriation program nor made the idea a priority. Even though González characterized his plan as moderate, to have brought it about would have required that the government place repatriation high on its agenda of the country's problems. The budget that he suggested to underwrite the return and resettlement of 450,000 people amounted to 366,345,291 pesos. The money would have been spent on lodging and other basic livelihood costs, tools, agricultural machinery, home construction, the drilling of artisanal wells, loans and credits financed through the Bank of Agricultural Credit, and various public services. González averred that while his figure might appear "exaggerated and extravagant," it was nonetheless based on a realistic assessment. Covering it would necessitate suppressing "superfluous expenditures," as well as reducing the budgets of the Ministries of War and Finance and suspending payment of the country's foreign debt for three years.[21] Simply put, the allocation that González proposed was little short of ridiculous when one considers that in 1936 and 1937 the government's investment in the public sector (industry, transportation and communications, agriculture, domestic livestock, fisheries, social assistance, as well as outlays falling within the category of administration, tourism, and defense) came to 168 and 192 million pesos, respectively.[22] In short, although González's proposal to bring back his compatriots from the United States abounded with goodwill, it had no realistic basis of support.

Wanting an unfettered look at the situation of their expatriates north of the border, the minister of the interior and other government officials toured the most important Mexican communities in the United States to evaluate firsthand the conditions under which their compatriots lived. Barba González interviewed a commission of workers that claimed to represent 600,000 Mexicans—clearly an exaggerated figure, since the 1940 U.S. census recorded a total of 377,000 Mexican natives residing in the country, of whom 60,000 were classified as indigent. The remainder was composed of the owners of small farmsteads or people prepared to invest in agricultural colonies on Mexican soil.[23] Two other members of the Mexican Chamber of Deputies, Ramírez Paulin and Torres Caballero, also traveled to San Antonio to examine the living conditions of their compatriots in that region.[24]

Although no information is available about reports they may have submitted, the two legislators doubtless noted that the return flow to Mexico was not as great as had been thought and that while many Mexicans found themselves in very difficult circumstances, others managed to get by thanks to public or private assistance or temporary jobs. Many others were not disposed to return to Mexico because family interests or work (or both) tied them to the United States.

Two additional Mexicans who took a strong interest in the situation of their compatriots in the United States were Vicente Lombardo Toledano, general secretary of the Mexican Confederation of Workers (Confederación de Trabajadores de México, CTM) and leader of the national organized labor movement; and Luis Islas, general secretary of the textile workers union in Mexico City. Lombardo Toledano and Islas presented several petitions and proposals to the government requesting that it mobilize to reincorporate Mexican migrant workers into the homeland. Lombardo Toledano expressed an interest in the "numerous" Mexican families, most of them indigent, then living in the United States.[25] In August 1937, he spoke with the foreign relations and interior ministers, as well as with the head of the Department of Labor, to urge that they take action on two fronts: repatriation of unemployed Mexicans in Texas, followed by their placement in agricultural colonies. In addition, Lombardo Toledano urged the government to prevent the emigration of Mexican nationals and Mexican associations in the United States and the AFL to work together to help Mexican nationals who could not obtain employment.[26]

For his part, Islas argued that the federal government needed to bring back the thousands of its citizens living abroad, who were devoting their energies to advancing the progress of other nations when they should be expending this effort in Mexico. He proposed that the government undertake a wide-ranging information campaign to underscore how beneficial it would be for the country if Mexicans and their families were to return. Moreover, the government should reach an agreement with industrial firms and businesses, resulting in the addition of five repatriated workers for every 100 employees.[27]

Islas also advocated that returning farmers and agricultural workers be given good quality land and ample resources. He further suggested the decommissioning of half of the property belonging to those who continued living abroad. Under his proposal, these individuals would have one year to return. If they did not, they would lose their nationality, though this would be automatically restored to them once they again took up residence in Mexico. In addition, Mexican citizens and their families would be granted special permission to travel abroad and remain in a foreign country only for the purposes of studying or of making short trips subject to the discretion of the federal executive.[28]

Like Lombardo Toledano and Islas, the directors of the National Union of Veterans of the Revolution, part of the politically influential upper corps of the army built up under Secretary of War Joaquín Amaro, requested that they be enabled to repatriate their companions now in the United States. Proposing to establish agricultural colonies, they asked for parcels of land large enough to allow people to earn an honest living. The group also made clear, however, that it rejected the idea of government handouts and "found dispossessions unacceptable," so they requested a period of twenty years in which to amortize the cost of the land and the legal instruments that would be needed to obtain loans and credit. In addition, they suggested that each settlement contain no fewer than fifty families and, jurisdictionally, have the status of a municipality with the complete freedom to elect its authorities.[29]

Like other officials, Lombardo Toledano and Islas expressed support for the idea that the government should help bring Mexican nationals back and find work for them in the country. Indeed, when the Mexican consuls in the United States held a convention in El Paso in October 1937, Lombardo sent them several communiqués requesting that they take measures as soon as possible to promote a process of repatriation.[30] Both Lombardo Toledano and Islas were eager to show solidarity with the Mexican population in the United States, and as we have seen, Islas's eagerness led him to take some extreme positions, such as promoting the return of all unemployed Mexicans living in Texas, dispossessing migrants abroad of their property in the homeland, and divesting them of their Mexican citizenship. To demand that the government do everything possible to organize the return of its migrant population was to demonstrate one's authentic nationalist spirit. It is thus unsurprising that in the mid-1930s various political and labor leaders—among them the directors of the National Union of Veterans of the Revolution—began to wrap repatriation in the flag of nationalism.

## Measures to Facilitate Return: The Border

The government took some measures to support the return of expatriates who reached the border. In the border cities that experienced the greatest passage of people (principally Ciudad Juárez, Nuevo Laredo, Matamoros, and Nogales), where the return of Mexicans both individually and in groups was a daily phenomenon, the federal government provided free rail passes to indigent citizens who had journeyed from the interior of the United States to resume life in Mexico. At the same time, it also took action to stem the flow of emigrants out of the country.

During the second half of the 1930s, deportees, whether individually or in groups, were constantly arriving on the border, and since the majority were indigent, the local authorities pressured the federal government to furnish them passage, so they could be transferred quickly out of the area and back to their home regions. Uppermost in these officials' minds was avoiding a repeat of what had happened in the first years of the decade, when large numbers of deported migrants got stranded, putting a severe strain on services and altering the balance and rhythm of daily life in the affected cities. The local authorities likewise favored a government policy that would impede these people from reemigrating, given the obstacles they faced in merely trying to survive.

As the year 1935 began, small groups of Mexicans unable to endure difficult living conditions in the United States began arriving on the border. They requested rail passes from the government so they could go back to their hometowns. Emilio Portes Gil, Mexico's minister of foreign relations, believed it was necessary to help his compatriots, but he also thought that the government needed to proceed cautiously, making sure to verify that the people awarded such benefits truly needed them. The practice of supporting the return of migrants with railway passes was not new; it had been inaugurated in the first half of the decade and continued to be followed during the Cardenista sexenio.[31]

Participants in the Third Convention on Migration, held at the end of 1935 in Mexico City, reaffirmed the government's approach to dealing with the issue: that is, it would render assistance for repatriation in exceptional cases only, by arranging to transport people from the border to some point inside the country. The Interior Ministry also underscored its support for the practice "of repatriation pure and simple," by which it meant offering assistance to some deportees in the form of railway passage from the border to their hometowns and villages.[32] Cisneros Canto, a member of the president's cabinet, and Óscar Peralta, the government's immigration representative in Ciudad Juárez, also furnished passage to some of their compatriots who had been deported and were completely destitute.[33]

At the same time that the federal government and authorities on the border helped transport indigent returnees back to their hometowns and villages, they also took pains to rein in emigration to the United States. Representatives from the Chamber of Commerce in Reynosa, Tamaulipas, who with their counterparts from Laredo and Ciudad Juárez had been forced to contend with the greatest number of returning migrants at the beginning of the decade, agreed to do what they could, "using all possible means," to prevent braceros from leaving in search of work. Their resolve on this score was in reaction to the xenophobic reception that these migrants experienced in the United States.[34] At the beginning of 1936, the Interior Ministry called for a cessation in the emigration of Mexican workers, in particular to the state of Colorado, and requested that the Department of the Federal District undertake a corresponding publicity campaign through various media.[35]

## The Government and Repatriation:
## Looking Outward from the Capital

The authorities in Mexico City acknowledged that they had no plan of action to respond to a large-scale return. Moreover, they openly feared the consequences that such a development could have for the country. Yet, for all their trepidation, they only budgeted small amounts of money to address the situation and only did what was absolutely necessary to reintegrate their compatriots who returned from the United States. Their efforts were largely directed toward promoting studies that analyzed conditions in different parts of the country where returnees might be settled. This was their way of preparing to receive hundreds of individuals.

*El Universal*, the newspaper founded in 1916 by Félix F. Palavicini, wrote that by the end of April 1936, the government would "at last" make known how it planned to come to the aid of those compatriots who made up "México de afuera (Mexico outside the country])," as well as how much it would invest in solving the problem.[36] This commentary was significant, since it underscored that the government still had not made clear just how it would act were a massive return of Mexicans to occur. Nor, despite the fear of new deportations, had it created a dedicated budget for such a contingency. Unofficially, some journalists understood that it was "possible" that Cárdenas, after meeting with some of his cabinet officials, might order that certain measures be taken, but as for a general, full-scale repatriation plan, nothing was known. For its part, the Interior Ministry had done no more than try to determine the simplest and most convenient way of helping Mexicans who had fallen into misfortune, whether in the United States, Cuba, Central America, or Europe.[37]

Luis I. Rodríguez, the president's private secretary, acknowledged that a massive return of migrants could be devastating for the country's economy. It was therefore necessary to prevent such a disaster and order the nation's finances in such a way that the country could go forward. He argued that the problem was national in its scope and significance and could not be brushed aside by the government. Nevertheless, he thought the level of investment suggested by some, such as Jesús M. González (more than 366 million pesos), was exceedingly high. Like others, he felt that the government—if faced with a large-scale return—should spend only the resources absolutely necessary and should do so gradually. For Rodríguez, needs inside the country demanded the special and continual attention that a potential return of migrants simply did not merit.[38] Hence he relegated repatriation to the secondary significance that it occupied for the majority of those in the government. Repatriation should not distract attention from other national priorities, especially the country's economic situation.

In a meeting with Cárdenas, Francisco Castillo Nájera, the Mexican ambassador to the United States, expressed the view that official support to enable people to return to the homeland should be "a cause for deep reflection and extensive study." He was keen that the government not take any hasty action, as it had some years before, when the precipitous return of migrants had not allowed time to examine the situation in depth. Castillo Nájera concurred with Cárdenas that, going forward, people who were repatriated should be given jobs identical to or "in line with" the ones they had held in the United States. As for farmers and agricultural workers, the government should have them settled where their abilities and aptitudes could best be utilized in the interests of the national economy. On their return they should identify with their work and be satisfied to be back in the country, and thus inspired "to join the collective labor for the betterment of the Republic."[39] High-minded goals, however, were one thing, practical considerations another. In actual circumstance, no project ever went forward to see that returnees were placed in jobs similar to the ones they had held in the United States, nor were they invited to be a vanguard settling a particular part of the country. The government went no further than to promote studies of different zones where irrigation projects existed and that could serve as sites to settle expatriate nationals.

In February 1936, a presidential entourage began a tour through the north of Mexico, during which it visited the Lower Rio Grande Valley, in the area around the city of Matamoros, Tamaulipas. The visitors surveyed the quality of the land and soil and the possibilities for irrigation. They proposed to study the viability of giving the land to groups of Mexicans now residing in the United States. In 1935 the federal government launched a program in this area that entailed the construction of defensive barriers to hold back and control the waters of the Rio Grande. The government intended to create a model agricultural region based on installing irrigation and on readapting the use of communal lands. The newspaper El Nacional, founded in 1929 as an organ of the governing party, exaggerated the impact that the project would have in resettling migrants coming back from the United States, claiming that "indifference and neglect would no longer await Mexicans who reincorporated themselves into the country. A plot of fertile land, a roof [over their heads], a helping hand to get things started awaited the repatriated."[40]

At virtually the same time that Cárdenas and his party were touring the north of the country, Mexico's National Irrigation Commission (Comisión Nacional de Irrigación, CNI) formally announced a project to construct a giant irrigation system in the San Juan River Valley (Tamaulipas). According to CNI officials, this system would constitute one of the federal government's largest public works projects to settle and employ both Mexican nationals returning from the United States and farming families already living in the region. The governors of Tamaulipas and Chihuahua expressed their willingness to assist people who returned to the country by employing them in highway construction and other public works projects. The governors' declarations, like those by other political and labor leaders in this period, had distinctly nationalistic overtones and were intended to convey empathy and support for expatriates. In practice, however, the steps taken to give the latter work and to set them up as agriculturalists were limited and sporadic, as was also the case in Baja California.[41]

## Baja California and the Repatriation That Never Was

If such declarations championing the return of migrants were not accompanied by actions to implement them, nor were a series of studies conducted in Baja California with the ostensible aim of resettling and creating work for Mexicans returning from the United States.[42] At the beginning of February 1935, the Ministry of Agriculture and Development agreed to promote a repatriation of Mexican migrants to Baja California. The plan was to resettle "groups of repatriated farmworkers" on land that would support and sustain their efforts at agricultural production. To carry out the project, it was determined that the funds—101,000 pesos—funneled from the National Repatriation Committee to an agency within the Agriculture Ministry, the Rural Population, National Lands, and Colonization Administration, should in the future be used solely to acquire land in Baja California on which to resettle impoverished campesinos who returned to the country without any means of subsistence. The National Bank of Agricultural Credit (Banco Nacional de Crédito Agrícola, BNCA) was charged with financing the colonization scheme and supporting the financial needs of the returned migrants.[43]

The executive branch was interested in this project for two principal reasons: first, it would provide a test for what were considered the "insuperable" agronomic conditions of the soil in Baja California; and second, it believed that establishing new communities in Baja would resolve a problem of national import, since the region was very thinly populated and had few native inhabitants.[44] And yet, there are no reports or news stories describing the opening of settlements for repatriated migrants in this region. Nor is there information indicating that the government took any other action to establish them or, for that matter, that a group of people ever arrived in the area.

During a meeting that he held with Cárdenas, General Agustín Olachea, the governor of Baja California, assured the president that Mexicans currently living in Los Angeles, San Francisco, and San Diego who wished to return would find work in the region's existing agricultural colonies. Cárdenas decided that Olachea and his technical advisors should examine how the area's agricultural settlements had been and were currently functioning and what types of problems they experienced. Olachea said he would be able to take in repatriated nationals who were experienced in agricultural work and had sufficient funds to meet their own needs, but he was opposed to bringing indigents to any part of the state. No place in Baja, he explained, was equipped to assimilate them. Existing supply and demand in the local agricultural market would not support them, and there was also a shortage of manufactured products. Impoverished returnees would thus become a burden for the current population.[45]

Nonetheless, planning for a projected resettlement continued. At the beginning of 1935, the secretary of agriculture sent several representatives to the region to study conditions in preparation for setting up Mexican nationals coming back from the United States. In early March, the manager of the BNCA reported that arrangements had been completed for establishing settlements in a region called Rancho del Arroyo del Tule, in the municipality of Mexicali, where a group of returnees—now having assumed the mantle of settlers—would be provided with parcels of land for growing cotton and pasturage. To assure that returnees would have the means to establish themselves, the land would be sold to them on an installment plan. The new colony, to be called México Libre (Free Mexico), would adjoin those of Zaragoza and Progreso, which had been established by former president Abelardo Rodríguez.[46] This was the stated plan, but whether a group actually settled in this spot or whether the government helped in its transport and financing is not known. What is clear is that accomplishing those tasks in the brief period since the bank manager's announcement would have been extremely difficult.

All the same, the government continued to state that it would analyze the possibility of giving land to Mexicans now residing in the United States.

An agency within the Agriculture Ministry, the Rural Population Administration, agreed to carry out a study of how water from the Colorado River could be utilized to irrigate land that colonists would occupy. The agency's commitment supported the proposals made by the executive branch to enable people to develop small landholdings in northern Baja California and to settle in this area the "increased number" of Mexican nationals expected to return to the country. At the same time, Tomás Garrido Canabal, then still serving as secretary of agriculture, led a study aimed at settling expatriates on haciendas south of Mexicali as well on lands along Sonora's eastern border with the United States. He met in Mexicali with both Manuel López, an Agriculture Ministry representative, and Salvador Guerra Aceves, director of the Department of Agriculture, to inspect the potential site for a program that would have two interconnected components: settling no fewer than 18,000 individuals and launching a large-scale irrigation project.[47]

Baja California was not the only territory that Cárdenas thought suitable for establishing agricultural colonies in which to resettle repatriated Mexicans; there were other areas of the country where the purchase of land for this purpose would be equally advantageous. He therefore ordered the Rural Population, National Lands, and Colonization Administration, based on studies, to acquire land appropriate for establishing groups of farmworkers who "return[ed] to the country to join their efforts to the dynamics of agricultural production." It was also decided that the Banco Agrícola would be in charge of financing the costs of colonization.[48] Despite these expressions of interest, no concrete progress was made.

At the end of 1935 and in early February 1936, there was continued interest in studying the possibility of founding settlements in Baja California for Mexican nationals who returned from across the border. During this same period, Saturnino Cedillo, the new secretary of agriculture, made several trips to the north of the country, in part to examine land on which to resettle hundreds of his compatriots who found themselves trapped in hapless circumstances in the United States. Among the states Cedillo visited was Baja California, where he assessed the conditions for resettling some 10,000 families Los Angeles County was said to be planning to deport. Cedillo also conversed at several points with representatives of a U.S.-based firm, the Colorado River Land Company, owner of more than 300,000 hectares of land deemed suitable for colonization, to conclude arrangements that would culminate in moving settlers onto the land. He also inspected the Rodríguez Dam and the countryside in its vicinity that could be adapted for irrigation and utilized to form settlements for repatriated nationals.[49]

The intended fruit of Cedillo's trip was a project outline he would present to President Cárdenas. The thinking was that by galvanizing repatriation to and colonization in Baja California, the government would help foster the "liberation," or opening up, of that part of the country, which would become "available, prosperous, and usable terrain" for the 50,000 Mexicans who supposedly would arrive to live in the region.[50] Given the importance of the project, the publisher of *Excelsior*, a newspaper founded in 1917 by the *poblano* (native of the state of Puebla) Rafael Alducín, editorialized that Cedillo deserved "the plaudits of the country," since up until this point nobody had assumed leadership for an effort of such magnitude.[51] Nevertheless, Cedillo's suggestions could not be implemented. The government's hesitant approach to confronting the return of its compatriots was manifest once again.

According to Cedillo, the difficulty of financing the return of 10,000 families could not be resolved short term, given that the region lacked the water needed for irrigation. To overcome this obstacle, he proposed the construction of dams in an area east of the Sea of Cortez. His plan was for the government to utilize the labor of Mexicans who returned from the United States. Once so employed, they would have a means of subsistence and would not become a burden to the public. At the same time, the plan had several other virtues: new sources of work would be created, new highways constructed, and the fishing industry would receive a boost, both for internal consumption and export to foreign markets, as would lime manufacturing and pearl farming. These initiatives in turn could yield sufficient resources to sustain settlers in the area.[52]

Cedillo's purpose, however, was simply to study the conditions in Baja California under which his compatriots might return to Mexico and to highlight the obstacles that needed to be cleared beforehand. As yet, the conditions were not ripe to settle a living, working population. For this step to be taken, more time was needed to adapt the land to its intended use. Despite such limiting factors, the secretary executed a contract in Baja California to colonize the Agricultural Valley of Mexicali, as it was known. In addition, he promised to study the conditions of certain parcels of agricultural land with a view to their being productively worked.[53]

On 14 April 1936, President Cárdenas signed with the Colorado River Land Company a contract stipulating that Mexican campesinos would settle lands in northern Baja California. Cárdenas's purpose in taking this action was to initiate agrarian reform in the Mexicali Valley. Under the terms of the contract, the company was to divide up, demarcate, colonize, and transfer into the exclusive possession of Mexican settlements all of its lands that could be productively utilized, an area covering 258,455 hectares (Piñera Ramírez 1983, 490).

The contract did not include any references to Mexicans residing in the United States. Nonetheless, Luis I. Rodríguez, the president's private secretary, stated that if individuals from that population were sent to colonize Baja California, the region's problem of underpopulation could be solved. This effort, it was foreseen, should be undertaken progressively, in stages, to help facilitate the "gradual absorption" of the Baja peninsula into national life.[54] By the end of 1936, however, the idea had all but disappeared from the conversation about Baja California. Studies carried out by the Ministry of the Interior on the economic problems of the state's northern district brought to light the stark, precarious situation facing large contingents of the area's workers. Many lacked jobs altogether, for which reason Cárdenas, who already feared that a large influx of migrants returning from the United States could worsen conditions for those who had not left the country, stopped displaying interest either in bringing people into the region or in shoehorning them into his broader plans for national development.

On 28 September 1936, the president delivered a radio message to the nation in which he set forth the administration's "Plan for the Recuperation of the Territories of Baja California and Quintana Roo," emphasizing that the endemic difficulties of these regions needed to be tackled with full "tenacity and force of action." This challenge would be met by settling people in the territories, thanks to the development of transportation links and irrigation systems, among other projects, to build and consolidate infrastructure and bind these regions, economically, socially, and culturally, to the rest of the nation. Cárdenas and his team thereby launched a national campaign on behalf of the territory of Baja California. The goal was to create sources of production that would both satisfy the needs of its population and give it a place in the country's internal market through the sale of its products outside the territory. To turn theory into practice, all types of transport would be established and tariffs adequate for the program would be instituted.[55] In contrast to its predecessors, the Cardenista government was committed to playing an active role in development work rather than ceding that function exclusively to private enterprise and foreign capital.

To carry out its plan, the administration came to various agreements with different ministries. Among the most important were those that it concluded with the Interior Ministry. The latter was tasked with sending a circular to the country's governors requesting that each state endorse the idea of serving

Mexico by coming to the rescue of Baja California, "repopulating it, reconstructing it, and making the most of it."[56] There was no indication of any kind that Mexicans residing abroad would be part of this campaign. Rather, the Cárdenas government preferred that people already in the country be the ones to relocate and settle in the region.

Changes took place during the Cárdenas administration that marked a new phase in the history of Baja, a phase that began with the implementation in the state of the country's agrarian reform program, which entailed conveying to campesinos the lands that belonged to the Colorado River Land Company. Two other measures of fundamental importance were the introduction of the Free Zone, designed by the government as a model to guide the economic development of the greater border region within the context of the country as a whole, and the government's desire that the state should have transportation links tying it to the interior of Mexico (Piñera Ramírez 1983, 485–86, 542, 571).

On 14 March 1937, Cárdenas decided to expropriate lands held by foreign companies such as the Colorado River Land Company, in Mexicali; San Isidro Ajolojol, in Tijuana; and Moreno and Company, in Rosarito. In addition, he defined and established the terms by which agrarian action plans for the territory of Baja California would be regulated, resolved, and executed. As a result, agrarian reform in the state took its first steps. An area totaling 90,500 hectares was distributed for the benefit of 16,000 families, and another 60,500 hectares was parceled out among colonists and small landholders. Twenty-hectare parcels were transferred to some campesinos and, in the Mexicali borough of Compuertas, land that had belonged to the Álamo Mocho group was divided up among 203 campesinos (Piñera Ramírez 1983, 491–93).

At the end of February 1937, a group of 103 campesinos, many of whom had lived for a period of time in the United States, arrived in Baja. They requested that they be granted *ejidos* (common lands) and identified land occupied by Moreno and Company in Rosarito as appropriate for this purpose. The president issued an order to the governor of Baja California, stipulating that he enable individuals and small groups that had come from the United States to settle in the Mexicali Valley.[57] One of those who benefited from Cárdenas's action was Zeferino Diego Ferreira, a Mexican national who had been deported after living for twenty years in Stockton, California. Ferreira emerged as the representative of a group of people who wished to resettle in Baja California, and he visited the municipal headquarters in Tijuana and Mexicali urging that the valley be declared a "federal zone." He acquired some land of his own out of a larger parcel that was divided up by an engineer who worked for the government. Ultimately, however, the number of people who returned from the United States and who managed to obtain a share of the lands being distributed was limited, and their frequency in doing so was sporadic. For example, when at the end of March 1937 Luis G. Alcérrega, an engineer and head of an agrarian affairs department within the Agriculture Ministry, bestowed various ejidos out of lands previously belonging to the Colorado River Land Company, there is no indication that returnees were among the beneficiaries.[58]

At the beginning of June 1937, fifty-eight ejidos had been formed, with the possession of land taken provisionally by the first thirty-eight and definitively by the remaining twenty. Each ejido covered 97,120 irrigated hectares. This change in the ownership and distribution of land brought an unparalleled increase in the population of the Mexicali municipality. But again, those moving into this northern strip of Baja came principally from within the country. Thus a kind of human mosaic was created that represented the full breadth of Mexico, as witnessed in the names that were given to the ejidos, based on where in the country the newly resettled campesinos hailed from: Sonora, Jalisco, Puebla, Michoacán, Nayarit, Guanajuato, Tamaulipas, Oaxaca, Yucatán, Sinaloa, Cuernavaca, Campeche, Hidalgo, Zacatecas, Nuevo León, Chihuahua, and so on (Piñera Ramírez 1983, 494, 496, 502). In similar fashion, the landless peasants who had arrived from other parts of the country to work seasonally, during the six-month growing period that began with the spring planting and lasted until the fall harvest, formed a swarm of unemployed and underemployed who became applicants for ejidos or turned into a kind of invading band. It became clear to Cárdenas that a wide-ranging and quickly implemented program of colonization and development could serve multiple ends. While the preference, in an ideal world, might be to gather in repatriated Mexicans as colonists because of the modern techniques they had ostensibly learned in the United States, moving campesinos from the heavily populated interior of the country was the more pragmatic option, since it would create an abundant workforce in a region that lacked one and, at the same time, serve as a safety valve to placate the demand for land that arose in areas where available land was scarce (Kerin 2001, 268).

Despite this initial wave of change, no data point to the arrival of a great number of Mexicans from the United States, although evidence does exist that a relative few, like Zeferino Diego, worked their way into the most important colonies that took shape at the time in Baja California and participated in the division and distribution of land. At year's end, it was reported that both the parceling out of 2,500 hectares to settlers and the acquisition by the CNI of 5,000 still-uncolonized hectares had gone successfully.[59] On this occasion, as had happened with the land distributions at the beginning of the year, only a small number of Mexican expatriates received any land or participated in settling this region. Consequently, they added little to the new centers of population.

Advancing the colonization of Baja California had been a stated objective of the Cárdenas government from the outset of its six-year term. To support this program, it agreed early on to promote the repatriation of Mexican nationals from the United States, and it conducted various studies of the conditions in this region of the country with the aim of resettling expatriates there. Yet, despite the studies conducted by civil servants in 1935, no program to organize the return of Mexicans residing across the border was ever fully fleshed out and put into effect. Nor did more than a small number of individuals manage to relocate to this area on their own. The government issued pronouncements and declarations, organized tours of the region by various officials, and above all, conducted studies to weigh the possibilities of moving returnees into the region, but in practice it did little. One of the underlying reasons for this gap between rhetoric and action was the tendency to funnel into Baja only Mexican citizens who had not left the country and to promote settlement projects with them. This preference underlay the policy of the Cárdenas regime. Later, when presenting a development plan for the territory at the end of 1936, references to Mexicans in the United States as a key group in furthering settlement were notably missing, even though building up settlements in the region was assigned a certain priority. As the sexenio wore on, mention of these people began dropping off the federal agenda for Baja California. The government allocated only a modest sum to assist a small number in getting established there and, very sporadically, supported the return of other individuals to whom it gave parcels of land.

## CHAPTER FOUR

# From the Creation of the Demography and Repatriation Section to the Elaboration of a Repatriation Project, July 1936–October 1938

After so many comings and goings and so many twists and turns, the repatriated will arrive in the capital and, on seeing the Río Consulado . . . will surely have to break into song, in a parody of *Gigantes y cabezudos* ["Giants and Big-Heads," a zarzuela by Spanish composer Manuel Fernández Caballero and librettist Miguel Echegaray y Eizaguirre (1898)]: "I see you again, famous river / much wider / much wider are you / and more beautiful. . . ."

—"THE CHORUS OF THE REPATRIATED," *EL UNIVERSAL*, 5 AUGUST 1936

In mid-1936, Cárdenas's power base had at last been consolidated. Calles's departure into exile that April marked the end of the Maximato (the six-year period, 1928–34, when Calles controlled Mexican politics), after which his partisans who still held positions that could possibly influence the exercise of power were replaced (González 1981, 41–47; Hernández Chávez 1979, 57–60; Dulles 1989, 585–93). The rule that the "Sonoran dynasty" had exercised for fifteen years had come to an end. The system of dual centers of power that had been inaugurated in 1929 suffered the same fate. The president now became the true axis around which the political process revolved. Definitive confirmation of this change came through several developments: when Cárdenas freed himself from the straitjacket of the Maximato; when all government ministers were compelled to act on the basis of presidential directives; when state-level *cacicazgos* (local political fiefdoms) were suppressed and governors forbidden to engage in practices that contravened or weakened the institution of the presidency; and, finally, when the legislative branch acceded to a genuinely collaborative, though not necessarily dutifully obedient, relationship with the executive. With these changes secured, the way was open for Cárdenas to pursue his regime's most important objectives. These had two distinctive features: the expansion of presidential authority and the incisive application of a slate of reforms in three areas of intense interest to the government: its relations with unions and its activities vis-à-vis labor conflicts; its agrarian policy, leading to a transformation of the business of farming and agriculture in general; and its position and policy on nationalization (Hamilton 1983, 125; Córdova 1974, 44–45; González 1980, 5–31; León 1986, 229).

As the radical period (1936 to March 1938) of the Cardenista regime gathered strength, the Mexican government—perhaps caught up in the reformist euphoria—established the first office, in the sphere of public administration, to assist the process of repatriation and incorporated this concern in demographic legislation. It also decided to undertake a repatriation project with very specific characteristics. These measures notwithstanding, however, official interest in the return of Mexican nationals remained tepid. Indeed, the voices heard in favor of containing and holding back support for repatriation were many and various. Mexican government officials thus focused their energies on measures to prevent the emigration of Mexican citizens to the United States and intervened to help returnees only when the urgency of the situation demanded it; that is, when Mexican nationals were being deported en masse.

## The Demographics Department

At the end of July 1936, two sections—Demographic Studies and Repatriation and General Population Records, were created within the Interior Ministry's Demographics Department. They were established with different work plans but served a common aim: fulfilling the objectives of the Plan sexenal (the government's six-year development plan) with respect to population and demography. The first section initiated an examination of the Immigration Tolerance Table for 1937, with respect to "acceptable immigration by race and characteristics of type." The second began its work by developing an obligatory general identification system that would cover all of the nation's inhabitants. In addition, the Demographic Studies and Repatriation section started to devise a plan to reintegrate into the country those Mexicans abroad, primarily in the United States and Canada, who found themselves in difficult straits. The intent was to set about this task systematically and in accordance with the allocated resources (SEGOB 1937, 27). Silvano Barba González, minister of the interior, stated that the Demographic Studies section had 1 million pesos to invest in repatriating and resettling Mexican nationals in agricultural zones prepared for this purpose.[1] He did not, however, indicate when or where this money would be spent.

Beginning in mid-1936, the Demographics Department clarified the guidelines that the government followed in this matter. Prior to this time, the measures the government had taken to deal with the return of migrants had been divided between the president's office and the Interior and Foreign Relations Ministries, with the Agriculture and Economics Ministries also occasionally engaged in the process. Now, with the creation of the Demographic Studies and Repatriation section, there was a single, specialized office that could advise Mexican nationals abroad who wished to return and sought information about the current situation in Mexico and the United States that might affect their plans (SEGOB 1939, 53–54). The way the department was constituted showed that official attention was constantly fixed on a possible return of migrants back and evidenced the government's interest in creating an office that would deal with the issue. The extent to which its plans were feasible was, of course, another matter.

## The General Population Law of 1936 and Repatriation

The general population law (*Ley general de población*) promulgated on 29 August 1936 replaced the migration law (*Ley de migración*) of 1930 and, in essence, reintroduced the elements of the Six-Year Plan that dealt with population-related matters. The migration policy of the Cardenista regime was now front and center. The new law highlighted a fundamental demographic problem faced by the country, namely, that its population increase must be based on natural growth, repatriation, and immigration. To increase natural population growth, the legislation proposed to spur more marriages, increase the birth rate, and offer greater protection to minors. It also encompassed the distribution of the population within the country, the return of compatriots, the intermarriage of different Mexican ethnic groups, and of these people with those of foreign origin, the protection of Mexican nationals, the education of the indigenous population, and the "general protection, preservation, and betterment of the people as a whole." To achieve these objectives, a General Directorate of Population was set up in the Ministry of the Interior (SEGOB).[2]

The law likewise included a section on emigration and repatriation that laid out an administrative structure to encourage the return of Mexican nationals and to impede their emigration. With the aim of preventing the shrinking of the population, the Interior Ministry was empowered to dictate measures that would impede or restrict the departure of Mexican citizens from the country. Stemming emigration was a basic principle of the general population law. A secondary purpose was to spur the return of nationals and to set these people up in places where they could apply "the knowledge and capabilities acquired abroad," providing them with the tools that would allow them to become agents of production. It would be the Interior Ministry's task to settle both Mexican nationals and immigrants in agricultural or industrial colonies founded expressly for this purpose. Returns would be facilitated systematically but only in justifiable cases and only for certain categories of people, above all those who worked in agriculture.[3]

The Ministries of Foreign Relations and the Treasury were also delegated to participate in placing and resettling Mexican nationals who might return from the United States. The contribution of the Finance Ministry, through its Customs Directorate, would involve exempting returnees from the normal requirement of having to obtain a Mexican consular certification and also assisting them in bringing in their personal belongings. The Interior Ministry would take charge of them from the border to their destination inside the country, with the Agriculture Ministry given responsibility for designating particular regions to take them in and help get them firmly established. Finally, to assure that their settlement was permanent, the law formalized the acquisition of land, machinery, work tools, and stores of seeds, together with the extension of loans and credits. Moreover, the law stipulated that the authorities should finance the return of people with experience in industry and trades, although in reality this provision was pushed into the background.[4]

Prior to 1936, legislation affecting migration had not incorporated repatriation, nor had it established how the government would act or promote it.[5] Despite the importance of the legislative precedent, government actions in respect to repatriation continued their modest path, as reflected by the fact that no specific group of individuals was selected to return and no project was developed to establish agricultural colonies. The idea that migrants represented a potential civilizing and developmental force for the country continued to hold sway, but no steps were taken to test this theory. Government outlays in favor of such moves were also kept to a strict minimum. In November 1936, Branch 4 of the Interior Ministry, which oversaw the repatriation of Mexican nationals residing outside the country, allocated 20,000 pesos for their passage and travel. The following month, on 28 December 1936, the Mexican Congress approved a budget of 32,000 pesos to cover the expenses of returnees. These sums represented a significant reduction in comparison to the amounts invested by the government prior to 1934.[6] This trend became even more obvious in 1937, as the actions carried out by offices in charge of the return of migrants weakened and the federal government's attention to the issue all but vanished.

## The Demographic Studies and Repatriation Section in 1937

From January to October 1937, the work of the Demographic Studies and Repatriation section was limited to two initiatives: (1) locating impoverished Mexican nationals in the United States who received public assistance and (2) devising a plan to form agricultural colonies. The section sought to locate its citizens who were receiving aid from social welfare groups and relief agencies in California and other parts of the United States. It expressed its interest in "knowing precisely the name and address of all Mexicans who resided in the United States," and in learning how many were living there illegally, so it could intercede on their behalf and offer them protection. In addition, it stressed two features that had consistently characterized the official outlook with regard to the return of migrants (SEGOB 1937, 28). On the one hand, the department believed that the solution to the economic situation of this Mexican population did not lie in bringing its members back to the homeland; that is, it recognized that promoting their return was not a high priority; on the other, it made clear that developing a program for establishing agricultural colonies was imperative. In other words, the department needed to fulfill the blueprint it had sketched out for itself: that of carrying out studies.[7]

In this same year, the government appropriated 50,000 pesos to aid Mexicans living abroad. Accordingly, the Agriculture Ministry put its branch agencies in the states of Nuevo León, Tamaulipas, and Coahuila in charge of locating lands on which various Mexican nationals returning from the United States, among them 3,000 families who had been living in Texas, could be established. No information exists, however, about whether any concrete steps were taken to further this plan and help these people get settled.[8] Since the flow of returnees in 1937 was minimal and the official priority vis-à-vis migration was to prevent the shrinking of the population, the government—in line with policy set forth in the 1936 population law—focused more on stopping the departure of its citizens than on organizing their return.

## The Concern over Emigration

Between January and October 1937, the Mexican government put greater emphasis on enforcing the existing regulations designed to impede the departure of the country's workforce. In addition to showing that they possessed a formal work contract, Mexican nationals who left as migrant workers were also required to deposit a sum of money as a guarantee they would be able to finance their return. The Interior Ministry's general policy was to make Mexicans dubious about migrating in light of the abuses to which foreign employers constantly subjected them. The ministry strengthened its efforts in this regard because, despite the adverse conditions that awaited them in the United States as well as the restrictions they faced in trying to cross the border, Mexican nationals continued to leave the country clandestinely (SEGOB 1938, 79; SRE 1937). To carry out the government's plan, the Interior Ministry called on its population offices and the country's governors to help it. While supporting the campaign against the emigration of Mexican workers, the Foreign Relations Ministry also took a different approach, focusing its attention on the Inter-American Conference for the Maintenance of Peace,[9] while also attending to the problem of Spanish Civil War refugees seeking asylum (SRE 1937).

Grounding his decision in the migration policy set forth by the Interior Ministry, Eduardo Hay, Mexico's minister of foreign relations, called for a campaign to prevent the departure of laborers whose contracts forced them to work under adverse conditions. At the beginning of May 1937, Hay called on border authorities in Chihuahua, Tamaulipas, Coahuila, and Sonora to deny the transport of Mexicans to Utah, Montana, or other states unless their contracts specified that they would earn a decent daily wage and that their recruiters would bear the expense of their return to Mexico.

Hay acted in accordance with the principles of Section 26 of Article 123 of the 1917 constitution, requiring that Mexican nationals who left the country to work abroad do so under a formal contract, as a way to guarantee both their rights and their return. The foreign relations minister also wanted to make workers aware of the risks they ran by placing themselves in the hands of unscrupulous smugglers who, through deception, got them into the United States and then left them to be arrested and deported. If the outward flow were to be stopped, Mexico's border authorities would have to work collaboratively and exercise vigilance in preventing illegal migration.[10]

Many government officials joined the effort to contain the departure of Mexicans, including people from the Foreign Relations Ministry, the consulates, and some of the ministers themselves, as well as both the official press and independent news outlets in the central and northern parts of the country. The crafty job recruiters, having assembled a group of Mexicans for various construction companies, now "went to ground," intent on evading the Mexican authorities who, learning of their operations, planned to prevent "this immoral flight." For their part, lacking the essentials to eke out a living, the workers denounced such interference and presented a complaint to the president. They had been enticed with the usual offer of good wages and payment for their travel expenses, but when they arrived in Mexico City, where their official hiring was supposed to take place, they were deserted by their would-be agents. Lending support to the government's attempt to impede the outflow of workers, migration authorities in Matamoros and Ciudad Juárez redoubled their efforts to dissuade workers from central Mexico from leaving the country.[11] In both these cities as well in other border communities a campaign was mounted against migration and in favor of the arrest of the middlemen and smugglers who descended on these parts in search of braceros.

A classic situation unfolded in Ciudad Juárez, where Oscar Peralta, an official with the country's immigration service, acted to secure the release of several Mexican nationals being held on the opposite side of the border, in El Paso. Peralta also requested that a radio station cease broadcasting advertisements for the hiring of braceros. The station had aired an ad requesting the services of 100 Mexican cotton pickers, who were led to believe that they could cross the border even though their documents were not in order, since it would suffice for them to have a "local passport."[12] This piece of misinformation led to the roundup of many of the unsuspecting Mexican workers.

Peralta managed not only to stymie the promotion of illegal migration but also to prompt the arrest of Joe Dearman, a rancher from Las Cruces, New Mexico, who owned extensive cotton fields. Dearman, who had arranged for the ad to be broadcast on the El Paso radio station, was apprehended by the authorities and forced to pay a fine of 500 pesos for having violated Mexican labor laws to the detriment of Mexican workers who picked and harvested cotton.[13]

## Support for Return

Although for the greater part of 1937 official interest in the return of Mexicans from the United States declined, and the subject received no more than sporadic discussion, the government nonetheless did promote and support the return of some individuals and small groups to advance its goal of colonization. To this end, José Castrejón Pérez, chief of the Population Service in the Interior Ministry, carried out several interrelated initiatives. He promoted the return of farmworkers to Matamoros; first organizing the Unión de Agricultores Mexicanos (Union of Mexican Farmworkers) in St. Paul, Texas, and, between September 1937 and December 1938, arranging the repatriation of twenty families who then formed a new agricultural colony, called La Esperanza, on lands belonging to the La Sauteña hacienda.[14]

Along these same lines, Francisco J. Múgica invited a former companion in arms, Pedro Sarabia, to return to Mexico from his current residence in

Alamo, Texas, to participate in farming the land around Matamoros, land that was "bearing great fruit" thanks to the improvements being made in the area by the government.[15] In addition, he asked Ramón Beteta, undersecretary of foreign relations, to use his influence so that better elements among the expatriate community who were eager to work could return to the country for this purpose.[16]

In mid-1936, Colonel Gabriel Leyva, the governor of Sinaloa, reported that a group of Mexicans who had come back from the United States were languishing in the small settlement of Caminaguato, because they had hoped to find work in the local mines but had not yet been hired. According to Leyva, they had ventured to Caminaguato at the direct encouragement of Cárdenas and thus were asking for assistance from the federal government.[17] In a somewhat parallel situation, Matamoros had become home to a number of discontented farmworkers who had arrived in the past two or three years, attracted by rumors that the federal government would give them land on which they could settle.[18] Within this group, the younger family members born in the United States were especially to be pitied, and many of the adults held the state responsible for their dismal situation, since they believed that the government itself had induced them to return to Mexico.[19] A committee of small and medium-scale farmers and agricultural workers who had returned from the United States to Mexicali, in Baja California, also found themselves in a difficult situation, since the promise made to them of land, farm tools, and housing had not been honored.[20]

From the beginning of the Cárdenas administration, various Mexican nationals and the children born to them in the United States had been regularly arriving back in Mexico, settling in communities or on lands distributed by the government. In a small number of exceptional cases, such as that of La Esperanza, the federal government was the instigator, assembling a small group in the United States and arranging their return to Mexico. The colonies in Caminaguato, Matamoros, and Mexicali, in contrast, did not form on the government's initiative or result from a publicized, organized government campaign. Instead, these colonies sprang up reactively, taking shape as a way of quickly accommodating people who landed back on Mexican soil after being deported or who had returned to the country of their own free will because they could no longer survive in the United States. In all cases, however, no systematic and detailed advanced planning had been done to assist returnees in getting successfully reestablished. As we will see in the particular case of La Esperanza, this omission led to their failure and abandonment. In addition, the Mexican government provided them with meager support.

## The Limits of Official Assistance and the Justifications
for Not Supporting Return

Paradoxically, the invitation to return to Mexico that the government extended to some individuals became intertwined with the measures it took to contain and resist the flow of its nationals back into the country. To serve the latter interest, it pursued a series of actions in the United States, including negotiating with U.S. authorities to avoid deportations, endeavoring to persuade its citizens to continue to live and work in the United States, and maneuvering so that U.S. migration initiatives and projects would not affect the entry of Mexican workers into the United States.

At the outset of the sexenio, Julián Velarde, who on Cárdenas's instructions had studied the question of repatriating Mexicans from the United States, intervened—in the name of the Mexican government—to stop the deportation of 4,000 indigent Mexican families who lived in Los Angeles. To this end, he met with Rex Thompson, a member of the Los Angeles County Board of Supervisors.[21] Velarde succeeded in halting the planned deportation.

In parallel fashion, even as he facilitated the repatriation of a few of his compatriots, José Castrejón Pérez of the Population Service agreed that those migrants who could renew their sharecropping contracts with Texas ranchers should do so, and that any further returns should be postponed until the following year. In Castrejón's view, Mexico's broad economic problems as well as a range of specific conditions then prevailing inside the country were the most immediate obstacles to an active, operable repatriation program.[22] According to Castrejón, Mexico's interests would not be harmed if its nationals remained north of the Rio Grande.

The government's justifications for withholding support for the return of its citizens ranged from citing the negative effects this would have on the nation's economy to setting it against a nationalist labor policy. The fear that the return of a large number of Mexicans would harm both the country's economy and local workers was constant and palpable. The response of Francisco Vázquez del Mercado, principal spokesman for the General Directorate of the Government, an office within the Interior Ministry, illustrates this attitude. In early 1937, representatives of the Mexican Honorary Commission of Cotulla, Texas, appealed to the government for assistance in returning to Mexico. Vázquez argued that settling returnees at the site of the Azúcar Dam, in Tamaulipas (where laborers and employees of the National Irrigation Commission were already working, though a presidential directive had put a temporary stop to the project), would create rather than solve a problem.

Importing more labor could harm the current employees, since it would probably aggravate conditions for local workers and perhaps even spark fights over jobs.[23] The view of Lombardo Toledano, general secretary of the CTM, was more nuanced. While he believed that his compatriots in the United States should not be abandoned, he also believed there could be no systematic move to organize their return until the matter had been duly studied and a plan approved that incorporated the conclusions reached by federal authorities regarding the best ways to proceed.[24]

The arguments made in official circles for not supporting more robustly the return of Mexican nationals also reflected a fear of bringing home people who had lost their rootedness and their sense of nationalism, people who now had children of another nationality and who were better organized, supposedly had greater knowledge, and had acquired superior practices and ways of operating. Moreover, Mexicans who had remained outside the country for a period of years were branded as traitors and opportunists who dodged the suffering of armed struggle by taking refuge in a foreign land. Participants in the Third Convention on Migration took the view that two problems had still to be resolved: (1) determining a suitable form of accommodating returnees and (2) managing their reintegration into Mexican society. An especially thorny subset to this latter issue was that of incorporating children who, as the offspring of Mexicans, "are [yet] not Mexicans idiosyncratically, either through their teaching, or their customs, or even the feelings that could awaken in them a [spirit of] friendliness that they do not find in the country of their parents" (Loyo 1935, 368).

Mexicans living in the United States were also looked on with suspicion because they were given to boast about the skills, customs, and practices they had acquired during their years in exile (Gamio 1930a, 230–37). The degree of organization and solidarity that they achieved in the United States was seen as posing a danger for Mexico's national workers organizations. Returnees, it was feared, might provoke splits inside the nation's unions and might come to occupy key positions in urban and rural workers movements, as they were doing in the United States. Faced with this incipient situation, national laborers' organizations would not give room to participate or award jobs to those who had sustained themselves by residing outside the country.

The general resentment that many people in Mexico had for migrants was still another justification for limiting government assistance to them. Special emphasis was also put on the negative consequences that their arrival would have for the country. According to Manuel Gamio, these clustered around three problems in particular, the first being that some portion of returnees did not go back to their hometown and region but, instead, made their way to the nation's capital or to another of the country's more populous cities. As a result, men who could otherwise have been first-rate farmers and agricultural workers became "mediocre" urban laborers who competed with workers who had not left the country. The returnees thus simply added themselves to the ranks of the unemployed. The second problem entailed "harmful elements" who attached themselves to criminals in the cities or became bandits and often rebels. Third, many in this population who failed to succeed went back to the United States, never to return to Mexico, but once safely across the border spoke out against colonization schemes for the repatriated, claiming that their own experience was proof that resettlement projects did not work, which discouraged other migrants from repatriating (Gamio 1930a, 238).

The Mexico City press took the same accusatory stance. An article in *El Universal*, for example, claimed that while the 110,000 Mexicans—clearly an exaggerated number[25]—who had returned from the United States during the last months of 1935 were dispersed across different regions of the country, the majority had gone to the capital in search of the comforts and conveniences to which they were accustomed. The inflow of this group, the article asserted, explained why the city's population had increased so sharply in just a few months. According to U.S. State Department reports and information supplied by U.S. immigration officials, of the total number of recent returnees, 11,000 were known lawbreakers and the source of most of the crimes committed in the capital. The police poured more fuel on this fire by asserting that the latest series of thefts occurring in the city had employed sophisticated techniques and a level of skill not possessed by Mexican malefactors. In a word, for *El Universal* the increase in criminality registered in Mexico was attributable to the presence of repatriated nationals.[26] The newspaper had stretched the truth because it wanted to use these returning migrants to divert attention from the real causes of the country's current social and economic problems, especially high rates of unemployment and poverty.

In a different part of the country, representatives of the Ciudad Juárez Chamber of Commerce likewise voiced concern over "the threat" that their repatriated compatriots presented. Their arrival and continued presence created a serious problem for the city's authorities and merchants, who were unable to give the repatriated basic provisions. Another factor that played into this concern was that many of the returning migrants came back with a prison record, prompting a request from municipal leaders to the president and the Interior Ministry that they help in removing this transient population from the city as quickly as possible. Within the group were not just criminals but people suffering from communicable diseases, especially tuberculosis, that already constituted a grave problem for the country. The encampment of these people in the city thus put the health and well-being of its citizens in danger.[27]

*El Universal* declared itself in favor of a policy that gave preference to citizens who had remained in the country over those who had chosen to leave. At the same time, one of its editorial writers expressed the view that the government should offer its citizens "a place under the Mexican sun" and, taking advantage of the nationalization of the railways, passage home free of charge. Nonetheless, the question remained: to what part or parts of the country should this stream of returnees be directed? It was a difficult problem to solve, since work and food were scarce in areas of the country with little population; while in areas where there was work and the means of subsistence, the needy, the unemployed, and jobseekers were already found in large numbers.

*El Universal* also made the point that if a return movement did materialize that brought large numbers of nationals back into the country's urban centers and other populated areas, the first line of resistance would come from the unions, because—even though workers maintained a united front to defend themselves—the fair slicing up of the "subminimal wage pie" was not a sure thing.[28] The newspaper further argued that it would be wrong to attend to the needs of "compatriots [who] moved away from their home" when campesinos and urban workers who remained behind were confronting circumstances no less difficult. The paper thus called for the application of radically nationalist principles, whereby Mexican citizens who had remained in the country be given preference over those who had migrated and returned with children of a different nationality.[29]

Despite these attitudes and the various arguments put forward to withhold support for an organized return, the arrival of Mexicans coming back from the United States did not touch off an extended debate within the government, or in the press, or among other elements of Mexican society. In this period, relatively few Mexican nationals entertained the desire to return or came back either with official support or on their own initiative. Consequently, the repercussions that returnees engendered in Cardenista Mexico were minimal. Across various strata of Mexican society, the reaction to the phenomenon was largely one of indifference. Ironically, the lack of support for the return of expatriate nationals was not grounded in the fear over the arrival of the unemployed, of criminals, of the sick and infirm, and of people whose national loyalties were in question, or in the justifications arising therefrom; instead, it derived from the fact that no urgent resolution to the problem was required as well as from the favoritism shown to workers who had remained in the country over those who had migrated.

## The Mexican Government and the Repatriation Project

At the end of 1937, while Cárdenas devoted the bulk of his time to resolving the campesino problem and to promoting agrarianism, the government made public its interest in implementing a repatriation campaign (Córdova 1996, 451; Meyer 1978, 229; Meyer 1995, 291–92; PNR 1933). Thus, that October, the Autonomous Department of Information and Publicity (Departamento Autónomo de Prensa y Publicidad, DAPP) announced that the country intended to bring back its citizens because they were needed to help further the progress of the nation. The department also indicated that these people would be furnished with what they needed to work in Mexico.[30]

DAPP's announcement reflected the government's intention to formulate the plan for a repatriation project, which consumed a full year (1938). Its reasons for doing so were connected to three events that took place during 1938 and the beginning of 1939: the president's decision to carry through with such a plan, an agreement reached with Los Angeles County authorities, and the arrival of Spanish refugees in Mexico.

The announcement delivered by the government at the end of 1937 marked a departure from the policies of previous administrations. The measures that they adopted had grown out of external factors, such as the mass deportations promoted and carried out by U.S. immigration authorities and labor leaders. Cárdenas, in contrast, had the inclination and interest to mount a pilot project, one that contained previously untried features. In his case, there was no emergency situation that demanded intervention and no immediate threat of any mass return of Mexican migrants.

## The Preparatory Work

As 1938 began, the Interior Ministry clarified that Mexican policy on migration should be concerned, first and foremost, with repatriating the country's nationals who lived in the United States. Not only were they forced to compete for jobs there with workers from other countries, but some had shown a yearning for the way life was lived in Mexico and for that reason wished to return. According to the Interior Ministry's calculations, there were 1 million Mexican workers north of the Rio Grande, the majority spread out across the border states, who had acquired knowledge and expertise that could and ought to be used to advance national progress (SEGOB 1938, 85).

The ministry did not attempt to retrace how, to that point, the government had confronted the issue of the return of its citizens. It merely sketched out the guidelines for an official repatriation project that needed to be designed and structured to assure its success. The core objective was to see that the country did not lose out on assimilating the particular virtues and competencies that some repatriated nationals would bring with them. Equally important, Mexico should avoid the definitive departure of this select group in the event that its members met failure because they were not sent to populated regions and channeled into activities that assured their success. In addition, assisting and looking out for the interests of Mexicans abroad was also indispensable, so they would keep alive their aspirations to contribute to "the program for the homeland" and would continue to view themselves as part of the Mexican people. The protection of "México de afuera," through raising that community's standard of living and defending its ties of citizenship, was a central feature of the plan (SEGOB 1938, 85). Yet the Interior Ministry's suggested approach to the return of its citizens was devoid of specific proposals and a detailed, deliverable plan of action. It wanted the project to be successful but did not spell out how that outcome would be achieved. Nevertheless, it began to spread the message.

In mid-February, *El Universal* reported that the Interior Ministry planned to organize a "large-scale" return of Mexicans living abroad and, as an initial step, was asking that the country's governors provide information on work possibilities in their states, so that repatriated nationals would not remain unemployed.[31] Around the same time, General Gildardo Magaña, who later would represent a wing of the Mexican Revolutionary Party in the presidential race, was sent by Cárdenas to San Antonio, Texas, to participate in the commemoration of the twenty-fifth anniversary of that city's daily paper, *La Prensa*, founded in 1913 by the journalist Ignacio Lozano.

In the speech that he delivered, in Cárdenas's name, in San Antonio's municipal auditorium, Magaña invited Mexican campesinos to return to "the bosom of the Homeland," declaring that the Mexican government was offering them not a windfall but instead something of more lasting value: land conquered by the revolution.[32] He also made clear that the government would lend a helping hand so that people who owned livestock, farm tools, automobiles, and household goods and furnishings but little cash savings might return, as might those who had the means to support themselves until the first crops could be harvested. In other words, the government was encouraging and would promote a selective return of its nationals.

In the wake of the newspaper notice about the Interior Ministry's position with respect to a large-scale repatriation plan, followed by Magaña's invitation narrowing the field to campesinos and people with the means of self-support, two versions emerged of how the government would treat the return of its citizens. *El Universal* had clearly distorted and inflated the government's intentions, since the latter planned not to promote a mass return but only, as Magaña noted, to help bring back individuals who met certain clear requirements.

An outline of the repatriation project had been completed by the beginning of March. It was refined over the course of the year, its main lines of action eventually coming into full focus through the efforts of Ignacio García Téllez, Mexico's interior minister, in cooperation with the Foreign Relations Ministry and the Demographics Department. As foreseen, it was directed at people who did not have work, with the further aim of identifying a pool of the most qualified workers, those with farming experience above all, who would be resettled in locations that had been stringently vetted. As a first step, Mexico's consuls were to take a census of their compatriots in the United States, noting if they were employed or unemployed and incorporating data about their economic circumstances, the number of people in households and whether, in each case, the family was financially dependent on a single member or whether separate family members had their own income, and finally, the age and birthplace of each person. To accomplish this task, the Interior Ministry, the SRE, and the consuls received assistance from the honorary commissions and other Mexican associations in the United States. The goal was to identify (within the eligible population) all people in need of assistance so they could exercise their right both to free transportation from the border to their in-country destination and to exemption from customs duties. In addition, the Interior Ministry would furnish work to each person according to his or her abilities and experience.[33]

The Interior Ministry, as part of the plan, would use the censuses to standardize migration policy, since the government had no intention of repatriating, as an entire class, people who were out of work or who at some point had latched on to a job. As noted above, the people it sought were people who could do specialized kinds of work, those connected to agriculture in particular. Moreover, once back in the country, these individuals would be sent to where they would find employment and could help train workers who were unionized or who belonged to cooperatives, to improve their efficiency and productivity. The official government outlook, then, was that preference in repatriation would be given to "the better prepared elements." People chosen in the initial round would be notified beforehand of their new place of residence and would depart for the homeland secure in the knowledge that their services would be put to use immediately. The rest of those selected for repatriation would be slowly deployed to productive locations where there was a demand for laborers.[34]

The Interior Ministry's suggested plan of action and its prospectus on the development of a repatriation project were very general and, on certain points, decidedly vague. At the same time, the results it expected to achieve were quite ambitious, given that all such previous schemes had ended in failure and, what is more, that the record of the Cárdenas administration in following through on plans in this sphere was notably weak. With the appointment of Manuel Gamio to the Demographics Department, however, the project would gain greater clarity and specific, attainable provisions.

## Manuel Gamio and the Repatriation Project

In the second half of 1938, after a period as director of the National University's Institute of Social Research, Manuel Gamio accepted García Téllez's invitation to become chief of the Interior Ministry's Demographics Department. Gamio's move into this new position overlapped with the government's intensified study and heightened discussion of a repatriation plan. Unsurprisingly, it also enabled him to influence the design of the last part of the project and, in large measure, to determine how it would be carried out. From this point on, Gamio put his own ideas and suggestions into practice.

Manuel Gamio put his stamp on Mexican migration policy throughout the 1930s and 1940s. The government sought his advice on how to deal more effectively with the mass repatriation of its nationals that occurred during 1930, and his suggestions regarding measures to protect Mexican braceros were also listened to carefully (Carreras de Velasco 1974, 19, 88). His research and work on the migration of Mexicans to the United States were done at the behest of Emilio Portes Gil, first when the latter was president and later when he served as interior minister, and also received the sponsorship and support of Dwight W. Morrow, U.S. ambassador to Mexico (1927–30), and the New York City–based Social Science Research Council (Gamio 1930a, 1930b, 1931).

Before taking up his post in the Demographics Department, Gamio had already made considerable headway in analyzing how a government repatriation plan should be developed. His understanding came primarily from his examination of the failure of a colonization project involving 300 people who returned to Mexico from La Laguna, California. Between April and August 1927, Gamio carried out a detailed study of their living conditions and general situation in Acámbaro, Guanajuato, where the group had been resettled (Gamio 1930a, 237–38).

Gamio noted that, from the very outset of the return campaign, these individuals had lacked any firm sense of or specific information about the agricultural and geographic characteristics or physical conditions of the land on which they were to be settled. They were uninformed about the roads, the topography, and the range of local products. On their arrival, they discovered that the land was unsatisfactory and that conditions were very unhygienic. As a result, many of them left, some setting off for different parts of the country, others to work on the nearby hacienda of La Encarnación (Gamio 1930a, 237–38).

The failure of the colonization scheme in Acámbaro led Gamio to rethink the dynamics of resettling Mexican nationals. He determined that in the future government assistance would be necessary, channeled through a frankly paternalistic program that included transportation, the provision of land, and coverage of the costs associated with getting people settled. In addition, he suggested the formation of a national commission to take charge of organizing repatriation and colonization efforts. Its immediate objective would involve surveying the features of potential sites, the existing modes of transportation, and prevailing market conditions. Next, commission members, or their representatives, would need to visit the sections of the United States that were home to large concentrations of Mexicans, in particular states in the Southwest and Mountain West, such as Texas, Arizona, California, Colorado, and New Mexico, with the purpose of promoting and organizing the return of farmworkers. The Mexican consuls could assist in this effort by spreading word in these communities of their government's offer of land for new colonization projects. The commission's third objective would be to circulate supplementary information and details, by word of mouth, about the founding of new settlements. Since difficulties and odd situations could arise that might threaten the successful implementation of either general plans or individual cases of resettlement, Gamio proposed the formation of a group within the government to intervene and stave off such eventualities. His final idea pertained to groups of fifty or more people who wished to return to the homeland. In these cases, Gamio suggested, the commission could travel to where people in the group were living to assist them in organizing and arranging their repatriation (Gamio 1930a, 238–40).

Gamio's proposed commission could thus engage and work with future settlers to ensure that their return was efficient and well-organized, serve as an intermediary in the discussions held between U.S. and Mexican authorities preceding the departure of Mexican nationals, plan their transportation back to Mexico as well as expedite their resettlement in the country, and investigate the advisability and prospects of extending bank credits to them. In addition, it could undertake a yearly study and evaluation of the development and progress of the pilot colony with a view toward improving conditions and streamlining organizational procedures for future repatriations on which the government embarked (Gamio 1930a, 240–41).

The experience of the Acámbaro project had laid the groundwork for Gamio's advocacy of this new approach, which he refined and amplified in his 1935 book, *Hacia una México Nuevo: Problemas sociales*. In this work, Gamio took the position that the government's actions should be confined to people who were recently repatriated since, in his view, those who had come back prior to 1934 were regressing from "the higher state they had reached" in the United States. In terms of diet, dress, housing, practical skills, personal ambitions, and ways of working, they had regressed to the state in which they had lived before migrating; everything in their lives had reverted to how and what it had been before (Gamio 1935, 58–59). The ease with which these returnees had slipped back into their former, tradition-bound way of life led Gamio to see earlier repatriations as failures, since—in his judgment—the country had not benefited from them.

Gamio put forward a new plan intended to exploit his compatriots' potential, so that the nation would not lose "the worthy activities of those men." A key component of his plan was that the settlements populated by repatriated nationals should be relatively distant from other villages and communities, located on agricultural estates already owned by the federal government or on land that it acquired for the purpose of colonization. In this way, the "regression" of returnees into old cultural practices and their "physical decadence" would be avoided, since whenever they were resettled into existing communities they drifted back into their former way of life, ineluctably pressured by the social environment and the weight of tradition. Of the population of the newly founded settlements, to be designated as "rural centers of the repatriated," 85 or 90 percent would be composed of farmworkers and agricultural laborers who had experience working in regions of the United States with a climate and range of agricultural production similar to those found in the rural centers. The remaining 10 or 15 percent could be composed of artisans or workers with industrial experience (Gamio 1935, 60–61, 58–60; Gamio 1930a, 236–37).

In essence, Gamio's ideas and proposals to implement and carry out a government repatriation project may be summed up in six points: (1) those who had come back to Mexico before 1935 were to be excluded, (2) the focus would be put on small groups of farmworkers and people experienced in planting and growing crops, (3) the repatriated should be settled in places rel-atively removed from other centers of population, (4) the return of nationals should be small-scale and promoted on a top-down basis, from within the government, deploying a modest outlay of resources for transportation, the provision of land, and the costs that people incurred in getting themselves reestablished, (5) the return should be promoted, organized, and arranged in the United States, where migrants currently lived and worked, and (6) this repatriation was to be an experiment that would help in designing and devel-oping subsequent government projects.

Gamio thus analyzed in full how, where, and through what particular means and measures a repatriation project should be mounted and carried out. As we will see, his ideas on this score were followed almost to the letter by the Cárdenas administration. Nevertheless, the ideas themselves were not new. Since the inception of the sexenio, indeed since shortly after the turn of the century, a host of such ideas had been expressed by government ministers, labor leaders, and demographers. Among others, Andrés Landa y Piña, Gilberto Loyo, Francisco Múgica, Ignacio García Téllez, José Castrejón Pérez, and Vicente Lombardo Toledano had advocated the establishment of agricultural colonies through the selective repatriation of Mexican nationals, agricultural workers above all, supported by minimal government funding. Their ideas, however, were general and vague in the extreme. None gave extensive thought to pre-cisely how the government should put a repatriation plan into practice. Gamio, in contrast, took these uncertainties into account and spelled out in detail how the government should proceed and what specific measures it should take.

During the second half of 1938, Cárdenas stepped up his pronounce-ments in favor of a repatriation plan, a stance that seemingly went against the grain, since the government was under political and economic pressure from the United States as the result of its nationalization of oil companies that March. It also faced internal challenges. Economic conditions in the country had worsened, causing a discernable drop in the regime's popular-ity. In addition, Saturnino Cedillo, the San Luis Potosí military and political cacique, had risen up in revolt against the central government. In October, Cárdenas again released a statement inviting Mexicans in the United States to return to Mexico. In line with this declaration, the DAPP announced that the government was putting the finishing touches on a repatriation program.[35] As one element in the program, Cárdenas issued an order that called for the formation of a commission to study the question of devel-oping and promoting federal lands as sites on which to resettle people. In overseeing this task, the commission needed to ensure that reports gathered on the climate, work and health conditions, and agricultural possibilities of these lands were executed with "the utmost methodical" care, so that their colonization would be anchored "on a solid foundation," and in a manner that yielded practical results.[36] The secretary of agriculture would be placed in charge of organizing the colonies based on the economic possibilities of each state.[37] Cárdenas did not restrict himself to intensifying and elevating the rhetoric in favor of a repatriation plan; he also took the first steps toward realizing it by forming a commission whose objective was to identify places where Mexican nationals returning from the United States could be resettled. Yet this sequence also underscored that the government's actions to support a return had been paltry at best. Four years after Cárdenas ascended to the presidency, they translated into the formation of a commission to look into the matter and devise a plan.

In mid-1938, still more official declarations were heard regarding the elaboration of a repatriation program, accompanied by calls issued to Mexicans in the United States to return to the homeland. The appeals made to Mexican nationals across the border were perhaps one way of distracting national attention away from the regime's reformist measures that day by day were drawing more criticism and condemnation. In similar fashion, the chief of the Demographics Department set forth his proposals for how to carry out the repatriation project. Cárdenas followed suit, making public his willingness to see the project through and undertaking certain actions as evidence of his commitment. The government came to the aid of various indigent nationals, helping them return to different places in the country and, in keeping with this objective, granting them land in some of the northern Mexican states. In the face of deep rumblings of discontent inside the country and of growing attacks on his government, Cárdenas tried to turn attention toward the Mexican community abroad as a device to bolster his flagging popularity and demonstrate his nationalist credentials.

## The Resettling of Some Repatriated Nationals inside the Country

During 1938, the government interceded to support the return of small groups that arrived in the states of Chihuahua and Tamaulipas. A Mexico City daily reported, at the beginning of June, that 100 families deported from the United States were set to begin agricultural work on 400 hectares of land that the federal government had granted them in the community of Villa Ahumada, in the state of Chihuahua, where they formed a community called the Local Agricultural Society of Deportees from the North. The families prepared the site to make it fit for living and dug wells to irrigate the land, on which they grew cotton, cereals, forage for livestock, and a variety of vegetables.[38] It is not known whether the colony proved successful or what range of difficulties it experienced. Nor do the available data permit one to gauge its accomplishments. Moreover, the number of families as reported by the press seems unduly high and was surely less than 100.

Another group of twenty-five families who had lived in Robstown, Texas, were resettled in the northern part of Tamaulipas, where they arrived either in automobiles or in trucks and with farm tools in their possession. They intended to grow grains, cereals, and cotton. Like their counterparts who had settled in Chihuahua, these families received land from the government, but there is no record of exactly what happened to them collectively. Some doubtless experienced serious difficulties, while others managed to adapt and establish themselves. Among the latter was Ambrosio Garza, who became the founder of the community of Río Bravo, Tamaulipas, where, in his recounting, "by order of President Cárdenas" he and other individuals received lots that covered twelve and a half hectares, on the condition that they work the land and did not sell it. During their time in Texas, these farmworkers had learned a good deal about growing crops and how to handle machinery, so, in Garza's telling, "in this place we could do a good job of planting, all the more because we were working land that belonged to us." Further in their favor was the region's abundant supply of water. Not long after they arrived, they opened irrigation canals, so that in some years they had good cotton harvests.[39]

The government also collaborated in setting up some families in Baja California. In mid-October, the Ministry of Finance and Public Credit (Secretaría de Hacienda y Crédito Público, SHCP) transferred 45,000 pesos to the governor of the state, Rodolfo Sánchez Taboada, to cover two tranches of repatriation expenses. Of the total amount, 30,000 pesos were used to support the costs of settling twenty-four families on the ejido of Guadalupe, with the remaining 15,000 devoted to resettling five families coming from Los Angeles.[40] The repatriated families in Baja suffered serious setbacks. In the following year, Sánchez Taboada requested additional financial assistance, since the group was bereft of funds, with the governor characterizing their situation as "truly painful."[41] President Cárdenas answered his call and signed an urgent accord so that the SHCP would quickly furnish the requested monies.[42] From time to time, then, the government provided sufficient support to enable some individuals to return and make a new start in their native country. The groups that received assistance were always small and, with rare exception, the sums of money approved by the government were never very substantial. The pattern of action followed by the Cárdenas administration thus differed little from that of its predecessors, who—apart from the times when they faced mass returns—had established a record of sporadically furnishing limited assistance to small numbers of Mexican nationals who wished to leave the United States and return to the homeland. Despite the outward appearance of reform—creating the Demographic Studies and Repatriation section in the Interior Ministry, promulgating its population law, and announcing its embrace of a repatriation project—the Cárdenas government's policy on the return of its citizens did not represent a breakthrough from the policies that previous governments had followed. Still, new situations arose that called on the government to respond in a new way.

## Difficulties in Providing Aid at the Border: Support from Organized Workers

During 1938, with the fall of the U.S. economy back into recession, the number of deportations again spiked, which in turn led Mexican border authorities to flood the government with petitions for free railway tickets so that returnees could travel back to their hometown or village. An accord emanating from the office of the president had stipulated that resources should be made available so that deportees who reached the border could continue on their way. At the end of April, the deputy representative of migration services in Ciudad Juárez, Ignacio H. Santana, held out hope that this policy would be put into practice. The Mexican National Railways, however, canceled the exemption that had been granted to repatriated Mexicans, which had allowed them to pay only a portion of the total cost of their passage.[43]

The suspension of this exemption created a difficult situation in cities and towns along the border, above all in Ciudad Juárez and Matamoros. A ragtag of unemployed and indigent men, women, and young people wandered the streets of the two cities. One of the ways used to obtain the money needed for rail tickets was to take up collections, but there had been so many of these since the deportees began congregating in these cities that few people were inclined to continue making donations. The situation was so grave that the Interior Ministry requested assistance from the Railway Workers Administration to transport people from the border to their final in-country destination.[44]

Matters were not resolved until October, when—on the initiative of the Ciudad Juárez Chamber of Commerce—various indigent families present in that city received passes to travel from the Mexican National Railways.[45] The willingness of President Cárdenas to intervene personally as well as his appeal to the country's organized workers for their collaboration also helped overcome the impasse.

In September, the interior minister reported that Cárdenas sought help from the country's workers organizations in the face of a threatened expulsion of 500 Mexican farmhands laboring on the tomato harvest in Indiana. Broadly speaking, he received the desired response, since many of these organizations supported the return of their compatriots, even going so far as to suggest both how their repatriation might be carried out in a systematic, organized way and how the nation might take advantage of their skills. On a similar note, the leaders of one of the country's largest labor federations, the General Confederation of Workers, announced that each of its member unions would contribute a sum in accord with its capacity to do so, a sum that would constitute a "respectable" amount to "make the life of their compatriots" in the United States, or their repatriation, "more bearable."[46]

Direct financial support from labor became more critical in October, when some 3,000 Mexicans were deported, through El Paso, in a precarious state. In response, the office of the president reiterated its request for collaboration on the part of workers and asked that, in this case, the unions reach deep into their coffers and contribute a considerably higher sum.[47] After the Interior Ministry and the Labor Department petitioned the majority of the country's unions and workers syndicates for this purpose,[48] funds arrived from around the country.[49] The union to which workers in the Terminal Company of Veracruz belonged sent in 100 pesos; the union representing the sugar refinery and associated workers in San Cristóbal (Veracruz) contributed 45 pesos; workers in the Superba Hosiery and Socks Manufacturing Union donated 35 pesos "in the hope," as they put it, "that this amount helps in part to relieve the very sorrowful situation of our class brothers."

The deportations that took place at the end of 1938 delivered a clear message to the Cárdenas administration. It was evident that the government had no concrete measures in place to deal with a sudden, unanticipated return of its citizens. As of mid-1938, apart from the announcement of a repatriation project and the assistance extended to indigent migrants, Cárdenas had taken few measurable actions to support the return of Mexican nationals. As their expulsion from the United States shot up, however, he was forced to respond in a novel way, by calling for assistance from a sector—the working class—that had helped secure his grip on power and now constituted one of the pillars of the government. At the same time, Cárdenas also entered into negotiations with officials of Los Angeles County to repatriate his compatriots.

## Bilateral Negotiations for Repatriation

At the end of 1938, some authorities in Southern California were still attempting to expel Mexicans from the country. The visit to Mexico City of a member of the Los Angeles County Board of Supervisors, Gordon L. McDonough, set off a chain of events. McDonough had come to the Mexican capital to discuss two repatriations—one general in nature, the other focused on Mexicans who were ill.[50] To initiate even tentative discussion of the latter group was difficult in itself, because neither side was willing to assume responsibility for tubercular Mexican nationals who lived in the United States.

Although they reached no specific agreement regarding sick Mexican migrants, García Téllez and McDonough nonetheless set a date—10 November—when they would meet in Los Angeles to discuss a general repatriation program. In that meeting, they reached agreement on four points. First, the Mexican government promised to begin carrying out a plan for the return of its compatriots. The plan called for the governors of several Mexican states to identify places where returnees could be resettled and also stipulated that the country's unions would incorporate returning workers into their ranks. Second, Los Angeles County would furnish the Mexican government with the address, number of family members, trade, city, and native state of indigent Mexicans listed on the relief rolls of Los Angeles County, so that the Mexican government would know the number and situation of those people who were to be repatriated. Third, the federal government in Mexico would pinpoint and designate large extensions of land on which to resettle these people. Fourth, the Mexican government, working through its immigration offices, could deny permission to leave to those of its citizens who requested admission into the United States to work but who lacked adequate means of self-support. On 17 November 1938, in a third conversation between García Téllez and McDonough, the four points were officially adopted (Hoffman 1974, 162–65).

The agreement negotiated between Los Angeles County and the Mexican government spotlighted some aspects of the latter's migration policy that it had already advanced since the beginning of the year. Other elements of the agreement by and large coincided with what the government had been in the process of formulating: support on the state level from governors to help resettle Mexican nationals who returned, obtaining help from workers organizations as part of a repatriation program, and the awarding of land and intensification of the central government's policy against migration. The existence of these multiparty commitments helped facilitate the signing of the pact by the Mexican side. In large measure, it represented an endorsement of long-standing Mexican government policy on the issue of migration and, in this way, enabled the Cardenista government to stay within the boundaries of its own broad goals respecting migration and repatriation. The pressures exerted and the demands made by the California authorities may have forced the Mexican government to accept (at least notionally) a flow of returnees, but they did not compel any fundamental recalibration of the Cardenista position.

This episode reflected the interest of U.S. authorities and, to a lesser extent, the Mexican government as well. But while it may have been shared, both parties acted on this interest from a different perspective. On the one side, in Mexico, the idea of a repatriation project had been under study since the beginning of 1938; on the other, the Los Angeles County authorities had shown a consistent desire to give new momentum to deportations. By the end of the year, both inclinations had converged, or intersected, but one—the Mexican project—gained the upper hand. The way the return of Mexican nationals was carried out would conform to the broad sweep of the Mexican plan, not to the objectives laid down by Los Angeles County officials. Cárdenas skillfully played the matter so as to realize two basic objectives: first, to develop his repatriation plan but roll it out in a way that avoided granting of large swaths of land to returnees; and second, to satisfy, on the surface, the expectations of the U.S. side yet stifle the California campaign to send back a large number of Mexican nationals. The latter objective would be realized by establishing a single colony on which to resettle migrants returning not from California but from Texas.

The agreement reached between the Mexican representatives and those from Los Angeles County spurred Cárdenas to expedite his plans for implementing a repatriation project. Again, he maneuvered to use the situation to his advantage. He acknowledged the assistance that the county authorities had extended to Mexican nationals, in return for which he committed to launch a program to bring home his compatriots. Moreover, Cárdenas demonstrated (or feigned) flexibility on the issue, because at that point he was trying to stabilize a delicate situation involving the expropriated oil companies (which had subjected the regime to strong political and economic pressures) and had no desire to fan the flames of conflict with local U.S. authorities.

The plan was presented by the president, the press (opposition as well as official), and various political figures as a wide-reaching, transformative one that would serve all Mexicans living in difficult circumstances in the United States. The stream of information and declarations that the subject generated from late 1938 into early 1939, as well as the interest that the government displayed in it (or made a show of displaying in it) contrasted radically with the scant attention it had commanded during the administration's initial years. Still, the government's limited actions on repatriation to this stage, the meager resources it had allocated for this purpose, and the modest assistance it had provided to support an organized return of its nationals immediately inspired doubts regarding how the project would be carried out.

In a population conference held in Mexico City at the end of 1938, participants discussed the question of why Mexico should "seek" and take in nationals from abroad when it could scarcely absorb the small number of those who had returned since 1935.[51] The response was that the government would support not a massive but a small-scale return, which would be economically feasible. Moreover, the president had already received reports that while various individuals wished to return to Mexico, they were fearful of doing so. The failure experienced by their compatriots in Pinotepa and El Coloso had undermined their confidence in coming back to the homeland. Others feared losing their right of residence or their personal goods and effects. For them, a return would entail great sacrifice, especially when they had managed to sustain themselves in the United States during the depths of the Depression. There were also reports that some Mexican American children preferred not to leave their country and return to the land of their parents.

Cárdenas had taken several firm steps toward realizing a repatriation plan. As we have seen, the head of the Demographics Department advanced a series of specific ideas about how such a plan should be implemented, and, in this same vein, an agreement had been worked out with the Los Angeles County authorities.[52] The president considered promoting a plan, one that was trimmed down, with precise objectives and through which he hoped to gain certain benefits that he could use to the government's advantage both inside the country and in its dealings with foreign powers. To initiate a campaign in favor of the return of Mexican nationals would be a way of responding positively to the agreement concluded with Los Angeles County (and might also serve to mitigate some of the tension that existed between the government and U.S. business interests resulting from expropriations of land in the Yaqui Valley, of the railways in June 1937, and above all of the oil fields). As events would show, the government would also use the repatriation campaign as a nationalist symbol, to generate sympathy and popular support for one of its policies at a moment when it found itself in open crisis.

Toward the conclusion of the sexenio, the reforms instituted by Cárdenas and his circle were severely criticized and bitterly opposed at various levels of Mexican society. The sectors that bore the brunt of his policies reacted by protesting angrily, petitioning for redress, and—in some instances—threatening violence. The Cardenista reforms as they affected the country's economic structure and organization, the political consequences stemming from the impetus given to large urban and rural workers groups, the displacement of the Callista faction in the management of national affairs, and the government's educational program as a pillar of the wider process of social transformation—all of these were deeply resented by a heterogeneous but powerful group of established interests. Large landowners, capitalists, ardent Catholics of average means, and, in general, all those who for various reasons did not subscribe to the aims of the Cárdenas regime, attacked it and its leanings (Knight 1993, 48–49; Medina 1978, 13–14; Townsend 1959, 341–48). The implementation of socially oriented policies produced a rift in Mexican society. At one end stood those who had benefited, at another, those whose interests had suffered, among the latter being some campesino and workers groups that, contrary to government intentions, had failed to benefit in any way during Cárdenas's years in power. Throughout 1939 and 1940, the divisive effect of the regime's policies fostered a tense social and politically explosive environment that served as a backdrop for carrying out a singular repatriation plan (Medina 1978, 13–14).

The widely publicized repatriation of Mexicans was a symbolic triumph of Cardenista nationalism. Together with agrarian reform and the expropriation of oil and the railways, the project to bring Mexicans back to the homeland was designed to animate patriotic pride within the populace and promote feelings of solidarity with the Mexican community in the United States. It lifted the government into playing an active role in this sphere and allowed it to cast itself as the engine of repatriation.

As 1938 came to a close, four years had passed since Cárdenas had ascended to the presidency. Little of a concrete nature had been accomplished in this time to support the return of Mexicans from the United States. The president, however, now took the position that the government response could not be limited to the support it had offered its citizens abroad in the past: giving free or subsidized railway passage to indigent deportees at the border so they could travel back to their hometowns and villages and granting land to small, select groups of returnees. It could not be limited to performing studies, to making repeated promises to free up sites where returnees could settle and successfully reintegrate, or to mobilizing the nation's workers so they would resolve the difficulties encountered by their migrant compatriots. Cárdenas now believed that the discussion in favor of returning Mexican nationals needed to be elevated and a formal campaign for repatriation begun.

## CHAPTER FIVE

# The Repatriation Project, 1938–1939

The work that I am doing is not intended to culminate in a repatriation campaign or crusade.

—RAMÓN BETETA, 5 MAY 1939

On 20 November 1938, as part of commemorations of the twenty-eighth anniversary of the Mexican Revolution, Cárdenas delivered a speech from the central balcony of the National Palace in which he announced the start of a repatriation plan. Addressing the crowd gathered below, he drew attention to the thousands of Mexicans who had migrated to another country in search of work, and he underscored his government's promise to help them return.

The changes "brought about by the Revolution," he stated, should benefit not only those who had lived through it within the borders of the republic but also those who had left the country, in quest of a better life and better circumstances. Consequently, Cárdenas laid special emphasis on his commitment to shower favor on the return of "his absent sons," as a way to help strengthen the population, pursue constructive actions, and confront problems afflicting the nation. Although the country faced a series of other social and economic challenges that needed to be met, these people, too, deserved every consideration (SRE 1939, 21–26l; Cárdenas 1978a, 1:335).

Cárdenas's address marked the point at which his commitment to implementing a repatriation plan went beyond the abstract and rhetorical. Moreover, while he expressed a desire to help "all" his migrant compatriots, he was careful to specify that such assistance would have to be provided gradually and selectively; that is, it would be tailored to resettle groups of Mexican farmworkers in areas of the country where their experience and skills might be usefully applied to advance social and economic development.[1] In focusing on agricultural workers as the target audience, and in the parallel belief that returning migrants would help propel the nation's development, the

Cárdenas administration repeated formulas and approaches that had been invoked and followed since the beginning of the century.

## Rejecting the Call to Return

The plan for a return that Cárdenas put into effect at the end of 1938 was generally greeted with either little interest or outright opposition by the Mexican community in the United States. Although many migrants lived under very difficult circumstances as a result of the U.S. government's employment policies, they were wary of the president's plan and were therefore reluctant to return. Others were gainfully employed or owned property, and now had ties to their host country.

At the end of January 1939, Ramón Beteta, undersecretary of foreign relations, circulated a message to the Mexican consulates in the United States requesting that they use all the means at their disposal to convey to the Mexican community in their jurisdiction the government's proposal to repatriate those who wished to return. More directly, Beteta told the consuls that they should help convince Mexican nationals of the advantages of returning home. In addition, he instructed them to carry out a census of individuals interested in returning.[2] By the end of March, the Foreign Relations Ministry had compiled a summary list from data gathered by the California consulates in San Francisco, Los Angeles, San Bernardino, San Diego, and Calexico; the Arizona consulates in Tucson, Phoenix, Nogales, Naco, and Douglas; the Texas consulates in Alpine, El Paso, Del Rio, Eagle Pass, Laredo, McAllen, Brownsville, San Antonio, Corpus Christi, Galveston, and Dallas; as well as consulates in New Orleans, Denver, Salt Lake City, Oklahoma City, Kansas City, Saint Louis, Chicago, Detroit, New York, and Mobile. The census indicated that a total of 565 families, comprising 2,785 individuals, had expressed an interest in returning to the homeland (see table 5.1).

According to Mexican consuls in San Diego and Dallas, a majority of their compatriots stated that they would resettle in whatever place the federal government chose for them. The consuls in the Texas cities of Del Rio and Beaumont told Beteta that the repatriation effort was urgently needed because Mexicans who had found employment with the Works Progress Administration had now been replaced by U.S. citizens.[3] The same urgency was expressed by the consul in Chicago, where Mexican nationals relieved of their WPA jobs now relied on public welfare. Within the group that indicated a willingness to return, laborers figured prominently. The Chicago area families included 151 children.[4]

TABLE 5.1 Repatriations requested by Mexican consulates in the
United States, 1 January–31 March 1939

| CONSULATE | NO. OF FAMILIES | NO. OF PERSONS |
|---|---|---|
| Beaumont, Tex. | 38 | 245 |
| Brownsville, Tex. | 2 | 12 |
| Chicago | 140 | 511 |
| Corpus Christi | 43 | 245 |
| Dallas | 34 | 191 |
| Del Rio, Tex. | 14 | 203 |
| Houston | 68 | 583 |
| New Orleans | 34 | 147 |
| Oklahoma City | 17 | 64 |
| San Diego | 175 | 584 |
| TOTAL | 565 | 2,785 |

SOURCE: APRB, exp. 308, leg. 8, Summary of repatriations requested by the
Mexican consulates in the United States, Mexico City, 3 April 1939.

A similar story emerged from Houston, where the Mexican consul reported that 68 families, totaling 583 individuals, needed to be repatriated
without delay because they had lost the jobs they had held working on federally funded projects. The consul in Corpus Christi reported that his compatriots were managing to survive thanks to public assistance. The group in
his jurisdiction that wished to return was comprised of farmworkers who
had lived in Texas for more than ten years. The families possessed a variety of
household items and the majority also owned a vehicle.[5]

The poor work conditions endured by most Mexican nationals and their
U.S.-born children drove them to consider returning across the border. In
many cases, however, that factor alone—important motivator that it was—
did not suffice. In Dallas, for example, families otherwise interested in returning lacked confidence in the Mexican government's plan. Before undertaking
the journey, they wanted to know where they would be sent and what employment opportunities they would find when they arrived. Other factors
also held them back. In Del Rio and Beaumont, Mexican children older than
twelve and younger than twenty were opposed to returning to Mexico because they had yet to complete their studies or because they believed they
would face a worse situation in that country.[6]

Many Mexicans living in Chicago displayed an interest in returning yet
resisted doing so, again out of a lack of confidence in the government's plan.
Mexico's consul in Brownsville, Texas, indicated that his compatriots in that

city and the surrounding area did not trust the arrangements that the government was making. Furthermore, the offer to return elicited little interest in itself because—barring unusual circumstances—the majority had regular employment working farmland in the Rio Grande Valley and no problem supporting themselves. Before making any decision to leave, they wanted to know what concrete support they could count on from the government. The same doubts regarding the Mexican government's capacity to carry out a project of this nature were voiced by some representatives of the Mexican community in San Antonio. And, like his counterpart in Brownsville, the consul in New Orleans reported that most Mexican nationals in his jurisdiction showed little or no interest in a return because they had jobs and faced no serious economic problems.[7]

In a visit in early 1939, Alejandro M. Bravo, chief secretary of the Brownsville consulate, heard similar sentiments expressed by his compatriots in San Benito, Harlingen, and Los Fresnos. They feared that, once back in Mexico, they would be left high and dry, without the help needed to survive and engage productively in agricultural work. What is more, many of them had finished tilling the soil and planting crops, which meant that they could not leave until the harvest months later, in September or October.[8] Bravo also observed that his compatriots who labored in the fields enjoyed certain creature comforts that gave them a feeling of well-being and fulfillment. They had developed particular interests and formed relationships or friendships that "brought them contentment." To these factors was added yet another, namely, that the children born in the region did not feel the same pull to return as did their parents. Returning to the homeland, Bravo remarked, "was a very serious and complex matter" for Mexicans who had lived for a long time in the United States. He concluded that Mexicans born and raised in the United States were for all intents and purposes lost to Mexico and that the repatriation would not happen unless Mexico's economy became stronger than that north of the Rio Grande.[9]

Based on all the information gathered, it appeared that fewer than 3,000 Mexican nationals wanted to repatriate because they could not find work in the United States. At the same time, however, these potential returnees harbored great doubts about the Mexican government plan. This lack of confidence was motivated in part by the much-discussed failure of the colony in Pinotepa, Oaxaca, as well as the hardship experienced by many families who repatriated when General Eduardo Hernández Cházaro served as head of the consulate in San Antonio. Many in the latter group had been part of the Pinotepa colony and, on returning to the United States, had let it be known that the Mexican government had failed to deliver on its promises. The letters that these people wrote to friends and relatives in the United States discredited whatever scheme the government might attempt to launch in the future.[10]

The circumstances surrounding the Cardenista campaign for return were fundamentally different from those that existed before 1933, when thousands of Mexican nationals found themselves pressured to leave the United States. In 1939, the government's repatriation plan faced a general climate of skepticism.

## The Organization of the Return in the United States

The first step toward implementing the Cardenista plan was taken at the beginning of 1939, when the president commissioned Ramón Beteta to examine the situation of Mexican nationals in the United States and organize the repatriation process. Beteta declared that plan operations would begin in Texas, conclude in California, and consist of two stages: a first, urgent phase that focused on people trapped in bad conditions and a second, selective phase that targeted Mexican nationals according to their occupation, but which at the outset would be limited to farmworkers. The latter might be sent to an agricultural colony, still to be founded, in Matamoros; or they might be incorporated into existing ejidos or placed on land that already had an irrigation system. As an exception to the general rule, allowance could be made to send those individuals whose circumstances were "extremely bad" back to their native village or town. Beteta believed that this latter group contained very few people and thus would not increase Mexico's unemployment rate. Moreover, he added, the type of repatriation they represented "has always existed."[11]

Beteta stated that the purpose of his mission was not to organize "a campaign or crusade for repatriation" but, instead, to set up a system that would permit, in a permanent way, "the gradual but definitive return of peasant farmers and agricultural workers who had left the country during the period of armed struggle." They should be given the opportunity to work in Mexico and contribute to the nation's development.[12] Beteta was much more than simply a high-ranking functionary. He wielded considerable influence within the government and maintained a singularly close relationship with Cárdenas. His rise to a position of power and the influence that he exerted during the Cárdenas sexenio were due in part to family ties as well as to a personal friendship and his academic training. Beteta had studied law in Mexico's National University and also earned a degree in economics from the University of Texas. Another factor that helped explain his standing was

Cárdenas's reluctance to discuss various matters with his minister of foreign relations, Eduardo Hay. Although Hay had the portfolio, it was an open secret that Beteta, not Hay, determined the policy of the ministry (Balderrama and Rodríguez 1995, 148).

As the plan spelled out, Beteta first went to Texas, where he spent most of his time promoting repatriation. He subsequently traveled north to cities including Chicago, New York, and Washington. The final stop on Beteta's visit was California, where he traveled briefly around the state but made nothing like the effort that he had in Texas to encourage the return of his compatriots.

## The Decision to Carry Through with Repatriation from Texas

The decision by the Mexican government to make Texas the focal point of its repatriation plan stemmed from how local labor leaders and migration officials in that state had handled the expulsion of Mexican nationals during the first years of the Depression. The decision was based on various factors, all of which Cárdenas doubtless evaluated in consultation with Beteta, García Téllez, and Gamio. One, however, had greater importance than the others: local authorities in Texas were less likely, in the face of an organized effort at repatriation, to unleash a wave of deportations.

Contrary to what took place in Los Angeles, Detroit, Chicago, and Gary, Indiana, welfare agencies in Texas had played no role in deporting hundreds of Mexican nationals. The public assistance agencies in Texas were not well organized and lacked the staff necessary to send foreign nationals to the border. In addition, when the Depression worsened in Texas, it became apparent that funds available for public assistance there were limited. Thus local agencies would not be in a position to help underwrite the costs of helping foreigners leave the country (McKay 1982, 147).

Given this history, as well as the more general "hands-off" policy followed by state government in Texas with respect to Mexicans leaving the state, it was less likely that officials there would decide to embark on a deportation campaign (or that public welfare agencies in the state would stop providing assistance to needy Mexican nationals) once they learned about the repatriation plan. Another mitigating factor was that the deportations that had begun in Texas in 1928 and intensified between 1929 and 1931 later tapered off, whereas in California, and Los Angeles especially, the expulsion of Mexican nationals that began in 1931 continued throughout the decade and were pursued more forcefully than in Texas or other states such as Illinois, Arizona, and New Mexico (McKay 1982, 147).

Simple geography—the proximity of Mexico—and the existence of a transportation network also dictated that Texas would be the easier state from which to organize and carry out a repatriation plan. From the outset of the Great Depression, a steady stream of Mexicans had returned to Tamaulipas and nearby states like Nuevo León. Their movement back across the border was continual, and the Mexican government essentially played no part in it. Many individuals had returned from Texas with relative ease and resettled in different areas of Tamaulipas and Nuevo León. The momentum that Cárdenas had given to return would not make it any more difficult for people to cross the border. The situation was very different in California, home to a large Mexican community, where authorities were still seizing on any pretext to deport Mexican nationals.

According to the official version, as enunciated by Beteta, the repatriation plan was initiated in Texas because Mexican migrants in that state, more than in others, needed and had requested immediate assistance. Furthermore, many of them were experienced in growing cotton, a factor on which the government leaned heavily in promoting the return, since it aimed to convert the area where it planned to resettle the returnees into a cotton-growing zone.[13]

According to Beteta, his compatriots in the central and western United States did not require urgent assistance because many had steady employment as day laborers. Others held jobs in factories or on the railroads or labored in the fields. At the same time, of course, these were the very people who would be most useful to Mexico, since their skill sets and training made them a force for progress in agriculture and industry. Moreover, they were the ones who remitted money to their families in Mexico. Still, not all Mexicans living in the United States needed to return to the homeland. Their residence across the border was not harmful either to them or to Mexico. Mexico, it went without saying, was unable to offer them work similar to that which they enjoyed in the United States, nor did it have the public assistance infrastructure of its neighbor to the north. In a sense, the repatriation plan sought to have it both ways. It held out the ideal of an integral return, so that all expatriates who wished to resume life in the homeland might do so, but it followed a pragmatic hierarchy, in which preference would be given to the neediest and, above all, to those who had the knowledge and experience to help advance the government's agrarian program for the northern region of Tamaulipas.[14] Two principles of the Cardenista repatriation policy thus maintained their primacy: Mexicans in the United States who had jobs should stay there and, of those who did not, only those believed to be the most qualified should return.

With his government's announcement of its repatriation project, Cárdenas clearly hoped that U.S. authorities would refrain from any large-scale deportation of Mexicans, since such a move would contradict the purposes of his plan. From this perspective, his decision to stage and organize the campaign in Texas augured well, since—as we have seen—the actions taken by the authorities in that state to deport Mexicans during the first half of the decade were relatively benign. Nonetheless, the Cardenista project could not escape analysis by interested parties in the United States.

While promotion of the return that Beteta intended to carry out in Texas was something that the Mexican government could act on unilaterally, the undersecretary could not set out on his travels around the United States without the approval, implicit or explicit, of the U.S. authorities. The matter was not negotiated, nor are there any indications that conversations were held to sound out the opinion of either the U.S. government or state officials in Texas. Officially, Cárdenas told Beteta that his task was discretionary, that he was only to issue statements about the government's interest in repatriating its citizens and about the progress it was making in furthering the nation's social and economic development. Unofficially, however, as part of his visits to Washington, D.C., and New York, Beteta helped Francisco Castillo Nájera, Mexico's ambassador to the United States, finalize the diplomatic package that had been negotiated with Donald Richberg, a key adviser to President Roosevelt and general counsel of the National Recovery Administration during the first New Deal. Richberg had been put in charge of negotiating with the Mexican government to settle claims arising from the oil expropriations. In addition, Beteta met with officials at the State Department.[15] All well and good, but how were Beteta's endeavors judged? To what degree could he intervene in U.S. internal affairs in his efforts to promote the repatriation plan?

Josephus Daniels, the U.S. ambassador to Mexico, had been criticized on various occasions for making observations about Mexican laws that affected the interests of his compatriots. For its part, the U.S. State Department conducted a quiet investigation to evaluate whether it might offer a critique of the repatriation plan. From reports issued first by the governor of Texas and subsequently by his counterpart in California, it was learned that Beteta had held broad discussions concerning the problems faced by Mexicans in the United States (in Texas especially), the government's plans to revitalize selected repatriation, and the possibility of securing employment for returnees in Mexico. Since Beteta had shown no indication of taking more aggressive or intrusive actions on behalf of his compatriots in the United States, U.S. officials concluded that he would not be interfering in their country's domestic politics; hence they did not try to obstruct his campaign or issue any statements that opposed it.[16] Moreover, U.S. labor leaders and migration authorities, who had spearheaded efforts to round up and deport Mexican nationals, undoubtedly cheered these developments, since—from their viewpoint—the departure of the unwanted Mexicans was now close at hand. Their attitude and that of the State Department gave Beteta full freedom to carry out his mission.

## Beteta in Texas

During April 1939, the undersecretary, joined by local Mexican consuls, energetically promoted repatriation among his compatriots in Texas. His approach was to call meetings, at which he and the consuls addressed the hundreds who attended, trying to instill enthusiasm among them for returning to the homeland and, in the process, explaining how the government intended to carry out its plan. Beteta's visits focused on San Antonio and communities in the Rio Grande Valley.

His first meetings were held on 9 April, with Mexican nationals who lived in Karnes City and Kenedy.[17] Beteta was accompanied by officials from the Mexican consulate in San Antonio, including the consul general, Omar Josefe; the assistant consul, Raúl S. Spindola; and the legal counsel, Manuel C. González. In addition to lending moral support and to reinforcing Beteta's message, the three officials had a tangible goal—to win commitments from as many prospective returnees as possible. In this effort they had some success, since more than a third of those in attendance, or some fifty individuals, indicated that they wanted to repatriate immediately. Others declared that they were interested in returning but could do so only after the harvest or after fulfilling their work contract.[18]

A week later, on 15 April, representatives from the consulate in San Antonio, together with Manuel Gamio, joined Beteta on his trip through the Rio Grande Valley, where a crowd of nearly 700 attended the meeting presided over by the group. The scene was repeated in Brownsville, where some 500 people gathered to listen to Beteta. Each person who repatriated, Beteta explained, would be offered ten hectares of land to work. The family would also be moved free of charge, along with their furniture and household goods, automobiles, livestock, and farm tools and implements. The land, however, came with one condition—it could not be sold or mortgaged. Each of the male children who began his own family, however, would also receive a ten-hectare parcel. The plan was that the newly resettled colonists would grow cotton as part of the government's development scheme in the area of the Lower Rio Grande Valley in Tamaulipas. The repatriation plan, Beteta informed his audiences, also allowed people to return to their hometowns or villages, in which case the government would pay for transportation. As a third alternative, returnees could elect to settle into certain ejidos available in the communities of Torreón, Coahuila; Navojoa, Sonora; Culiacán, Sinaloa; Nueva Italia, Michoacán; or Ciudad Victoria and El Mante, Tamaulipas.[19]

Beteta's offer to incorporate people into these ejidos was related to a rural financing project, set up by the National Bank of Ejido Credit (Banco Nacional de Crédito Ejidal, BNCE), designed to attach 1,000 repatriated Mexicans, or some 435 families, to various local ejido-based credit associations (see table 5.2). The plan stressed that participants should have expertise in some branch of agriculture. There are no indications, however, that the program ever attained anything close to its projected size. At its height, it included some seventy people.[20]

The reports that came out of Texas indicate that Beteta's audiences reacted positively to his proposals, since many families expressed a desire to return to Mexico as quickly as the official agreement could be drawn up. A group from the community of Raymondville, located in the northern part of South Texas, on the lip of the Rio Grande Valley, exemplified this sense of urgency. When Beteta met in Corpus Christi with a group of Mexican nationals living in the city as well as in communities surrounding it, his address and appeal were greeted with "resounding enthusiasm." Although the number of people recorded as participating in this event was never officially announced, the San Antonio Spanish-language newspaper *La Prensa* reported that it exceeded 500 families.[21] The undersecretary also organized an assembly in San Antonio that drew more than 3,000 people from rural areas across Central and South Texas. The news reports that emanated from this meeting reinforced the view that the repatriation plan was being embraced enthusiastically. Local newspapers and radio stations had cooperated in this venture, with *La Prensa* giving it vigorous support. Many who attended the San Antonio meeting expressed a clear desire to return to Mexico.[22]

On 20 April, Beteta delivered an address at the Rusk Settlement School, in Houston, in which he declared that he bore a message of hope, since he carried President Cárdenas's invitation to his compatriots to take up work and receive the fruits of the Mexican soil, because "now, indeed, Mexico is forged by Mexicans." They would improve their living conditions through this avenue of work. Beteta told his audience that he was offering them this opportunity because times had changed and the ideals that animated the country

TABLE 5.2 Data on the project to distribute 1,000 returnees among local communal agricultural (ejido) credit associations

| AGENCY | NO. OF ASSOCIATIONS | NO. OF ASSOCIATES | NO. OF LAND PARCELS | PLACE OF ARRIVAL | EXPERTISE REQUIRED OF SETTLERS |
|---|---|---|---|---|---|
| Torreón | 290 | 31,000 | 20 | Torreón | cotton |
| Navojoa | 70 | 8,000 | 30 | Navojoa | wheat and garbanzos |
| Culiacán | 103 | 5,000 | 30 | Culiacán | garbanzos and vegetables |
| Nueva Italia | 2 | 2,000 | | Uruapan | rice |
| Ciudad Victoria | 271 | 9,000 | 25 | El Mante | rice and fruit |
| Monterrey | 92 | 5,000 | 15 | Monterrey | fruit |
| Celaya | 443 | 29,000 | 30 | Celaya | wheat |
| Córdoba | 120 | 7,000 | 40 | Córdoba | coffee |
| Jalapa | 178 | 11,000 | 40 | Jalapa | fruit |
| Guadalajara | 190 | 17,000 | 30 | Guadalajara | wheat |
| Morelia | 178 | 16,000 | 30 | Morelia | wheat |
| Cuautla | 64 | 5,000 | 10 | Cuernavaca | rice and sugarcane |
| Matamoros | 57 | 3,000 | | Matamoros | cotton |
| Los Tuxtlas | 220 | 12,000 | 30 | Los Tuxtlas | plantains |
| Tepic | 133 | 11,000 | 30 | Tepic | tobacco |
| La Barca | 98 | 8,000 | 25 | La Barca | wheat |
| Chihuahua | 150 | 11,000 | 30 | Chihuahua | wheat |
| Oaxaca | 79 | 12,000 | | Oaxaca | fruit |
| Colima | 36 | 1,500 | 10 | Colima | fruit |
| Tabasco | | | | Villahermosa | plantains |
| Iguala | 138 | 11,000 | 10 | Iguala | |

SOURCE: APRB, exp. 306, leg. 5, Correspondence with other departments, Office of the President, and state governments, General repatriation to Mexico, Ignacio García Téllez to Ramón Beteta, Mexico City, 18 April 1939.

had evolved. A new order had arisen that affected everything in Mexico; the country, he assured them, awaited its returning migrants with open arms.[23]

Beteta then went on to thread the needle. The repatriation plan, he explained, was designed to provide an opportunity to work to "all" Mexicans who might need it. Those, however, who had jobs along interests that tied them to the United States could just as well go on living there. Strictly speaking, that is, the offer being held out did not include everyone but only those in difficult circumstances who were Mexican by birth, Mexican "in their blood," people whose origins lay in Mexico and who felt genuine affection for "the land that gave them their name as Mexicans." Moreover, Beteta hastened to assure them, once back on Mexican soil they would possess the same rights as their "blood brothers" in Mexico and would not be treated in a high-handed way; their opinions would be heard and would carry weight.[24]

Beteta stated that the National Bank of Agricultural Credit (BNCA) would furnish them with cash advances, so they could immediately begin working their plots. The money would have to be paid back when the first harvest was complete, although the bank would try to leave them enough to meet their needs and continue working the land—the sole condition being that they could not sell or mortgage it. To jumpstart the return, Beteta invited those who wished to go back to make their way to the nearest consulate, where they could obtain needed information and submit their request.

Beteta also claimed that many of the Cárdenas administration's enemies were spreading the word that the government lacked the funds to repatriate Mexican nationals, that it was bankrupt, and that if people returned they would only suffer. In fact, Mexico *was* passing through difficult economic and political times. In addition, the government had taken few concrete measures and allocated few resources to support an organized return, so no sooner had it launched the project than it ran into problems financing it.[25] Indeed, difficulties arose at the very outset with respect to the Interior Ministry's appropriations for repatriation. García Téllez received an urgent appeal from Beteta to step in and resolve the matter, since, after promoting the repatriation plan in the president's name, the latter would be made a fool of if he "came out saying that we have to wait for the Chamber [of Deputies] to approve transfers [of money] in September or for [the Ministry of] Agriculture to find water in the subsoil."[26]

The question of financing the program was quickly resolved by presidential action. In April, Cárdenas ordered the undersecretary of finance to make a special transfer of funds for the express purpose of assisting the considerable number of Mexicans who would be returning to the country. Other projects, he suggested, could be temporarily suspended if that proved necessary. Subsequently, Hay informed Cárdenas that he had allocated US$6,000 to assist Mexican nationals in the United States who found themselves in dire circumstances and to help transport them back to Mexico. As related by Beteta, the Mexican consul in Houston received an additional $300 to repatriate a group of eleven families. In this same context, Agustín Leñero, Cárdenas's private secretary, held discussions with Interior Minister Ignacio García Téllez, Foreign Relations Minister Eduardo Hay, and Undersecretary of Finance Eduardo Villaseñor to resolve the posting of funds to Beteta.[27]

In Houston, Beteta ended his 20 April address by affirming that the government was extending to his listeners the hand of friendship, giving them the opportunity to become financially independent and their own masters by enjoying the fruits of their labor.[28]

The undersecretary also made a trip to Austin, where he met with Texas's governor, W. Lee O'Daniel, spoke before the state senate, and visited the campus of the University of Texas.[29] In going about the city, where many Mexicans lived, Beteta found that his compatriots there were doing reasonably well "under the circumstances," since some of them had taken the place of black workers in the fields.[30] He noted two poles, or two extremes, of the Mexican migrant population: those who were destitute, and therefore desperate, and those who did not need assistance because they already had work.

Together, Beteta and Mexico's consuls in Texas toured different communities to promote the repatriation plan and record the names of possible returnees. The San Antonio consul visited Oilton, Mirando City, Hebbronville, Benavides, and San Diego. In addition, he distributed hundreds of leaflets that described the repatriation program. Efraín G. Domínguez, the consul in Laredo, retraced his colleague's steps, visiting the same communities, exhorting his compatriots to submit a request for repatriation. In early May, McAllen consul Lauro Izaguirre held a meeting with 300 Mexican nationals from the communities of Los Ebanos and Donna who had gathered in the main hall of the Workers Protective Society.[31]

The Mexican press in San Antonio exclaimed that Beteta's efforts to bring "the stray sheep" back into the fold had achieved excellent results. "Mr. Beteta's deliberate way of speaking and his inviting and eloquent language" had stirred the "hearts of Mexicans . . . patriotism responded; faith was placed in the homeland." For all the glowing reports, however, Beteta well knew that many of his compatriots would hold back until seeing "how it is going for those who went on ahead." On 10 April he had written to the president that "the urgent and desperate cases have up to now been few." Later, he reported that the dearth of requests for repatriation was explained by the great lack of confidence people had in the word of the government. Some of their compatriots, Beteta asserted, were "extremely wary because of all the attempts that have been made to repatriate them," particularly since the prior repatriations— (in Pinotepa, Oaxaca; and El Coloso, Guerrero)—had turned into scenes of starvation, of households plunged into poverty, of small fortunes dried up in the collective failure, and of the able-bodied left unemployed, desperate, and disaffected. Others hoped that this time events would take a different course, that the actions taken to help them would be tangible, so that those "who wanted to have bread to put in the mouths of their children" would not be pulled down into complete destitution.[32] The reaction by some members of the Mexican community in Texas was one of interest. Nonetheless, in the end, few among them actually wanted to return.[33] Ultimately, disbelief in the plan prevailed over its acceptance.

Mexicans in the United States could still envision earlier failures and, overall, did not believe that future conditions would be any more "appealing." "The unsettled prospects held them back," as did a residue of distrust. In general, despite the diplomatic reports and newspaper accounts highlighting the enthusiasm shown by many individuals, the Cardenista call for return generated a rather muted response on the part of the Mexican community in Texas. All the same, Beteta managed to convince 5,000 people to accept the Mexican government's offer.[34] Beteta's efforts, given the context and the number of individuals he was able to persuade, were noteworthy, all the more so when one considers that the majority of people he convinced were U.S. citizens who previously had intended to remain in their adopted country.

In a confidential report that he sent to Cárdenas, Beteta pointed out that virtually all the prospective returnees were either U.S. citizens of Mexican birth or had lived in the United States over a period of years. A list compiled by the Mexican consul in San Antonio of the people interested in repatriating showed that their average time spent living in the United States was between ten and fifteen years (see table 5.3). Most had U.S.-born children, but Beteta did not view this as a barrier to the repatriation plan.[35]

As a rule, neither the Mexican consuls nor Beteta placed any great emphasis on the difference between Mexican children born in Mexico and children born to Mexican parents living in the United States. In order to avoid controversy and hew close to the Mexican constitution, children in both categories were seen to be Mexican, regardless of where they happened to come into the world. Nevertheless, for those who had been born outside of Mexico, the legal implications of taking up the government's offer were not always crystal clear. For example, Elena Zúñiga, a Mexican American in Houston, expressed her fear to Beteta that, although her parents were Mexican, she—as a U.S. citizen—would be deprived of her rights if she returned with them to Mexico. The undersecretary assured her that she need not worry, because, as the daughter of Mexican nationals, she would enjoy the same rights in Mexico as they did. She also need not worry, he explained, about preserving her status and privileges in the United States, because the Mexican government had no objection to her doing so. In Beteta's words, "the privileged legal position into which those with dual nationality fall should not, in my opinion,

TABLE 5.3 Data on Mexican citizens and family members seeking repatriation to Mexico to settle land furnished by the Mexican government

| HEAD OF HOUSEHOLD | BIRTHPLACE | POINT OF DEPARTURE | LENGTH OF U.S. RESIDENCE (YEARS) | IMPLEMENTS OR VEHICLES | LIVESTOCK | DESIRED LOCATION IN MEXICO | NO. OF FAMILY MEMBERS |
|---|---|---|---|---|---|---|---|
| Guillermo S. Menchaca | Múzquiz, Coah. | San Saba, Tex. | 24 | automobile | none | Matamoros, Tamps. | 4 |
| Antonio B. Baca | Belén, N.M. | Albuquerque, N.M. | 10 | none | none | Baja California | 0 |
| Martín Pérez | Lampazos, N.L. | San Antonio, Tex. | 50 | none | none | Ciudad Juárez, Chih. | 0 |
| Genaro Ramos | Georgetown, Tex. | New Braunfels, Tex. | 10 | none | none | Matamoros, Tamps. | 4 |
| Télilo Cortez | Had. Peotillos, S.L.P. | Kyle, Tex. | 15 | automobile | none | Tamaulipas | 1 |
| Manuel Hernandez | Santa María del Río, S.L.P. | New Braunfels, Tex. | 30 | automobile | none | Matamoros, Tamps. | 2 |
| Cipriano Vargas | Teremendo, Mich. | Karnes City, Tex. | 21 | none | none | Matamoros, Tamps. | 3 |
| Eduardo Muñoz | Lagos de Moreno, Jal. | Ben Arnold, Tex. | 25 | automobile | hens | Matamoros, Tamps. | 4 |
| Reinaldo Vega | Villa Allende, N.L. | Ben Arnold, Tex. | 19 | none | none | Matamoros, Tamps. | 4 |
| Jose Ambriz | Monterrey, N.L. | Ben Arnold, Tex. | 26 | none | hens | Matamoros, Tamps. | 5 |
| Jesús Muñoz | Lagos de Moreno, Jal. | Ben Arnold, Tex. | 25 | automobile | none | Matamoros, Tamps. | 8 |
| Pablo Robledo | Nuevo Laredo, Tamps. | Ben Arnold, Tex. | 14 | automobile | hens | Matamoros, Tamps. | 6 |
| Eleuterio Robledo | San Carlos, Coah. | Ben Arnold, Tex. | 25 | automobile | none | Matamoros, Tamps. | 3 |
| Francisco Menchaca | Penjamillo, Mich. | Ben Arnold, Tex. | 28 | automobile | none | Matamoros, Tamps. | 7 |
| Ildefonso Vásquez | Dr. Arroyo, N.L. | Seguin, Tex. | 24 | automobile | domestic animals | Tamaulipas | 6 |
| Jose Vásquez | Zaragoza, Coah. | Seguin, Tex. | 24 | automobile | domestic animals | Tamaulipas | 4 |
| Jose Jiménez | Saucillo, Coah. | San Saba, Tex. | 19 | Implements | none | Matamoros, Tamps. | 7 |

| HEAD OF HOUSEHOLD | BIRTHPLACE | POINT OF DEPARTURE | LENGTH OF U.S. RESIDENCE (YEARS) | IMPLEMENTS OR VEHICLES | LIVESTOCK | DESIRED LOCATION IN MEXICO | NO. OF FAMILY MEMBERS |
|---|---|---|---|---|---|---|---|
| Jesús Barajas | Menar, Tex. | Menar, Tex. | 22 | implements and truck | none | Ocotolán, Jal. | 11 |
| Gumersindo, Valadez | Ojuelos, Jal. | New Braunfels, Tex. | 49 | none | none | Comarca Lagunera | 5 |
| Anastasio García | Acámbaro, Gto. | San Saba, Tex. | 10 | automobile | none | Matamoros, Tamps. | 6 |
| Valentín García | Acámbaro, Gto. | San Saba, Tex. | 10 | none | none | Matamoros, Tamps. | 2 |
| Isaac Trejo | Acámbaro, Gto. | San Saba, Tex. | 19 | automobile | none | Matamoros, Tamps. | 9 |
| Manuel Flores | Zacatecas, Zac. | San Antonio, Tex. | 27 | none | none | La Sauteña, Tamps. | 1 |
| Fernando Moreno | León, Gto. | San Antonio, Tex. | 25 | automobile | none | La Sauteña, Tamps. | 7 |
| None | Ramos Arizpe, Coah. | San Antonio, Tex. | 28 | truck | domestic animals | La Sauteña, Tamps. | 5 |
| Nazario Martínez | Ramos Arizpe, Coah. | San Antonio, Tex. | 26 | none | none | La Sauteña, Tamps. | 5 |
| Féliz Juárez | Chihuahua, Chih. | San Antonio, Tex. | 27 | none | none | La Sauteña, Tamps. | 7 |
| Eulogio Hernández | Moctezuma, S.L.P. | San Antonio, Tex. | 11 | none | none | La Sauteña, Tamps. | 4 |
| Concepción Martínez | Ciudad Mier, Tamps. | San Antonio, Tex. | 20 | none | none | La Sauteña, Tamps. | 7 |
| Victor Badillo | Santa María del Río, S.L.P. | San Marcos, Tex. | 21 | none | none | San Luis Potosí | 0 |
| Antonio Vargas | Monterrey, N.L. | Cameron, Tex. | 21 | none | none | Matamoros, Tamps. | 3 |
| Leopoldo Almazán | Matehuala, S.L.P. | San Antonio, Tex. | 28 | none | none | Tamaulipas | 7 |
| Tiburcio García | Cualepec, Gto. | Temple, Tex. | 25 | automobile | none | Ciudad Juárez, Chih. | 7 |
| Segundo Botello | Rancho Nuevo, Coah. | San Antonio, Tex. | 26 | truck | none | La Sauteña, Tamps. | 8 |
| Refugio Martínez | Tierra Nueva, S.L.P. | Cameron, Tex. | 15 | none | none | Ciudad Juárez, Chih | 6 |
| Francisco Enciso | Villa Nueva, Zac. | Cameron, Tex. | 21 | plows | domestic animals | Ciudad Juárez, Chih | 2 |

| Name | Origin | Destination | Age | Transport | Livestock | Location | Years |
|---|---|---|---|---|---|---|---|
| Sixto R. Martínez | Had. Tapatilla, S.L.P. | San Saba, Tex. | 26 | covered wagon | none | Baja California | 0 |
| Buenaventura González | Matehuala, S.L.P. | Dilley, Tex. | 30 | automobile | none | cattle lands | 10 |
| Inés Hernández | Mexico City | Lockhart, Tex. | 30 | none | none | agricultural land | 5 |
| Aurelio Márquez | Guanajuato, Gto. | Round Rock, Tex. | 19 | none | none | Matamoros, Tamps. | 7 |
| Francisco Muñoz | Zaragoza, Dgo. | New Braunfels, Tex. | 17 | automobile | none | Matamoros, Tamps. | 1 |
| Marcelo Arredondo | Parras, Coah. | New Braunfels, Tex. | 17 | automobile | none | Matamoros, Tamps. | 5 |
| Francisco Hernández | Tepic, Nay. | New Braunfels, Tex. | 27 | none | domestic animals | Matamoros, Tamps. | 1 |
| Francisco Machorro | China, N.L. | New Braunfels, Tex. | 27 | none | none | Matamoros, Tamps. | 7 |
| Marcos Díaz | Torreón, Coah. | New Braunfels, Tex. | 20 | automobile | none | Matamoros, Tamps. | 1 |
| Juan Rivera | Silao, Gto. | Maxwell, Tex. | 15 | automobile | none | Matamoros, Tamps. | 5 |
| Pablo Casteñón | Torreón, Coah. | San Antonio, Tex. | 19 | automobile | none | Matamoros, Tamps. | 7 |
| Jesús Ramírez | Matehuala, S.L.P. | Seguin, Tex. | 37 | automobile | none | Matamoros, Tamps. | 5 |
| Zacarías Flores | Villafuente, Coah. | San Antonio, Tex. | 29 | tools | none | Matamoros, Tamps. | 4 |
| Jose Jesús Zárate | San Martín, Jal. | New Braunfels, Tex. | 22 | none | domestic animals | Matamoros, Tamps. | 5 |
| Vidal Cantú | Agualeguas, N.L. | Cameron, Tex. | 18 | none | none | Matamoros, Tamps. | 1 |
| Eulogio Rangel | San Francisco, N.L. | Cameron, Tex. | 38 | none | none | Matamoros, Tamps. | 5 |
| Francisco Castellano | Cherokee, Tex. | Thomdale, Tex. | 21 | truck | none | Ciudad Juárez, Chih | 4 |
| Silvestre Macías | Tlalpa, Zac. | San Gabriel, Tex. | 19 | automobile | none | Ciudad Juárez, Chih | 2 |
| Jesús Rocha | S.P. Colonias, Coah. | Kennedy, Tex. | 19 | truck | none | Matamoros, Tamps. | 4 |
| Francisco Rocha | S.P. Colonias, Coah. | Kennedy, Tex. | 19 | automobile | domestic animals | Matamoros, Tamps. | 3 |
| Baltasar Martínez | Monterrey, N.L. | San Antonio, Tex. | 39 | none | none | Monterrey, N.L. | 2 |
| Enrique Acosta | Guadalupe, S.L.P. | Seguin, Tex. | 26 | none | none | Tamaulipas | 1 |
| Aurelio Peña | Noriega, N.L. | San Antonio, Tex. | 30 | none | none | Tamaulipas | 2 |

| HEAD OF HOUSEHOLD | BIRTHPLACE | POINT OF DEPARTURE | LENGTH OF U.S. RESIDENCE (YEARS) | IMPLEMENTS OR VEHICLES | LIVESTOCK | DESIRED LOCATION IN MEXICO | NO. OF FAMILY MEMBERS |
|---|---|---|---|---|---|---|---|
| Agustín Martínez | Monterrey, N.L. | San Antonio, Tex. | 30 | none | none | Matamoros, Tamps. | 11 |
| Esteban Ornelas | San Juan, Gto. | San Antonio, Tex. | 16 | tools | none | San Juan, Gto. | 9 |
| Luis Villagrán | Taran-dácuaro, Gto. | San Antonio, Tex. | 19 | none | none | Matamoros, Tamps. | 9 |
| Francisco Moreno | Marín, N.L. | San Antonio, Tex. | 28 | none | none | Matamoros, Tamps. | 10 |
| Guillermo Nuñez | Monclova, Coah. | San Antonio, Tex. | 11 | none | none | Monclova, Coah. | 1 |
| Julián Cruz | Carnale, N.L. | San Antonio, Tex. | 15 | truck | none | El Azúcar Dam | 5 |
| Vicente Castillo | Rosita, Coah. | San Antonio, Tex. | 14 | none | none | El Azúcar Dam | 3 |
| Jose Salas | Parras, Coah. | Seguin, Tex. | 35 | none | none | Tamaulipas | 5 |
| Pedro Castañeda | Esperanza, Coah. | San Antonio, Tex. | 14 | none | none | El Azúcar Dam | 4 |
| Santiago Ibarra | Mezquital, Zac. | San Antonio, Tex. | 30 | none | none | Jalisco | 6 |
| Jose Medina | Tepezala, Ags. | San Antonio, Tex. | 31 | plows | none | Comales, Tamps. | 6 |
| Tomás Salazar | Santa María, S.L.P. | New Braunfels, Tex. | 27 | automobile | none | Matamoros, Tamps. | 9 |
| Zacarías Marfil | Monclova, Coah. | New Braunfels, Tex. | 21 | automobile | domestic animals | Matamoros, Tamps. | 11 |
| Crescencio Rodríguez | Rinconada, N.L. | San Antonio, Tex. | 34 | none | none | La Sauteña, Tamps. | 10 |
| Jose Ramos | Ciudad Porfirio Díaz, Coah. | San Antonio, Tex. | 43 | tools | none | Coahuila | 6 |
| Inés Villareal | San Nicolás, N.L. | San Antonio, Tex. | 25 | none | none | Tamaulipas | 6 |
| Jacinto Vásquez | Piedras Negras, Coah. | Seguin, Tex. | 24 | none | none | Tamaulipas | No data |
| Pedro Vásquez | Zaragoza, Coah. | Seguin, Tex. | 24 | none | none | Tamaulipas | No data |

| Feliciano Chapa | Agualeguas, N.L. | Lockhart, Tex. | 28 | none | none | El Azúcar Dam | No data |
|---|---|---|---|---|---|---|---|
| Mateo Maldonado | Had. La Mesa, Tamps. | Lockhart, Tex. | 21 | none | none | La Sauteña, Tamps. | No data |
| Jose Oyervides | Saltillo, Coah. | McMahan, Tex. | 29 | truck | none | La Sauteña, Tamps. | No data |
| Pardomiano Alonso | Mier y Noriega, N.L. | Cameron, Tex. | 15 | plows and automobile | none | Matamoros, Tamps. | No data |
| Pablo Bustamante | Pueblo Nuevo, N.L. | Cameron, Tex. | 12 | automobile and trailer | none | Matamoros, Tamps. | No data |
| Dimas Llamas | Mier y Noriega, N.L. | Kingsbury, Tex. | 20 | truck | none | Matamoros, Tamps. | No data |
| Juan Velarde | Bustamante, N.L. | Cameron, Tex. | 16 | automobile | none | Matamoros, Tamps. | No data |
| Jesús Martínez | Zaragoza, Coah. | Cameron, Tex. | 18 | none | none | Matamoros, Tamps. | No data |
| Juan Moreno | Torreón, Coah. | Cameron, Tex. | 20 | automobile and plows | none | Matamoros, Tamps. | No data |
| Onésimo S. Ibarra | Had. El Pañuelo, N.L. | San Antonio, Tex. | 27 | automobile and plows | none | La Sauteña, Tamps. | No data |
| Feliciana S. Vda. de Mendoza | Had. El Pañuelo, N.L. | San Antonio, Tex. | 25 | automobile and plows | none | Tamaulipas | No data |

SUMMARY TOTALS: Head of household: 88; other family members: 368; grand total: 456.

SOURCE: APRB, exp. 312, leg. 6, "Relación de ciudadanos mexicanos y sus familiares que desean repatriarse a México para radicarse en las tierras que el gobierno les proporcione en calidad de colonos," Mexico's consul in San Antonio, Texas, San Antonio, 8 April 1939.

be undone by Mexico."[36] The question of nationality was not discussed inside the Cárdenas administration, nor was it a source of great concern among the country's legislators.

## Beteta in the Northern United States

After spending considerable time in Texas, Beteta turned his sights to the north, traveling to the East Coast and the Midwest. He spent little time in those regions, however, neither bothering to hold meetings, as he had done with Mexican consuls in Texas, nor speaking publicly on the repatriation plan. Rather, he confined his activities to helping compatriots plan their return and to ensuring that the main criterion governing repatriation—its selectivity and exclusive focus on people with experience in the agricultural sector—was understood.

The latter message, for example, came through in a session Beteta held in early May at Columbia University, where he made clear that the objective of Mexico's repatriation plan was simple and straightforward: to promote and arrange a gradual and systematic return of Mexican agricultural workers who found themselves in difficult circumstances in the United States and who, by returning to Mexico, could help improve its agricultural productivity. As part of this campus visit, he spoke with a group of faculty on a number of topics related to Mexico, focusing especially "on matters connected to the repatriation." On 5 May, he met with a group from the city's Mexican community, to whom he explained "the [Mexican] government's forward-looking socioeconomic policy" without mentioning that, for the moment, it was unable to offer laborers stable employment. Beteta reported to Cárdenas that he received few inquiries about and requests for repatriation in New York and none at all from farmworkers.[37]

In Chicago, in contrast, the undersecretary received "a considerable number of requests." A total of 140 families without work expressed to him their wish to repatriate. The majority of the unemployed men in these families, however, were foundry workers who had become naturalized U.S. citizens. Although their requests to repatriate may have been heartfelt, Beteta had no choice but to remain true to the plan, so he left instructions that the consulate needed to explain to them that the government's offer applied solely to agricultural workers. Nonetheless, he indicated that as soon as new industrial jobs could be developed, the government would attempt to find positions for those who still wished to return to Mexico.[38] Beteta received only sixteen requests during his stop in St. Louis and even fewer in Pittsburgh, where nine unemployed Mexican nationals who had worked in foundries petitioned him for repatriation. The St. Louis and Pittsburgh cases typified the pattern across these regions of the United States, where, as Beteta pointed out, there was "no real, collective intention on the part of Mexicans to return to the homeland." He observed that his compatriots grew emotional when they spoke of Mexico, but they had no clear need to return to their native country, "only the desire." Moreover, they were not living in the poverty experienced in other states.[39]

In sum, the Mexican community in the northern United States showed little interest in returning home, a disposition that aligned well with the central purpose of Beteta's visit to that region—to promote the return of a particular class of Mexican nationals—farmworkers—and to otherwise act discreetly, so as not to give false hopes to others. His trip to the East Coast and across the Midwest was brief and had a second objective: to help advance the negotiations taking place between the Mexican government and the oil companies whose fields in Mexico had been expropriated. For the undersecretary, promoting and explaining the repatriation plan to Mexicans living in the northern United States, and recruiting returnees in that region, was distinctly less important than his comparable mission in Texas.

## Reactions in Mexico

Few people in Mexico were interested in the Cardenista repatriation plan. While it did have its critics and provoked some negative commentary, it failed to spark any widespread debate. Mexican society was focused on other concerns, such as the presidential succession and the country's economic situation, and had little time for polemics over the return of compatriots from the United States.

Typical of the response was the position taken by an editorial writer for the Tampico newspaper *El Mundo*. In his opinion, the importance ascribed to repatriation "was decidedly exaggerated," with respect to both the number of Mexican workers who found themselves in difficult straits and the alleged urgency of bringing them back. According to this editorialist's assessment, which was supported by one of Beteta's reports, fewer than 200 Mexican nationals, spread across different places in the United States, were in urgent need of assistance. In addition, many of those who had expressed the desire to return did not really want the government's help, and since they formed such a small cohort, Mexico would derive little benefit from their return.[40] A similar view was expressed by Alfonso Romero, a columnist for the Nogales, Sonora, newspaper *Acción*.[41]

Neither the Tampico editorial writer nor the Nogales columnist was impressed by the government's pronouncements on behalf of its repatriation project. On the contrary, both criticized Cárdenas's overhyped publicity for a plan whose objectives were highly selective and limited. They also reported the views of those in Mexico who spoke out against the return. The *El Mundo* columnist averred that the pool of possible returnees consisted of people who would return only because they were out of work and who subsequently would make their way back to the United States. Thus, in the event they repatriated, they would be tantamount to tourists, mere visitors as it were, who kept their residence across the border so as not to surrender their rights.[42]

Salvador Novo, a Mexican man of letters known for his heated criticisms of Cárdenas administration policies, as voiced in his column "La semana pasada," was bitingly skeptical about the results of the repatriation program. He viewed it as an undertaking that would be carried out "provisionally, while later they would swim across the river they preferred to call the [Rio] Grande rather than the [Río] Bravo." He also had little faith that "the repatriated *pochos*" [Americanized Mexicans living in the United States], who had shown themselves incapable of staying in Mexico, would readapt successfully to Mexican society. He wrote sarcastically that Beteta's repatriation plan demanded of Mexican nationals who lived on U.S. soil a greater demonstration of their feelings for the homeland than those they displayed when jubilantly celebrating 16 September in a way that mimicked Fourth of July celebrations; or when they went into a California movie theater "even though" it showed Mexican films, "or when they admitted that in certain restaurants they called quesadillas 'tacos' and *hot cakes* with *catchup* 'enchiladas'" (Novo 1964, 596–97).

Other writers, in Chihuahua and in Mexico City, sympathized with the assessments of both the Tampico editorialist and Novo. Their view, expressed in one form or another, was that many Mexican nationals would not return with the right outlook and orientation, since their children's upbringing and education had been suffused with the ways and customs of U.S. culture and society. Moreover, in the judgment of these critics, some who opted to return did not honestly want to do so, because fundamentally they had adjusted to life across the border. They were motivated to return, and made a show of wanting to resettle in the homeland, out of fear of being deported from the United States because they did not have legal status there. The population of prospective returnees, such writers argued, also included people with illnesses whom local welfare agencies wanted to send back, people without any resources, manual laborers as well as some with special skills, children, the unemployed living off relief rolls, and people disabled by workplace accidents.[43]

These judgments and opinions reflected the anxiety felt in some quarters that the repatriation plan was ill-conceived and posed a threat to Mexico, because it opened an avenue for the return of the unemployed and the infirm.

Still, the topic did not provoke widespread discussion, and some even applauded the government's initiative. For example, *El Popular*, a Mexico City daily identified with working-class interests, celebrated the repatriation plan as a resounding social and economic triumph, equating it with the country's nationalization of oil and the railways and the awarding of land to peasant farmers in the ejidos of La Laguna and Nueva Italia.[44] This and other such readings were exaggerated. The campaign to repatriate Mexican nationals could not realistically be compared with the more radical measures taken by the Cárdenas government (the expropriation of oil and the railways, and of land for agrarian reform), in terms of either the investment in it, the interests affected by it, or the challenges the government faced in defending it against controversy and political opposition. It was indeed the case, however, that Cárdenas exploited the repatriation project for symbolic purposes, manipulating it as a nationalist emblem. By making such a public show of support for the Mexican community in the United States, he hoped to unite the country behind him and rally support for his presidential initiatives.

## Finding a Place for the Repatriated

The second stage of the repatriation project involved selecting a site on which to found an agricultural settlement, a task that Cárdenas farmed out to state governors, the National Irrigation Commission (CNI), and the Ministry of Agriculture, whose representatives and officials proceeded to gather essential data from around the country.

At the beginning of 1939, the president assigned Manuel Gamio, who was still serving as chief of the Demographics Department, to do two things: first, identify and locate across the entirety of Mexico federally owned lands that were empty and lying idle; and second, undertake studies with the aim of bringing back Mexican nationals. Assisted by an interministerial committee, Gamio investigated and pinpointed four regions in the state of Tamaulipas: the Lower Rio Grande Valley, Colombres No. 1, La Sauteña, and the San Fernando River area. The first region was considered to be the most favorable for launching a project for two reasons: the potential lands belonged to the BNCE and they offered the best conditions for establishing a settlement. Gamio reported that the land was of good quality and could be irrigated almost immediately. In addition, it was close to both rail lines and to the Matamoros-Monterrey highway, which in turn connected it to the larger national markets as well as to those in the United States. These factors, Gamio stated, guaranteed the success of the settlement scheme.[45]

A second party, the BNCE, also looked for places where the repatriated could be settled. Its managing director was assigned by Cárdenas to examine how they could be assisted, given work in Mexico, and placed into the different ejido-based credit associations that operated in the country. The bank would also provide such "credits and financial assistance" as might be needed so the returnees could get their agricultural endeavors off the ground, and it would otherwise furnish them with whatever resources were required so the repatriation program under design could be fully realized. Other committees also analyzed the conditions in various places where settlements might be established and determined steps that needed to be taken so that the groups that returned could get resettled. According to the press in Chihuahua, the government had a reserve of 50,000 pesos for this purpose.[46]

A frontline committee, the Tamaulipas Colonization Commission, was sent by the CNI to the state of Tamaulipas and, specifically, to the La Sauteña and Río Bravo properties. Headed by Mario A. Grajales, the commission was composed of engineers from the Ministry of Agriculture's Agrarian Department.[47] Its objective was to begin drilling wells in both Río Bravo and La Esperanza (the latter located in the municipality of El Mante) and to start preparing these lands so that no fewer than 150 families could be established and resettled on them. In addition, the engineers were to supervise the construction of houses and other buildings and have tents set up as temporary living quarters for the incoming population.[48] It is not known, however, if these plans came to fruition.

With the intention of undertaking a study similar to the one carried out by the Tamaulipas Colonization Commission, a team was also put together and sent to the Mapimí Basin region, in Sinaloa. The team developed plans for installing a system of wells that would cover 10,000 to 15,000 hectares, where some 500 families could be resettled and grow cotton. In addition, a representative of the Ministry of Agriculture, José D. Báez, and an envoy from the BNCE, were also dispatched to this area to identify for the agricultural team specific sites where people returning from the United States could be settled. The government also hoped to establish a work center for repatriated migrants on the La Sauteña hacienda, for which purpose these two officials carried out a preliminary study.[49]

For its part, the Ministry of Agriculture directed its agents to report on and document any sites that they believed would be suitable for resettling Mexican nationals who should decide to return from abroad and, as part of the report, outline what the costs would be to prepare the land and make it usable. The chief engineer of the irrigation system in Pabellón, Aguascalientes, was similarly instructed to report on the suitability and conditions of a twenty- to thirty-hectare lot that, with irrigation already in place, could serve as the site for a group of returnees who desired to resettle there.[50]

Subsequently, on 12 April 1939, Cárdenas sent a communiqué to the country's governors underscoring that their cooperation was vital to the repatriation program. The administration's immediate objective was to intensify the study phase and, with the help of governors, determine the site on which to resettle both repatriated Mexican nationals as well as laborers from Spain who, fleeing that country's just-ended civil war, would soon be arriving to live in Mexico. In the view of the executive branch, both migratory flows "would inject energy" into the country. The addition of "new hands" would lead to an increase in production and consumption; that is, it would boost "the country's economic potential."[51]

In Chihuahua, Governor Gustavo L. Talamantes announced that he would support the project and, at his request, Saucedo Montemayor, one of the Agriculture Ministry's agents in the state, called on the representatives of several businesses and properties (the Palomas Land & Cattle Company, the Northern Agricultural Company of Mexico, Ojo de Federico, the Estate of Pedro Zuloaga, and the haciendas of Corralitos, Babícora, and Santa Clara) to meet with him to discuss the particulars of resettlement of those returnees whom the federal government intended to send to the state.[52]

Montemayor's initiative produced tangible results. Representatives of the Santa Clara hacienda offered 70,000 hectares of land, to be distributed among 150 families, or a total of 40 hectares for each settler. Ojo de Federico offered to provide 10 hectares of optimal land to each of the 150 settlers. The Northern Agricultural Company in turn offered 1 million hectares of land to be used for grazing cattle. In this same vein, it was reported that the Babícora hacienda, part of a company owned by the U.S. corporate magnate William Randolph Hearst, could take in 1,000 families, with each settler receiving thirty hectares on which potatoes, corn, wheat, and oats could be planted. In addition, each settler would receive a subvention of 3,500 pesos, to construct a house, as well as tools, two cows, four hogs, twenty-five hens, and four mules.[53]

In addition to gathering information about areas containing communally farmed lands and different sources of work in the region, Governor Talamantes indicated that there were 30,000 hectares of workable land near Bachimba, located in Irrigation District No. 5, on which 3,000 families could "easily be settled." In the governor's opinion, assuming some investment by foreign business interests, the territory pertaining to Laguna de Casas Grandes and to the Boquilla de Plazuela irrigation system, in the municipality of Buenaventura, would furnish sufficient land to settle repatriated nationals who wished to work in agriculture.[54] With respect to other sorts of work, Talamantes suggested that returnees could also be deployed on the construction of the highway running from Ciudad Juárez to Chihuahua City. Moreover, some members of the ejidos situated in the municipality of Galeana had expressed an interest in placing small groups of agricultural workers.[55]

Some days after President Cárdenas had disseminated his 12 April communiqué, the governors of other states, such as Guanajuato, affirmed their interest in cooperating to help advance the repatriation of Mexican nationals. The general secretary of the government of Nuevo León, for example, informed the federal executive that the state's authorities had made 70,000 hectares available for settlement. The area included the ranch lands of La Mediondilla, El Peñuelo, and Margaritas, in the municipality of Galeana, and could accommodate 300 families.[56]

The members of ejidos located in the Comarca Lagunera also lined up behind Cárdenas's appeal, committing themselves to find a place for their repatriated compatriots within their complex of agricultural cooperatives.[57] The governor of Tamaulipas, Marte R. Gómez, said he had no objection to cooperating, since his state had taken in repatriated nationals at various times, certain that they were good workers.[58] Not all the governors were able to offer aid, however. Elpidio Perdomo, for example, regretted not being able to cooperate because his state, Morelos, was very small, and any new influx of people would only create problems for it.[59]

The number of hectares and sums of money cited—sometimes highly exaggerated—by private firms and individuals and by the governors of Chihuahua, Guanajuato, and Tamaulipas, as well as the proposals of ejido members of the Comarca Lagunera, failed to materialize, for the simple reason that these plans did not correspond to Cárdenas's goals or interests. The president never intended to deliver the land and financing they mentioned. Instead, he sought only to carry out studies, as had been his wont since assuming the presidency, and not to see a repatriation project through to completion. His plans were more modest than some governors had believed. He would not embark upon a series of projects in different states but, instead, select only a single site in the north of the country on which to settle one group of people. Another event, however—the arrival of Spanish Civil War refugees—was closely linked to the repatriation campaign and, indeed, was a principal reason that Cárdenas promoted it.

## CHAPTER SIX

# Spanish Refugees, the Repatriated, and the Lower Rio Grande Valley

When Mexicans have bread for their children and when the country's citizens abroad are officially supported and repatriated, then the government can afford itself the luxury of helping, on the people's behalf, all the foreign refugees it wishes to.

—*LA OPINIÓN*, LOS ANGELES, APRIL 1939

## The Mexican Government, the Spanish Refugees, and the Repatriated

The repatriation campaign and the effort to locate sites on which to resettle returnees largely coincided with Cárdenas's actions to grant asylum to refugees fleeing the Spanish Civil War. In both Mexico and the United States, the president's opponents used the admission of Spanish Republicans against the president. These criticisms were one of the factors—along with the personal interest that the president had displayed since the beginning of 1938 as well as the accord signed with the Los Angeles County authorities—that led the administration to put its plan for an organized repatriation into effect.

In 1936, the main body of Spanish army troops, led by Francisco Franco, had risen in revolt. Supported initially by conservative forces in Spain and later by the fascist and national socialist governments of Italy and Germany, the rebellion sought to unseat and overthrow the Spanish Republic which—since the elections held earlier that year—was controlled by a government of the Left. In light of the direct support that Franco's insurgency received from Italian and German "volunteers," the government of Mexico took the position that the Spanish government had fallen victim to aggression and therefore had the right to receive moral, political, and diplomatic protection as well as direct material aid from other member states of the League of Nations.[1]

The support extended by the Cardenista regime to the Spanish Republic was viewed as the touchstone, the clarifying act, of Mexican intervention in foreign affairs. Cárdenas would offer assistance to the legitimate government of Spain by furnishing it with arms manufactured in Mexico. He adhered unwaveringly to his administration's policy in favor of the government presided by Manuel Azaña. In this same spirit, he granted asylum to hundreds of Spaniards. Along with France, Mexico became the refuge for these "exiled" Republicans. Their exodus began in 1937 and culminated during the first months of the Second World War. The first group to arrive in Mexico was comprised of approximately 500 children. They were followed by a contingent of prominent Spanish intellectuals, and later, by Spanish Republicans en masse (Lida 1994, 33, 48–49; Pla Brugat 1994, 218–30; Fagen 1973, 29–30; Matesanz 1995, 119–70).

Mexico's assistance to Spanish exiles came in two phases. The initial phase involved efforts to house nearly 25,000 people who had crossed into France. In the second phase, Narciso Bassols, Mexico's ambassador to France, negotiated with both the French government and representatives of the Spanish Republic in exile to bring out of France thousands of additional Spanish refugees, of all ages and classes, and to oversee their resettlement in Mexico.[2]

Cárdenas's actions with respect to the Spanish exiles were motivated as much by practical as by altruistic and humanitarian considerations. In his September 1939 report to the Mexican Congress, he drew public attention to the advantages that would accrue from welcoming the Spanish: Mexico, he declared, would benefit from the contribution made to it by a group of people who, in race and spirit, were closely connected to the Mexican people. This was a population of immigrants well suited to assimilation, "in accordance with language and blood," in contrast to other migratory flows whose members generally kept themselves "separate" from the country's native inhabitants, whom they displaced economically. They tended to concentrate in urbanized areas and engaged in speculative business ventures without tying themselves to the fate, or higher purposes, of Mexico itself. In sum, between 1936 and 1940, the Spanish Civil War unleashed a current of politically based immigration, constituted by Republican exiles who, in Mexico's case, were officially granted asylum by the government (Lida 1997, 33, 140; Mexico 1940, 15–17; SEGOB 1939, 11).

## The Reaction in Mexico to the Arrival of the Spanish

Upon their arrival in Mexico, the Spanish exiles elicited quite varied, even contradictory, reactions. The government, led by Cárdenas and some of his closest associates, as well as the cream of Mexico's intellectual class, welcomed them warmly with demonstrations of support. Such sympathy was not as evident in other sectors (Lida 1997, 117). Many prominent and well-recognized Mexican professionals, such as Ignacio Chávez, Salvador Zubirán, Enrique Arreguín, and Gustavo Baz, went to extraordinary lengths to ensure that the Spanish expatriates could be recredentialed and thus made eligible for important posts. Two organizations—the Frente Socialista de Abogados (a lawyers' group) and the Legión de Precursores de la Revolución (an association of progressive intellectuals and former combatants in the Mexican Revolution)—likewise supported the government's decision to take in the exiled Republicans (Matesanz 1995, 386; Lida 1997, 117).

For organizations representing campesinos and urban workers, however, the official welcome extended to the Spanish exiles was more problematic. During a decade of crisis and economic depression, in a country marked by poverty and negligible financial resources, a country only recently removed from the upheavals of its own revolution, competition for jobs and daily bread with the newly arrived refugees from Spain was the last thing that was needed. Three groups, the Comité de Unificación Revolucionaria (Committee for Revolutionary Unification), the Frente Constitucional Democrático (Constitutional Democratic Front), and the Centro Social Demócrata Mexicano (Mexican Social Democratic Center) organized mass meetings at which their leaders railed against the threat that the Spanish would pose to public order and peace and the burden they would place on the nation's economy. The Unión Nacional Sinarquista (National Syndicalist Union) and the Confederación de Cámaras Nacionales de Comercio (Confederation of National Chambers of Commerce), both strong opponents of Cárdenas's government, also protested against the arrival of the Spanish exiles.[3] Aquiles Elorduy, a member of the national committee of the Partido de Acción Nacional (National Action Party) and Eduardo J. Correa followed an "antirefugee" line because, in their judgment, Mexico was inviting in communists or "reds." Cárdenas's political adversaries fought the acceptance of the Spanish Republicans. Among this opposition were the country's two most important newspapers, *Excelsior* and *El Universal*, both of which were openly hostile toward Republican Spain (Reyes Nevares 1982, 68; Correa 1941, 560–62; Pérez Montfort 1992, 124, 148; Pérez Montfort 1994, 115).

The Catholic and corporatist right fulminated against the "reds," who, in its view, had come from Spain only to revive the discord earlier sowed by Mexico's revolutionaries. Similarly, with few exceptions, long-time Spanish residents in Mexico, the *gachupines*, had from the outset felt no affinity for the Republican cause and now showed little sympathy for the exiled Spaniards.

Paradoxically, it was the attitude of some of Mexico's creole elite and their militant brand of Hispanophilia, in opposition to the indigenist principles of the Revolution, that caused the recently arrived Spaniards to be seen in a sympathetic racial and cultural light. At the same time, the most nationalist groups—which had sprung from the Revolution expounding a militant ideology that sought to reassert the claims of the country's pre-Hispanic origins and heritage—time and again invoked the memory of the conquistador's sword as a new form of xenophobic reaction against the newly arrived Spanish (Lida 1997, 117–18; Márquez Morfí 1988, 146–47). When we assess the opposition in terms of its constituent groups and where these fell along the socioeconomic and political spectrum, it is clear that the critics of the open door extended to the Spanish exiles were anything but homogeneous. In a number of instances their interests and motivations merged, but on the whole, the declarations and expressions of protest were disparate and contradictory.

## Refugees and the Repatriated: The Reaction in Mexico

In Mexico, the subject of the braceros served as a sharp point of contrast that the "antirefugees" did not hesitate to use in their verbal attack on Cárdenas. These protests began sporadically in April and intensified at the end of June 1939. In the majority of cases, they followed a course of indirection; that is, they were couched as pronouncements favoring the repatriation of Mexican nationals from the United States, rather than the arrival of the Spanish refugees.

The stance taken by Salvador Novo is an excellent example of how some in Mexico compared and contrasted the arrival of the Spanish exiles with repatriation as a way of attacking Lázaro Cárdenas. Novo had spoken out against the repatriation project, expressing skepticism over its probable results and the migrants' ability to successfully readapt to Mexican society. Yet Novo made a point of asserting that in his presidential address of 1939, Cárdenas had devoted "two hundred words" of his speech to underlining how, by granting asylum to Spanish exiles, Mexico had fulfilled its duty to honor the universal rights of refugees. Cárdenas's words, Novo wrote, had provoked rounds of applause "lasting twelve, ten, and seven seconds (twenty-nine in all) that those who repatriated had not merited from the audience" (Novo 1964, 410).

The Tampico newspaper *El Mundo* was equally opposed to the repatriation project, editorializing that the country would derive little benefit from the return of its nationals. In another editorial comparing the subject of repatriation to that of the Spanish refugees, it seized the opportunity to criticize Cárdenas by arguing that the government helped reintegrate its own citizens into the country only if they had independent financial means and a secure job, "whereas the reds [get] whatever they ask for." In the newspaper's account, while the government facilitated the entry into Mexico of hundreds of Spaniards who had left their own country, taking them in without any major requirements—which was untrue—and "even extended them generous help," there was "the painful case" of "extreme urgency and injustice" confronting thousands of its compatriots who suffered hunger and misfortune in the United States but were blocked from returning by the government when it insisted they arrive with money and assured employment.[4]

*El Mundo* was guilty of exaggeration with respect to both the amount of aid that the government gave the Spanish refugees and the requirements that it imposed on Mexican nationals who wished to repatriate. All the same, its commentary did not deviate from the truth entirely. The newspaper's argument hung on Ramón Beteta's interest in helping a certain type of person repatriate, preferably smallholders and agricultural workers who knew how to plant and harvest different crops and who possessed work tools and sufficient means to produce a yield from the land that would be assigned to them; a type of person, that is, drawn from among those who qualified as "capable and prepared." In the eyes of the newspaper's editorial writer, there was a disconnect between the policy on repatriation and that governing the entry of Spanish refugees. The criticism leveled was severe because, according to the writer, the conditions placed on the repatriated "did not square with the liberality shown by the government toward the Spanish fugitives." Furthermore, the government also pursued a misguided and distorted policy with respect to the latter, since, when granting asylum, it betrayed an interest in selecting the best prepared and most highly qualified refugees.[5]

*El Universal*, which had also published several articles in opposition to the repatriation, complained vociferously that the government invited in Spanish extremists and revolutionaries when it had failed to resolve the situation of its citizens abroad, in the United States in particular.[6] On this note, the *tabasqueño* Alfonso Taracena, who cofounded the paper with Féliz F. Palavicini, took the view that Mexico's political leaders were not taking care of their own house [*eran candil de la calle y oscuridad de la casa*], because they had forgotten the braceros even as they set up a canteen for the refugees near the Monte de Piedad (national pawn shop) in Mexico City (Reyes Nevares 1982, 68–69).

Rafael Zubarán Capmany, a *campechano* from the generation of Mexican revolutionaries born between 1875 and 1890 and avowed opponent of Cardenismo, expressed his sympathies with a caravan of compatriots who returned from the United States, proposing—tongue in cheek—that they be serenaded by the Lerdo de Tejada orchestra, since the Republic's leaders had been greeted by military bands. "Goodness gracious!" he exclaimed, the repatriated "have to be given a reception, even if they are Mexicans" (in Reyes Nevares 1982, 68–69).

For its part, the Confederation of National Chambers of Commerce and Industry believed that the arrival of Spanish refugees would only worsen the general situation of the country. In its view, the favors shown to the exiles would be better extended to those Mexican nationals who wished to return to the homeland.[7] Still, while these statements and declarations called on Cárdenas to demonstrate a more conciliatory attitude toward repatriation, their main objective was not to support the return of Mexican migrants. On the contrary, the opposition interests and groups plainly feared the negative effects that, in their judgment, repatriation would have. Instead, the objective behind this critique was to assail the Cardenista regime.

## Refugees and the Repatriated: The Reaction of Mexicans in the United States

It was not only in Mexico that the regime's opponents criticized Cárdenas for welcoming Spanish exiles rather than Mexicans seeking to repatriate. Various people in the U.S. Mexican community reacted similarly. The critics rallied under the banner of the urgency of greater effort by the administration on behalf of an organized return. Just as in Mexico, however, the real intention was to attack Cárdenas, not to inspire him to build greater support for repatriation. The critics called for Cárdenas to attend to the needs of Mexicans, and asserted that his preoccupation with the problems of the Spanish refugees had led him to overlook Mexicans, squandering public monies and expending them to the detriment of local workers and the Mexican people in general.

An editorial writer for the San Antonio newspaper *La Prensa* suggested that only Spanish laborers and professionals should be admitted to Mexico, since to accept everyone would be prejudicial to migrants who were going to repatriate. The columnist requested that the Spanish return to their own country to avoid creating resentments in Mexico, as the government needed to protect "the thousands of unemployed nationals over and above all its sympathies [for the exiles] and all partisan political interests." The piece stressed that the government was generous with these foreigners but deprived "our own." For this editorialist, the "peaceful invasion of refugees" was "pleasing to our classic creole hospitality," but it was necessary, first and foremost, to help "our own, the children of Mexico."[8]

Along these same lines, Eliseo Valle Cortés, a Mexican national who lived in Los Angeles, sent a newspaper cutting to Cárdenas which maintained that, so far as "displaying generosity" toward the Spanish refugees was concerned, few governments had outdone Mexico's. Mexico's generosity, the article insisted, was praiseworthy. Nonetheless, it was important—Valle Cortés added with more than a trace of irony—to know what the thousands of Mexican families mired in poverty, for lack of government assistance, thought about these acts of generosity. The same question applied to the many hundreds of expatriates, living in the United States, who experienced great hardship but were unable to return to the homeland for lack of money. Hence Valle Cortés faulted the government's "magnanimity," since it "made a show of being generous" toward foreigners but forgot about the destitution within its own country in its eagerness to "win plaudits and praise from abroad."[9]

The author of the newspaper article believed that the government's charitable actions, the ideological affinity it felt toward the Republican cause, and the racial bonds that tied Mexicans to Spaniards explained but did not justify the squandering of the public treasury. Above this situation were the needs of Mexicans themselves, because they were the ones who contributed to building up the national treasury. Thus, the first priority was to meet the country's internal needs, after which the government could strike out on a course of generosity buoyed by its "air of self-congratulation." The article's author believed that when Mexicans in their own country had bread enough to give to their children and when their compatriots abroad were supported and repatriated, then the government could afford the luxury, on behalf of its people, of assisting all the foreign refugees it might wish to help.[10]

Two newspapers, *La Prensa* (San Antonio) and *La Opinión* (Los Angeles), founded in 1913 and 1926, respectively, by the journalist Ignacio Lozano, who often commented on the state of affairs in Mexico and celebrated Mexican culture in the U.S. Southwest, featured an editorial titled "Consumatum Est" lambasting the preference that the Mexican government gave to Spanish refugees over its own citizens residing in the United States. In a four-square attack on the Cardenista administration, the editorial maintained that it was not the Spanish who should be blamed for their being in Mexico but those who had brought them there: Lázaro Cárdenas and Narciso Bassols, ambassador to France. The majority of newspapers in Mexico adhered to this same line and began to direct their criticism toward those Mexican leaders and officials who had determined the processes that governed the selection and admission of Spanish exiles.[11] Another piece in *La Opinión*, titled "Down with the Mexicans! Long Live the Spanish!," similarly took the Cárdenas government to task for displaying a more favorable attitude toward the Spanish than it did toward its own repatriated citizens.[12]

This paper published an article by Adolfo Gómez, from Piedras Negras, Coahuila, titled "Candil de la calle . . . ," in which Gómez averred that the popular saying *candil de la calle, oscuridad de su casa* [roughly, to be helpful to strangers but unhelpful to one's own family] fit the Cardenista immigration policy perfectly, since it promoted the entry of "thousands of Spanish refugees," even as many of its own citizens in the United States remained without work, lived a pitiful existence, and were forced to depend on public charity to survive. On Mexican soil, by contrast, the Spanish were fêted and immediately established, in many cases displacing Mexicans or at least causing the redirection of funds that Mexican citizens required to meet their immediate needs for food and housing. According to Gómez, both the federal government and state and municipal governments as well as the CTM and other workers' unions fought for the honor of being the first to take in and accommodate the Spanish, granting them more rights and privileges than their host citizens and showing greater generosity to them than to "our own people."[13]

Both in Mexico and in the U.S. Mexican community the arrival of the Spanish refugees was contrasted with the lagging effort at repatriation as a way of heaping criticism on Cárdenas. To answer its critics, the government announced the organized repatriation of its migrant nationals from the United States (Hoffman 1974, 157; Balderrama and Rodríguez 1995, 147). Robert K. Peyton, a U.S. vice-consul stationed in Chihuahua, thought that the government's undertaking was clearly motivated by political interest, the need to counter the criticisms unleashed by the government's warm welcome of the Spanish refugees.[14] Indeed, in short order, Cárdenas directed Ignacio García Téllez to carry out the repatriation program in two phases: the first, to take place "before the first Spaniard arrived," was to be accomplished without complicated bureaucratic formalities or a rigorous process of selection. The only criteria were that returnees be capable of working in agriculture and desirous of returning to Mexico. In the second phase, the returnees would be sent to an area in the Lower Rio Grande Valley, a few kilometers from Matamoros, in the state of Tamaulipas. The plan was executed accordingly. The first ships that arrived in Mexico with refugees onboard were the *Sinaia*, the *Ipanema*, and the *Mexique*, which docked on 13 June, 17 July, and 27 July 1939, respectively.[15] The repatriation project got underway in April. If the criticisms directed against Cárdenas played a role in jump-starting repatriation, however, they were not the core reason he decided to launch the program; rather, they were one factor intertwined with others.

In the first place, the plan for an organized return dated to early 1938. It was rooted in Cárdenas's personal interest and accelerated by the agreement concluded at the end of that year with authorities in Southern California. In other words, the government's decision to implement a repatriation project and the preparatory work associated with it predated the large-scale arrival of Spanish refugees. Second, the mass entry into Mexico of Spanish exiles only began, as we will see, in mid-June 1939, by which time the repatriation plan had been fully executed. In this sense, the project to bring Mexican nationals back to the homeland and the arrival of the refugees were events that unfolded during the same period but not simultaneously. Each developed in its own way but, for tactical reasons, was played off against the other by various people out to attack Cárdenas. In short, at least two supranational factors (the accord reached with authorities in California to implement a return of Mexican nationals and the campaign on behalf of Spanish refugees) coincided at the very time that Cárdenas had decided to undertake a repatriation program, although for him the repatriation program—unlike the move to admit Spanish refugees—was of secondary importance in Mexican foreign policy.

The numbers of refugees admitted into the country and those of repatriated nationals are a partial indication of the importance that the government attached to each of the two migratory currents. From the outset of the Spanish Civil War to the end of the Second World War, "Mexico possibly" took in more than 20,000 Spanish Republican refugees or, on average, 1,500 per year. This extended immigration was deeply political. Furthermore, the Spanish immigrants were highly trained, intellectually and technically, and predominately from cities (Pla Brugat 1992, 119; Pla Brugat 1994, 226–27, 230; Lida 1997, 75, 84, 92–93, 141).

There are no precise figures for the number of Mexicans whose return was supported by assistance from the government. In 1939, however, some 3,750 people were repatriated and subsequently resettled in the northern part of Tamaulipas. The federal government also helped various individuals and small groups of people who returned to their native villages and towns as well as other people who went to places suggested to them (around 2,000 individuals in all). Broadly speaking, although the support given to the repatriated was meaningful and unprecedented, given that nearly 6,000 people returned to the homeland with official help, the entry—and all that attended it—of Spanish exiles in Mexico certainly overshadowed that of the repatriated nationals. Moreover, the repatriation project lasted a mere three months (from April to June 1939), whereas the arrival of the Spanish refugees took place over a span of years. Indisputably, then, the government was focused more on admitting the refugees than on promoting and furthering the return of its citizens from the United States.

## The Lower Rio Grande Valley and the Repatriation Project

At the end of April 1939, as various people in Mexico and the United States compared the arrival of the Spanish refugees and the repatriation of Mexican nationals, Cárdenas set about implementing the second stage of his project: selection of the region in which to resettle those chosen for repatriation so they could form the nucleus of an agricultural colony. In the end, a zone in the Lower Rio Grande Valley, around the city of Matamoros in northeastern Tamaulipas, was viewed as the most suitable. In both population and productive output it was growing significantly.[16] Covering approximately 98,000 hectares, the zone was bordered on the north and northeast by the Rio Grande, on the east and southeast by a straight line that joined the La Burra and El Consuelo ranches, on the west by the El Culebrón lagoon and the Canales mesa, and on the south and southwest by a line that ran along the side of the Tío Fernando, Mogotes, San Pedro, and La Purísima ranches.[17]

The site was selected on the basis of a study that President Cárdenas requested of Marte R. Gómez, the governor of Tamaulipas, to which contributed Manuel Mesa, general manager of the BNCA, and the engineer Eduardo Chávez, the official in charge of the irrigation flood control barriers and the Rio Grande Commission. Their study analyzed and proposed different zones in which to resettle the repatriated, areas of land where climate, irrigation, and soil conditions guaranteed that they could make the most "of their efforts."[18]

The zone eventually chosen had also been suggested by Manuel Gamio, who believed that the valley offered certain advantages to the people who repatriated. Here they would encounter a higher cultural level than in the center and south of the country (shoes, slacks, shirts, etc. were commonly worn); tortillas, wheat, and meat formed a steady part of the local diet; and though the differences might be minimal, the men in this area "have better physical features than those of the center and south." In addition, the newly resettled would not experience problems with the local residents "on account of troublesome rivalries and competition."[19] It was also proposed that the initial settlement take the form of a pilot project, located in an area relatively removed from other centers of population—ostensibly to avoid the loss of the returnees' skills or run-ins over existing jobs with people already established in the region—and of modest size. As Gamio, head of the Demographics Department, suggested, only a small part of the zone was designated to found the settlement.

On 22 April 1939, Cárdenas held discussions with Ramón Beteta in Matamoros to finalize details for the colony and familiarize himself with the site and the irrigation infrastructure where the returnees were to be settled.[20] Cárdenas spent two days there, in order to study agrarian problems and issues surrounding repatriation. He was accompanied by a group of prominent officials, among them General Juan Andreu Almazán, a candidate for the presidency; the engineer Melquiades Angulo, then serving as minister of communications and public works; and the governor of the state. In his meeting with Beteta, Cárdenas wrestled with the question of how the government should proceed and what arrangements needed to be made so that those chosen for repatriation could establish a functioning agricultural settlement.[21] Following the suggestion of the undersecretary of foreign relations, he decided to centralize the administrative work of the repatriation. Beteta would therefore be responsible for all activities carried out on U.S. soil—the selection, transport, and training of returnees. These operations in turn would be delegated to the Mexican consuls, thereby remaining under the aegis of the Foreign Relations Ministry. Eduardo Chávez was placed in charge of repatriation activities on the Mexican side.

Chávez's remit involved transporting the repatriated from Matamoros to the new settlement, lodging them, helping build their houses, providing them with general economic assistance, giving them their plots, and ensuring that the settlement proved a success. It was determined as well that the costs of the repatriation effort would be covered with funds from the Ministries of the Interior, Foreign Relations, and Agriculture and Development; while—going forward—matters of "financing" would be carried out by the BNCA and the BNCE.[22] In this way, by assigning specific tasks, Cárdenas carried out the second phase of his project, creating a structured means of proceeding in which different departments of the federal government assumed some defined responsibility. He spread out the cost of the project so that no single department would be unduly burdened.

Local authorities and the federal government also took advantage of Cárdenas's visit to sign an agreement aimed at accelerating ongoing work to improve the conditions of the land in the valley. On 24 April 1939, at the field camp of the Tamaulipas [Public] Works Office of the Lower Rio Grande, Lázaro Cárdenas, Marte R. Gómez, and Melquiades Angulo approved the agreement, with the dual goal of promoting the area's agricultural development and solving the problem of lost harvests that beset the local population because the river often overflowed its banks. Although nearly two years earlier, on 14 July 1937, Cárdenas had expropriated certain lands and taken other actions, mainly through flood control and irrigation projects, to promote the area's development, little tangible progress had been made. He therefore ordered that the minister of communications carry out required river barrier work as well as other operations to prevent flooding and assure that both long-established residents of the region and the incoming repatriated Mexican nationals would be able to earn a living. Specifically, the proposal called for preparing an area of production that, according to official sources, contained exceptionally high quality land capable of furnishing food both to the local population and to "all groups of people" in other parts of the country or to the repatriated.[23]

In addition, the proposal also outlined programs for cash allowances, for irrigation, and for improved sanitation. It called for modifying the existing division of farmlands, to replace an "anachronistic" system of "parceling out" plots of land that was unsuited to the reorganization of the locality; for granting deeds to land; for setting up schools; and for instituting a policy on extending credit such that the region could be productive, have irrigation, and, overall, enjoy a self-sustaining, developed economy.[24]

Cárdenas agreed that paving the way for "new human contributions" would hinge on the government's economic prospects and possibilities and on solving the problems of the region itself.[25] The project's objectives were ambitious and without precedent: to assure the well-being of the repatriated families—up to 500 spread over 10,000 hectares—and of the campesinos who made up the community of Anáhuac, in which some 150 people had settled.

Since the region's climate and soil were particularly suited to the cultivation of cotton, the plan called for the area's farmers to specialize in this crop. To this end, a program was carried out aimed at maintaining pest-free plants, avoiding the use of poor quality seeds, and pursuing a forceful policy to safeguard plant health. The same approach was to be followed to protect the local cattle ranching industry (Secretaría de Agricultura y Fomento 1940, 53).

In announcing the president's decision to spur the return of Mexican migrants and the selection of a site on which to resettle them, Gamio judged that the valley would in the future become Mexico's most important agricultural area, since it covered 300,000 hectares and represented an investment of 13 million pesos, of which, as of April 1939, only 4,000 had actually been released.[26] For his part, Chávez asserted that the various works under way had contributed in large measure to the emergence of Matamoros as the most prosperous cotton growing region of the republic and that, as a clear indicator of the economic boom, the population of the city and environs would grow from 12,000 in 1935 to 120,000 by 1940.[27]

Minister of the Interior García Téllez believed that the settlement in the region of repatriated nationals would not only directly benefit the national economy but would be transformative for Mexico's future because it would impede the flight abroad of hundreds of braceros, whose "energies, much-needed in our midst," could be retained and utilized.[28] He also stated that when the new irrigation system was completed the region would become the leading center of agricultural production in the country.

The lofty expectations trumpeted by Gamio, Chávez, and García Téllez applied to the broad development of the zone and to the projected effect of the repatriation of hundreds of Mexican nationals. These agricultural and public works programs, which the government had decisively promoted in this region since the middle of the decade, had indeed boosted its population and development. The repatriation project, in contrast, was the focus of government attention for only a few months in 1939. The wider development scheme for the region had been high on the government's agenda since 1935 and formed part of the general Cardenista plan for broad agrarian reform that, among its other features, emphasized improved irrigation systems. The repatriation of Mexican nationals, meanwhile, was a low priority within the government's development scheme for the region and was not devised until the Cárdenas sexenio had all but ended.

After the 24 April 1939 presidential agreement had been signed to ratchet up the works carried out by the Lower Rio Grande Commission, the plan to establish a new settlement was quickly set in motion. Accordingly, Cárdenas took the unprecedented step of approving a budget of 800,000 pesos to fund it.[29] Seeking to prevent future complications and understanding the failure of earlier projects, whether carried out by people acting on their own or with government support, Gamio suggested that the new settlement be limited to 100 families. In this way, the mistakes made and deficiencies experienced by this group could be corrected so that future settlements might avoid them.[30] Those chosen in this first wave of repatriation had to be farmers and agricultural workers, and the return "would be conditioned by the possibilities that the settlement offered and by the feasibility of enlarging it in the immediate future."

The plan was an experiment in which the government invested a substantial sum of money to repatriate hundreds of families of Mexican origin and nationality then living in the United States. Moreover, within the long history of Mexican migration to its immediate neighbor north of the Rio Grande, the plan had no forerunner. To this point, with the exception of the actions pursued by presidents Álvaro Obregón, Abelardo Rodríguez, and Emilio Portes Gil—in response to mass deportations from the United States—no Mexican government, minus the threat of large-scale returns, had activated a special program to support an organized return of its nationals and invested significant monies to accomplish it. Still, these official measures taken by the Cárdenas regime had their limits, since the help that the government tendered to Mexicans who had been repatriated at an earlier time and to hundreds who had returned to the homeland on their own, without receiving any assistance, continued to be meager at best, a cause for which the government had little appetite.

## The Hope . . . and the Reality

In April 1939, in the settlement of La Esperanza ("The Hope"), Santa Teresa, located on the lands of the former hacienda of La Sauteña, in Tamaulipas, twenty families, 110 people in total, found themselves living in precarious conditions. They had been repatriated by the government between September 1937 and December 1938.[31] When they reached La Esperanza, Cárdenas offered to divide the land up among them and support their work with money and tools, but these promises were never kept. In April 1939, the president's office sent a commission to La Esperanza, composed of representatives from the Interior and Agriculture Ministries, the National Health Department, and the BNCA, with the objective of solving the myriad problems that the colony confronted, problems of internal organization, of insufficient or nonexistent credit, of agricultural production, irrigation, health, housing, and raising livestock. Cárdenas instructed the bank to extend credit to the settlers and told the Agriculture Ministry and the CNI to resolve the pervasive irrigation problems.[32]

As part of this directive, the engineer Mario Grajales, assistant head of the Office of Population in Matamoros, joined a representative of the Agriculture Ministry in trying to help these repatriated families grow crops and see to their own welfare. In addition, the two officials were to improve the settlers' housing and living conditions and get them the tools they lacked.[33] Grajales's trip also had another purpose, that of analyzing whether it would be feasible for the government to invest in the La Esperanza lands and provide "moral" and material "support" to the people who had settled there. In the event that the answer was yes, geologists, physicians, and workers from the Department of Agriculture and Communications would be sent to the settlement. A school would be constructed on the property, along with a telegraph and post office, and improvements would be made to a road to facilitate transport of people and goods.[34] None of these projects, however, came to pass. The impoverished living conditions and the inferior quality of the land caused the settlers to abandon La Esperanza, moving to different small communities where, for the most part, they joined existing groups of ejido-based farmers. Of the original twenty families who settled La Esperanza, only seven braved the poverty and stayed behind.[35]

Beteta, who at the time was one of the people most identified with the repatriation project, believed that the desperate state into which La Esperanza had fallen constituted a "thorough repudiation of everything I have been saying." Consequently, Cárdenas should order that the settlement be salvaged and turned into "a center of attraction, not of expulsion, for the repatriated." Beteta, however, was on the losing side of the argument. The government took no other measures to rescue and preserve the settlement. Moreover, La Esperanza was not the only place of resettlement where returnees experienced problems or where the government's official efforts revealed their limitations.

During the second half of April 1939, Beteta reported that a group of 115 families living in the settlement of Anáhuac, located in Ramírez, Coahuila, faced a critical situation because the BNCA had suspended the financing intended for land-clearing operations. This action had deprived the Anáhuac, Progreso, Valle, and Porvenir farmers' associations of needed aid. The four associations were composed of men who had repatriated to Mexico before 1935 and who now—without the resources they required—requested that Beteta allow them to reemigrate to the United States. Beteta, of course, recognized that such a move on their part would reflect badly on the repatriation project that had just gotten under way. He therefore asked that the BNCA address the matter and cut through the bureaucratic obstacles, but little advance was made on this score.[36]

At this same time, in "disorderly fashion and to no good end," numerous repatriated families were wandering through Mexico City, going "from door to door" asking for work. With the purpose of organizing this itinerant collectivity and getting its demands heard, a committee asked the capital city newspaper *Excelsior*, in its pages, to call on all of Mexico's unemployed repatriated citizens to gather in the offices of the Interior Ministry and request that it consider them for the settlements being planned for different areas in the country.[37]

The situation of some 2,000 other repatriated nationals who had arrived in the capital at the beginning of 1939 produced another crisis rooted in the government's failure to deliver on its promises. The people in this group had come from various parts of the United States, including Illinois, Wyoming, Iowa, Nebraska, and Michigan. They had submitted a request to the Agriculture Ministry that they be granted the right to settle and work the lands belonging to the settlement of Río Grande, in the state of Oaxaca. A heavy-handed, creaking bureaucratic process, which had slowed down their request to and within the ministry, had led to their current difficulties. They had not been able to gain any relief or support. The same problem arose in Baja California, where many repatriated Mexican migrants were now expressing anger and disillusionment because, despite the promises they had been given that they would receive "everything and more," they had in fact received nothing and were now destitute.[38] To make matters worse, García Téllez made it known that the Interior Ministry's funding for repatriation was exhausted because it had been used to help bring back to the homeland a group of men who had fought in the Mexican Revolution.[39]

In short, many repatriated Mexican nationals who had returned to the country either before April 1939 or at some point during that year—with official support or on their own initiative—experienced considerable difficulties both in getting resettled and in simply surviving. Those who arrived in various places in the north of the country, such as La Esperanza or the Anáhuac settlement, or in Baja California, received little support. The promises they had been given were not kept and such assistance as they did receive was suspended. Similarly, those who came to Mexico City were ignored by the government; the petitions they submitted for the right to settle particular lands led nowhere, and no steps were taken to provide them with jobs.

That the repatriated were forced to endure such trying and painful conditions was due in the main to two factors. First, official, state-sponsored measures to help them were largely absent, since the government had not set aside and directed resources to assist these people once they were back in the country, nor did it develop any firm plan in this regard. The Cárdenas administration was not inclined either to furnish emergency assistance or to push for projects that would relieve the distress of the repatriated. The country's weak economy, whose difficulties were compounded by inflation, reinforced its reluctance. The immediate cause of Mexico's economic problems lay in the type of financing adopted to fund public expenditures. Because the latter were so high, given the government's broad social programs, the treasury had to keep increasing the money supply, a pattern worsened by a lack of confidence on the part of investors and savers, only fueling a steady rise in the price of goods (Smith 1955, 224; Nathan 1955, 345). Second, government attention was narrowly focused on the repatriation project and on the suggested courses of action proposed by the officials in charge of carrying it out. Gamio concentrated on the importance of official support being selective—directed solely at those people enrolled in the organized program of return and not at those who had already come back to Mexico. Paradoxical or contradictory as it might seem, the Cardenista administration took a clear interest in developing a repatriation project while simultaneously showing very little interest in supporting its citizens who had already returned, such as those who massed in front of the National Palace to ask for land on which they could resettle. The government likewise gave little help to the colony of La Esperanza, whose members were perishing from hunger just a few kilometers from the site of its new project. This last case, like those of Mexico City and Baja California, demonstrates that the government's actions to aid its citizens who had repatriated from the United States were limited and, in many instances, barely registered. At the beginning of 1939, governmental action centered on founding an agricultural colony.

**CHAPTER SEVEN**

# The 18 March Agricultural
# Colony in Tamaulipas, 1939–1940

My wish is that we are always remembered.

—GUADALUPE MUÑOZ GRANADOS, MEXICAN NATIONAL REPATRIATED
TO THE 18 MARCH AGRICULTURAL COLONY, 20 OCTOBER 1939

## The 18 March Agricultural Colony

On 8 May 1939, Lázaro Cárdenas agreed to the establishment of the 18 March agricultural colony as part of his government's larger development scheme for the Lower Rio Grande Valley in the area of the Tamaulipas city of Matamoros. Situated twenty kilometers north of the Victoria-Matamoros highway and covering approximately 25,000 hectares, the terrain abutted the colony of La Independencia, which was comprised of settlers from District No. 4 (aka Don Martín), in the state of Nuevo León, and also lay east of the colony of Los Ángeles and south of the colony of Anáhuac. Its name was chosen by Cárdenas in honor of the date when the country's oil fields were nationalized, as one way to maintain the nationalist ethos that inspired and underpinned the expropriation.[1]

The project was divided into two stages. The first entailed the expenditure of some 800,000 pesos, to be used to repatriate and resettle 500 families and grant farmland to each of them, as well as to construct windbreaks, roads, and to purchase right of way. The work of surveying the land and planning the layout of the zone was to be accomplished during the second stage, along with the work of clearing the land, which—as one of the basic elements of the program—the members of the new settlement would themselves do. The Department of Water Works and the Lower Rio Grande Valley Commission determined that the colony should contain 500 families, each of whom would receive ten hectares.[2]

Engineer Eduardo Chávez, the director of the government's public works program for the Lower Rio Grande Valley, was given administrative responsibility for the colony. Five buildings, each having ten separate units, were to be installed to serve as provisional housing for the incoming families.[3] Three teams of surveyors were to be employed to create a plat that would incorporate 500 kilometers of rough dirt roads and other minor roads and also demarcate property lines for the settler families. As noted above, the clearing of the land would be delegated to the returnees themselves. The compensation they received for this work would enable them to be self-supporting until they could begin farming their parcels. In addition, funds would be provided for the purchase of equipment and livestock (each family to be given a team of mules and farm tools), but with a limit of only 50 percent of what the entire community was projected to need, since the government believed that many of the repatriated would come back with their own implements and tools. With respect to permanent dwellings for the settlers, once a family's parcel was assigned, work was to begin on the construction of a modestly sized house built to an adequate standard, for which assistance would be provided in the form of building materials and a sum of 200 pesos per family.[4]

The overall development plan included the construction of a twenty-five kilometer road that would extend from the Victoria-Matamoros highway and cross through the community of Anáhuac before reaching the new 18 March settlement. Additionally, other work would bring in potable water, install drainage, sink a well to provide a ready supply of water together with a pump motor and a tank in which to store the water, accompanied by a small network of pipes to distribute it. The plan also called for the construction of a school and other facilities necessary for the welfare of community members.[5]

The total amount required for the work to establish the colony came to 786,450 pesos, which according to Chávez would cover the needs of the repatriated from May 1939 to January 1940 (see table 7.1). This sum included the costs of provisional and permanent housing, division and clearing of the land, equipment and administrative expenses, and other general outlays. It is not known what portion of this budget was released and expended. The documentation surrounding the project as well as later events suggest that the government only directed small sums of money, cumulating in a modest total, that helped partially meet the settlers' needs.

At the end of April 1939, the sinking of the wells and preparation of plots began, along with the construction of both the road to connect the colony with the Matamoros-Reynoso highway and the provisional housing units. In addition, Chávez secured tools and equipment for clearing the land as well

TABLE 7.1 Planned monthly distribution of funds allocated for the 18 March colony

| CATEGORY | MAY | JUNE | JULY | AUG. | SEPT. | OCT. | NOV. | DEC. | JAN. | TOTAL AMOUNT |
|---|---|---|---|---|---|---|---|---|---|---|
| Provisional housing | $7,500 | | | | | | | | | $7,500 |
| Division of land | 8,000 | | | | | | | | | 8,000 |
| Land clearing | 65,000 | $65,000 | $65,000 | $65,000 | $65,000 | | | | | 325,000 |
| Equipment | 4,000 | 2,000 | 2,000 | 2,000 | 48,000 | $48,000 | $48,000 | $48,000 | $48,000 | 250,000 |
| Permanent dwellings | 20,000 | 20,000 | 20,000 | 20,000 | 20,000 | | | | | 100,000 |
| General outlays | 36,000 | 17,500 | 5,000 | | | | | | | 58,500 |
| Administrative expenses | 5,450 | 4,000 | 4,000 | 4,000 | 4,000 | 4,000 | 4,000 | 4,000 | 4,000 | 37,450 |
| TOTALS | 145,950 | 108,500 | 96,000 | 91,000 | 137,000 | 52,000 | 52,000 | 52,000 | 52,000 | 786,450 |

SOURCE: AGN, FC, exp. 503.11/3–1, President of the Republic, concerning the establishment of the 18 March colony for repatriated nationals, marginal note of the president approving the distributions, Torreón, 8 May 1939, Eduardo Chávez, Tamaulipas, 24 April 1939.

as other items needed so that returnees could begin work without delay. The arrangements pertaining to customs and migration, to certifying the health of the returnees, and their transport from the border to the site of the new settlement were taken care of. Chávez also worked with Florencio Cuéllar, the official in charge of tax collection for the state of Tamaulipas, concerning the process to be followed so that repatriated families could register and acquire legal title to their land. Cuéllar estimated that the various steps in this process could be completed before 20 May 1939. To keep matters as organized as possible, Marte R. Gómez, Tamaulipas's governor, recommended that none of the repatriated be dispatched to the new settlement until all bureaucratic formalities had been completed. On the basis of these advances, Chávez announced that he was prepared to begin receiving families as of 1 May, although within a few days he requested a postponement until 22 May.[6]

## The Mobilization in Texas and the Return to Mexico

At the end of April 1939, Ramón Beteta began to transport individuals and small groups toward Mexico. Some set out for their native town or village, others went to ejidos, and still others were directed to the 18 March agricultural colony. The repatriated migrants came mainly from rural areas of Texas, and a smaller number from the state's urban centers. After getting organized, some in the group set off to familiarize themselves with conditions in their intended locale; others made the trip as an organized unit directly assisted by the government; still other families returned on their own without any support. Uniformly, however, all of the repatriated returned to the homeland with their personal belongings, in their own vehicles or in those furnished by the U.S. government. The motivation for returning varied from family to family. In some cases it was lack of work and ensuing poverty; in other cases it sprang from the wartime climate that began to grip the United States, compounded by the fear that the head of the family might be subject to military service; and in still other cases it was the lure of the land that was being offered.

The first person to repatriate was an agricultural worker, Jesús Barajas, who returned to Cojumatlán, Michoacán. He had left Mexico during the Cristero Rebellion, due—in his telling—to the violent and inhumane conduct of General Joaquín Amaro. Barajas returned with his wife, an adult son, and five minor children. He had family and friends in Mexico and came back with his tools, an old Ford automobile, and a trailer in which he carted his family and all their belongings. The government, through Beteta's efforts, furnished him with tires, gasoline, and some money for the road trip.[7]

Beteta also helped organize the return, by both railway and truck, of 1,997 Mexican nationals who went back to their town or village of origin. They came from the Texas cities of San Antonio, Beaumont, Brownsville, Dallas, Del Rio, Corpus Christi, Eagle Pass, and Houston, as well as from New Orleans, Los Angeles, and Oklahoma City.[8] With respect to those selected to populate the new agricultural colony, Beteta's timetable called for the majority to arrive in Matamoros during the second half of May. A group left Texas for the colony in the middle of the month. Its thirteen families, sixty-five people in all, came from San Antonio and several small communities near the city. Their economic situation was dire. A second group, composed of fifty-three people from the South Texas city of Kenedy, left for Mexico at the end of that month. Around this time, the first families coming from Beaumont, Richmondville, and San Antonio had crossed the border and within days were helping clear the colony's land.[9]

One area from which a considerable number of Mexican nationals repatriated at this time was Karnes County, located southeast of San Antonio. At the end of April 1939, a group of agricultural workers in the Karnes County city of Kenedy began to discuss among themselves whether they might find it worthwhile to return to Mexico. Their next step was to form a repatriation committee, headed by Moisés Z. Reséndez. In early May, the committee visited the site of the 18 March colony to inspect conditions there. In general, they came away with a favorable impression of the opportunity being offered by the Mexican government and indicated that the quality of the land marked off for settlement was similar to that found on the Texas side of the Lower Rio Grande Valley. Its soil was amenable to the cultivation of cotton, corn, beans, and other vegetables.[10] Following the committee's return to Kenedy, several groups were organized to initiate a move to the colony, and at the end of May, thirteen families, seventy-three people in all, left Karnes County.

As the summer progressed, the 18 March colony continued to attract more settlers, drawing in small groups from around Dallas, Houston, and also additional people from Karnes County.[11] A report from McAllen, Texas, indicated that groups of Mexicans who lived in the nearby Rio Grande Valley communities of Donna and Weslaco were making arrangements to return to Mexico and, at the end of May, forty people from Beaumont and Port Arthur likewise left for Mexico, determined to join ejidos in Guadalajara and elsewhere. In this same period, several families living in the towns of San Sebastian, Brady, Raymondville, and Robstown also left for Mexico.[12] Thus, two streams of repatriations occurred at this time: one directed toward multiple locations in Mexico, the other targeting a single destination—the 18 March agricultural colony.

Although the majority of returnees made the trip as part of a group, some traveled by themselves and relied solely on their own resources. In both instances, the repatriated made their decision to journey back to Mexico once they had become aware of the promises Beteta was making or because a senior family member faced the prospect of being conscripted into military service. The case of Bartolo Loera Castillo exemplified the latter situation. A Mexican national who lived in Hop, Texas, he undertook the return trip with his immediate family—his wife, who was a U.S. citizen, and his three children, all of whom had been born in the United States. Loera Castillo's decision to return to Mexico turned on the fact that he had received notice of his obligation to present himself for induction into military service. To avoid doing so, he used such resources as he had to pay the costs of his trip back to the homeland.

Since January 1938 a tense calm had prevailed in the United States, as the likelihood increased of its being drawn into the European conflict. Despite President Roosevelt's assurance that the nation would maintain its neutrality, events in Europe (Germany's annexation of Austria, Adolf Hitler's invasion of Czechoslovakia, and the threat that hung over Poland) impelled the country to enlarge its armed forces. Roosevelt would soon fight for a conscription law, with the result that in the following year, for the first time in its history, the United States had a peacetime draft. The war created tensions not only between generations but within families as well. The fear caused by the conscription, or threat of conscription, of the father in a family carried serious social repercussions. In Matamoros, a rumor was rampant that Mexican citizens were returning because war was about to break out.[13]

During May 1938, the 18 March colony welcomed no fewer than 408 families and a total of 1,498 people, including 506 adult men. This influx accounted for 82 percent of the total settler population planned for the colony. As such, the government set 22 October 1938 as the deadline for new arrivals.[14] Nonetheless, people continued arriving after this date, both those whom the government had approved for the colony and many others who simply turned up on their own.

Several people representing the Mexican Honorary Commission of Kyle, Texas, headed by its president, Telésforo Galván, also traveled to Matamoros to examine local conditions. When they reached the area, however, heavy rains impeded their movements and made it difficult for them to assess the quality of the land and soil. The administrators of the 18 March colony nonetheless assured them that the land was excellent for agricultural purposes and that the settlers' needs would be covered by the Mexican government. On returning to Kyle, the group reported favorably on the opportunities that the future settlement would provide. A short time later, a delegation from El Granado, Texas, traveled to the 18 March colony to learn more about the community and assess its prospects.[15]

In early June 1938, another forty-five people departed from Houston. Among them was the family of Elena Zúñiga Rosales, a twenty-five-year-old citizen of the United States. She reached Mexico with her father, Inocencio Zúñiga, who had been born in San Luis Potosí; her mother, Tomasa Rodríguez, a native of Cerralvo, Nuevo León, and four brothers. Elena's father had decided to return to Mexico because he could not find work in the United States. He served as the group's leader and was in charge of recording the number of families that left, how many members they included, and their age, sex, and other data. Zúñiga's group returned in a twenty-four-family caravan that included several young people and children who spoke English as well a good many women and infants. The night before leaving, the group had gathered at the Rose School, where crackers, coffee, bread, sugar, cans of Carnation milk, and other provisions were handed out and families were informed that they would be transported to Matamoros with their belongings, including the furniture that many were bringing. The caravan reached the border on 17 June 1939. From the time they met in Houston until they arrived at the 18 March colony, the families received assistance from the government. Their progress along the way had stalled for several days, however, due to rains that made the roads impassable. Until conditions improved, they were lodged temporarily in the warehouse of a cotton ginning mill.[16]

Other contingents of returning migrants continued to leave Texas, with the 18 March colony as their destination, during the middle of June: 60 people from Sebastian, for example, and 65 from San Antonio. According to a report published in San Antonio, by 13 June more than 500 Mexicans who lived in Texas had left the state, heading to Tamaulipas. A week later the reported figure had climbed to 849, or 185 families from across Texas. At the beginning of July, various families residing in Kyle, San Marcos, and New Braunfels were taken to Brownsville, Texas, along with their personal belongings, farm tools and livestock; while still other families from San Antonio left for Matamoros. To this point, according to official calculations, the Mexican government had expended US $10,000 on repatriating people from Houston, Sebastian, Raymondville, Robstown, and Corpus Christi.[17]

The trend continued. At the end of June and during July, more than sixty Mexican agricultural workers coming from the Texas communities of Donna and Von Ormy were transported to Matamoros so they could set themselves up in the colony. Similarly, their counterparts left twice a week from San Antonio,

New Braunfels, and San Marcos, taking their cows, sheep, pigs, and goats with them. At the end of July, the 18 March colony received families that the government had helped transport from Dallas, Malakoff, Terrell, and Harlingen.[18]

May 1939 was the month in which the greatest number of people left Texas for Mexico—approximately 1,500, the majority of whom with the 18 March colony as their destination. On the scale of importance, this group was followed by those who returned to their native village or town—some 2,157 people fell into this category. In the end, very few returnees—only around 70—reported that they had returned to or joined an ejido. In his year-end report to the thirty-seventh legislature, Cárdenas announced that the colony had been established with 627 heads of household; 3,750 individuals, 900 of whom were older than sixteen; that each family had received a ten-hectare plot suitable for growing crops; and that 464,000 pesos had been expended on transporting these people and getting them settled.[19]

## The Significance of the Return

As we have seen, the number of Mexican nationals who, under official government sponsorship, either settled in the 18 March colony or returned to their own town or village continued its upward trajectory, eventually reaching 6,000 people. This organized movement was unprecedented because it entailed voluntary repatriations channeled through a program planned and promoted by the Mexican government. In 1939, Mexican immigration authorities registered 15, 925 repatriated nationals. Thus, almost a third of those who returned had done so under the auspices of the government's official program.[20] The program's great success in 1939 seems, then, to have been spurred by Cárdenas's decision that year to promote it actively and aggressively. The president's intervention was important because, when it is removed from the equation, the level of interest displayed by Mexican migrants in returning to the homeland appears generally to have declined.

In Tamaulipas, the repatriation and resettlement of nearly 4,000 people significantly increased the population of the region. In mid-June 1937, the Lower Rio Grande Valley was inhabited by 16,500 people, which meant that the soon-to-arrive returnees would boost the area's population by 25 percent. The overall population increase was also influenced by the establishment of other settlements; among them the colony of Magueyes, founded by 800 families of agricultural workers from Irrigation District No. 4 in Nuevo León, that covered 10,000 hectares (Secretaría de Comunicaciones y Obras Públicas 1940, 151).

Together, the Magueyes and 18 March settlements extended over 50,000 hectares. They were complemented by other agricultural settlements that totaled 30,000 hectares. These new areas of colonization, when added to a similar 20,000 hectares earlier freed up, brought the total land designated for such settlement to 100,000 hectares, a land area that gave the region preferential status among the country's principal agricultural zones. Mexico's communications and public works minister reported at the end of 1939 that the region was undergoing a "frenzy of development" (Secretaría de Comunicaciones y Obras Públicas 1940, 151–52). The inflow of repatriated nationals, along with the move of people from District No. 4 and other areas in the interior of the country, had visible short-term impacts on the Lower Rio Grande Valley, notably the sharp increase in its population. Other effects, such as the level of agricultural production, were more long-term, not felt until sometime after the founding of the 18 March colony.

## The Colony during the First Years of Its Existence

From May 1939 until the end of the year, the groups of people being transported from Texas to the 18 March colony poured their energies into helping construct the settlement and creating a new, livable home for themselves. Over the first year of the colony, both Eduardo Chávez, the man immediately responsible for administering its development, and the undersecretary of foreign relations claimed to be optimistic about its progress, their statements drawing attention to some settlers' solid, visible achievements. Nonetheless, the settler population as a whole endured numerous setbacks.

## Optimism

The process of getting the settlers established was simple and streamlined. Each group that arrived in Matamoros was met by representatives from the National Irrigation Commission (CNI). The latter delivered to each family its allocated 12.5 hectares (2.5 more than the amount stipulated by Cárdenas in his 1939 annual report) and also gave them a set of tools: a machete, an axe, a hoe, and a pickaxe-like tool with which to clear and prepare the land they would be cultivating. The tool kit also included files to keep the other implements sharp. Chávez declared that each family received 65 pesos for each hectare it cleaned and cleared. Every week employees of the CNI took stock of the progress made on each parcel of land and extended credit to families, consonant with the work they had accomplished, for use in the local stores. According to Chávez, such basic goods as the settlers needed could be purchased in the immediate vicinity, making long trips to other communities unnecessary.[21]

As temporary lodging, some families were given tents; others received galvanized metal sheets that they used to put up provisional structures. For several months this latter type of dwelling was the only one constructed. Each family received an allotment of lumber, valued at 200 pesos, to build its house. In addition, the CNI launched a public works program that included the construction of a school, an infirmary, a post office, small shops, roads, and drainage. Wells were drilled and sunk at strategically placed sites so that the settlers could count on a regular supply of water. Four wells were completed in 1939, followed by others in the early 1940s. A plan to provide the colony with electricity was also devised (McKay 1982, 429–30).

On 14 July 1939, Cárdenas learned from Chávez that the first crops had been planted. Some two weeks later, at the beginning of August, Beteta paid a visit to the colony to observe firsthand the work being done and to learn of any problems that the settlers were experiencing in getting established. After making the rounds of the colony and viewing the work under way, he proclaimed the project an overall success and praised its initial achievements. According to the information he sent Cárdenas, the majority of people in the colony had expressed to him their satisfaction in being there. What is more, he had personally witnessed them working "enthusiastically" in clearing the land and further reported that "only 34 of the 600 heads of household were much below what had been hoped for in terms of productivity."[22] Many, clearly, were pleased with their lot, while "few felt otherwise." Beteta's encouraging report was not unique; some of the letters sent by the repatriated settlers to their friends conveyed a similar tone of satisfaction.

In this vein, Ignacio de la Cruz sent a letter to "his buddies" and relatives in which he wrote that what had been promised to him had been delivered. Five other members of the new community, José Tenorio, Pedro Traigo, Guadalupe Moreno, Juan Galindo, and Pablo Casares expressed gratitude to the authorities of both countries because they had received all of the basics they needed. Cipriano Cirlos wrote to his friends in Texas that "we are all very happy, we aren't lacking anything that they promised to us, we are already working our plots and are very content eating deer, wild boar, rabbit, and beef, because all this meat is here and lots of it." He noted that the soil was very rich and that "for us, the poor, there is happiness here." Elena Zúñiga remarked that she and her family received assistance from the government as well as various provisions, enabling them to survive. In addition, her family, like others, boosted its income with the wages earned by its children, who had been born in the

United States and who worked during the week in Brownsville, in laundries and bakeries and as welders.[23]

Beteta's confident assertions regarding the smooth functioning of the colony were but one version, and a one-sided version at that, of what was taking place there. The views expressed by certain repatriated nationals showed that some of the settlers were perfectly satisfied with what they had received, as they were with their decision to return to Mexico. In general, however, the first days and weeks of life and labor in the colony were anything but easy for the settlers, requiring sacrifices and bringing setbacks.

## The Crisis

Living conditions for the inhabitants of the 18 March colony reached a crisis at the end of 1939 and in 1940 due to various factors, among which were the colony's poor organization, shortage of water, overpopulation, insufficient financing, and the attitude of some of those in charge. Despite Chávez's cheery statements about the colony's advances and the support given to its families, the families themselves were facing the typical difficulties of a new settlement in the throes of construction where the only sure thing was the land itself, accompanied, in this case, by modest government support. Everything else— houses, harvests, drainage works, construction of rough dirt roads, clearing of the land, and more, had to be built or done by the settlers themselves. For the colony to get ahead, their efforts and work were essential.

Nature did not cooperate. Over the summer of 1939 the area was flooded by heavy rains and the roads became impassable. The downpours were followed by periods of intense heat and plagues of insects that made it difficult to do sustained work. Food was frequently in short supply, as were other basic necessities. Medical care was limited and settlers' houses were only half-built. Some of the new returnees scribbled letters to Mexican consuls in the United States, describing the strained conditions in the colony. Many of the problems that afflicted it were caused by the premature arrival of large groups, which created a disorderly horde of settlers. Chávez was prepared to absorb and provide accommodation to 100 families per month, but during the first ten weeks of the program, nearly 600 families had arrived (McKay 1982, 430).

As early as mid-1939 people began to record and document the colony's difficulties. At the beginning of July, Miguel Flores Villar—a member of the Chamber of Deputies—declared, after traveling through the United States and northern Mexico, where he visited the colony, that the situation in which the repatriated settlers found themselves was "simply indescribable": they were forced to sleep under the trees and endured no end of suffering. When Beteta visited the community to find out how it was functioning, he too noted that it had serious problems. In general, the work plans for the colony were not being followed; everything was delayed and the housing was poor. Sickness was spreading among the population; potable water was unavailable and its installation had suffered "natural setbacks."[24] As the days passed, the difficulties only mounted; it was unclear how the colony could succeed.

The provisional dwellings had tin roofs and wooden walls lined with the same material; the excessive heat that built up inside them, combined with the dust, caused numerous cases of conjunctivitis among the colony's children. These families had to live or camp away from where their permanent houses were to be located. Some, to protect themselves from the elements, were forced to make do without even enclosed tents; their "dwelling" was the space beneath a canvas strung between trees or an improvised hut made of sticks, with tree branches for a roof. Others hung lengths of canvas from the trees and tied them to their ancient automobiles. Still others were fortunate enough to have tents that Chávez had furnished them. At this early stage, the houses being built with proper materials, as called for in the plan, were far from the total needed—and these had been only half-constructed.[25]

The most serious problem was water, because the wells that had been sunk were found to contain salt. Thus more wells continued to be drilled in the search for potable water, and while this went on, the government provided the community with water from outside at a cost of approximately 9,000 pesos per month. Not only was this an unforeseen expense, but the quality of the imported water turned out to be very bad. Each parcel had a barrel filled twice a week by tanker trucks that brought water in from farms several kilometers from the colony. In a situation made worse by overpopulation, the needs of families exceeded the amount of water available, so it was strictly conserved and used only for essential purposes. Furthermore, since it was not potable, numerous cases of typhoid, dysentery, and diarrhea broke out. Although this health problem never reached epidemic proportions, it posed serious difficulties, and there seemed to be no solution on the horizon. It was compounded by a general lack of medical care, the victims of which were primarily the colony's children.[26]

The shortage of food led the settlers frequently to go hunting at night, and also to spend time fishing, thus supplementing the meager rations doled out to them by CNI representatives. Luckily, the area had abundant game, including deer, rabbits, "white-bellied" rodents, snakes, wild boar, badgers, armadillos, and wild pigs, which together served as the main sources of meat for some families. Others ate nopals and other edible cacti.[27]

The pace and scale of work directed toward installing irrigation in the valley were insufficient to meet the needs of its inhabitants. The plan called for constructing canals capable of irrigating 20,000 hectares of communally farmed land plus small family plots, but this target was missed by 10,000 hectares because the government failed to provide funding to construct many of the canals. Vitally needed irrigation was thus only partially completed. Problems also arose with respect to the division and granting of land, as it had not been possible to make good on the promise that all repatriated nationals would receive their own designated parcels. Unsurprisingly, this situation caused protests and contributed to the deplorable conditions in which some settlers found themselves.[28] The miscalculation on delivering land, as well as the insufficient housing, water, food, medical care, and the like, clearly showed how poorly the government had organized the back end of the repatriation project, rushing the settlement into operation without first equipping it with proper infrastructure, financing, and a network of support.

The majority of complaints made by the settlers pertained to the distribution of food and other supplies (or lack thereof). Moreover, and contrary to the assurances that Chávez had earlier given, there were no businesses nearby where people could obtain the things they most needed. Due to these escalating problems, Chávez decided, in August 1939, that it was time to take "a breather," so that the administration could correct these deficiencies. That, in turn, meant not taking in more repatriated nationals. Given conditions in the settlement, to accept any more large groups would be to jeopardize its potential for success.[29] Although Chávez sought constantly to demonstrate that the colony was functioning well, he had no choice but to confirm that it was beset by serious problems during its first months in operation.

Taking stock much later, however, Chávez held that the majority of setbacks—undeniable as they were—had been of short duration and that within several months he had been able to overcome them. According to him, furthermore, within a year many of the settlers had brought their land under cultivation and harvested excellent yields of cotton, corn, and beans, such that following the 1940 harvest, few of them continued to need assistance. He maintained that only 10 percent of the settlers abandoned their land and that conditions in the colony improved. At the same time, he acknowledged that, as economic conditions in the United States strengthened in the 1940s, many of the settlement's younger members, who had been born in that country, returned to it (McKay 1982, 434–35). Chávez's account of the number of such people who emigrated was confirmed, in part, by several of the repatriated. Some insisted that the number who returned north of the border was high, while others said it was low, but in either case, they said, such movement occurred during the early days of the colony. Subsequently, the majority of settlers remained on the land.[30]

Predictably, perhaps, Chávez chose to focus more on the colony's achievements than on its reversals. His way of seeing things clashed with what some of the settlers reported to Marte R. Gómez, the governor of Tamaulipas, complaining about the difficulties they faced and the inability of the CNI authorities to satisfy their needs. According to their declaration, the government's efforts to get them settled in this agricultural center had been fruitless. They thus asked to be sent to parts of Mexico where conditions were less adverse (McKay 1982, 433).

In expressing their disenchantment and describing the woeful conditions that obtained in the colony, some settlers tried to reach the desk of the president himself. Writing on behalf of comrades from Gregory, Ingleside, and other Texas communities as well as those from Aransas Pass, where he had led the local Mexican honorary commission, Marcelino Sepúlveda sent a letter to Cárdenas, beseeching him to consider the everyday needs of each settler family. Sepúlveda noted that despite the governor's personal visit to the colony, at which time he was presented with a list of more than 500 complaints, nothing had yet been done. In Sepúlveda's view, the settlers confronted three most serious problems. The first related to the provision of food and the payment they received for clearing the land. Sepúlveda described his own experience as head of a large family that needed a minimum of 80 pesos per month to cover the costs of food, but for the work he did on a full hectare of land, he was paid only 65 pesos. The second problem was the deficient building material furnished to settlers for their houses. The third was the shortage of water, which was "pretty bad" and only distributed twice a week in a barrel that held approximately forty-five gallons. Sepúlveda pleaded with the president to find some way to get them out of the colony and send them back to their native communities. The group he represented had given up on staying in the 18 March settlement.[31]

The colony also had a women's association whose representatives likewise appealed to Cárdenas to do the right thing by attending to the flagrant needs of the settlement's female population.[32] Aurora B. Cuéllar and Elena Zúñiga, president and secretary, respectively, of the Unión Femenil 18 de Marzo (18 March Women's Union), requested that Cárdenas immediately visit the colony so that he could personally witness the shortage of medicines and the scant attention being paid to the sick. They expressed the opinion that "within a very short time, if we continue like this, instead of raising worthy citizens for our beloved homeland, we will become a graveyard." They added that the water in the community was "really disgusting" and in short supply, and that food, too, was lacking. For these reasons, they were writing to him, since they were sure he was unaware of such details.[33] The troublesome situation persisted through 1940. Francisco B. Múgica, a delegate from the colony's settlers league, stated that their sole food consisted of "cactuses and mesquite," for which reason he requested that they be paid for the work they were doing to construct the irrigation canals and that they also be paid in advance for work they were yet to do in clearing more land. Furthermore, added Múgica, the canal work itself was tardy; the credit that settlers were supposed to receive was not as robust as promised, and the colony's regulatory regime was deficient.[34]

In short, the inhabitants of the 18 March settlement confronted a series of nagging problems once they reached the site and began to live there. In contrast to the systematic and, to a certain degree, well-ordered way in which Beteta organized the return flow in and from the United States, the reception and resettlement of the repatriated in Mexico was hasty and disorganized, the victim of inadequate planning and preparation.

The dismal conditions that prevailed in the colony were hardly novel, since people living in the surrounding region had suffered privation for the past five years. Moreover, this situation was the norm in many places, with respect both to colonization projects that involved Mexican nationals who returned from the United States and to other projects that drew in people coming from various regions inside the country. During the 1930s, the best-known cases were the settlements of Pinotepa, El Coloso, La Esperanza, and Ciudad Anáhuac. The lack of drainage, potable water, transport and communication, supplies, irrigated land, and the proliferation of gastrointestinal illnesses, a high infant mortality rate, and deficient medical care were the predominant features of communities throughout Mexico. Put another way, the strained situation of the 18 March colony was not exceptional.

## CHAPTER EIGHT

# The End of the Project, 1939–1940

My assignment has become much less plain in California. . . . Here I decided
to speak personally with the groups of Mexicans who wanted to repatriate
so as to accomplish the impossible task of not leaving them discouraged and,
at the same time, convincing them that they should certainly not try to go
back to Mexico.

—RAMÓN BETETA TO FRANCISCO CASTILLO NÁJERA, 15 JULY 1939

## The End of the Government's Plan and the
## Change in the Promotion of Return

After Ramón Beteta promoted repatriation in Texas, his presentations quickly
lost their emphasis on the advantages of return. Indeed, three months after
the program was launched, the government terminated it. It had no plans
to develop another such program but, instead, planned to resume acting
as it had since Cárdenas first assumed the presidency—that is, conducting
studies of areas where repatriated citizens could be resettled, but with two
long-standing qualifiers ever present: the government would support the return only of those whose circumstances most warranted it, and it would seek
to contain any large-scale repatriation.

In mid-June 1939, in San Antonio, Beteta announced that the plan for an
organized return, over which he had presided, was now over. The reasons
behind this decision were straightforward; the government's intention all
along was merely to carry out an experiment, one with two main objectives:
to promote the return of a few hundred agricultural workers from Texas and
to establish a settlement in northern Tamaulipas.[1]

On the basis of reports from San Antonio, Beteta considered it likely
that halting the flow of arrivals into the 18 March colony would provoke a
negative reaction, since Mexico's consulates in the United States were still

holding hundreds of requests for repatriation. Some of these had been fully processed, with the people submitting them poised to leave, expecting at the earliest opportunity to be transported back to Mexico. Nevertheless, the die had been cast, as Beteta made clear to Omar Josefé, Mexico's consul in San Antonio, explaining to him that the government had to suspend the repatriation program "for the time being," yet without discouraging altogether Mexican nationals who wished to return to the homeland. It was a delicate balancing act because, above all, the consuls had to ensure that they did not instill false hopes that might lead their compatriots to walk off their jobs, sell their belongings at a loss, or worse still, abruptly leave home and take to the roads, heading for the nearest consulate. Beteta's assessment was that the termination of the program might spark isolated protests and that San Antonio's Spanish-language newspaper *La Prensa* might use the opportunity to attack the administration.[2]

To neutralize the critics and forestall demonstrations against the government, the undersecretary of foreign relations suggested a modification to the new policy, under which the government would continue to support repatriation, and subsidize passage back to Mexico, but only for those people who wanted to return to their native town or village. In this way, Beteta believed, cutting off the flow of people to the 18 March colony would be less noticed and the risk of "a sense of dismay and excessive criticism" could be contained. As part of his new message, Beteta also made it known that, for now, the government would not promote repatriations from other U.S. states, and especially not California, until Cárdenas agreed to the formulation of a plan aimed at this region. He predicted that the effort could start up again the following year, 1940, when the government would be in a better position to resolve the difficulties of this "momentous enterprise."[3]

## Beteta in California

When Beteta visited California during July 1939 and spoke about repatriation, he was careful not to promote it. Following instructions from Cárdenas, Beteta avoided addressing mass audiences, so as not to produce "counterproductive outcomes"—that is, a large-scale return. He spent three days in and around San Diego and another three in the Los Angeles area. He headed north on 20 July, to visit Santa Barbara, San Jose, and San Francisco. Reflecting Beteta's new approach, the Los Angeles newspaper *La Opinión* carried no news of any presentations made by him in front of large groups. The *Los Angeles Times* paid scant attention to his visit.[4] The undersecretary remarked that in California his task had turned more difficult "and become much less plain." Significantly, while Beteta had spent almost a month in Texas promoting return, he was in Los Angeles proper for a mere two days. The short stay is explained by two factors: first, he did not want to stir up interest in the program since that could lead to an increase in the number of requests for immediate repatriation, "which at the present time we are unable to accommodate"; and second, he did not want to trigger the expulsion of a large number of Mexican nationals, something that it was thought could happen if Los Angeles public welfare agencies witnessed the Mexican government undertaking a project to repatriate its citizens, as such a move would allow city authorities to rid themselves of a costly expense.[5]

To avoid promoting repatriation, Beteta told Castillo Nájera that the fall in the price of silver had hurt the government's economic situation. The purpose of his visit, he said, was not to propagandize but to provide guidance to the Mexican consuls so that, "without discouraging our compatriots who are of a mind to return," the consuls could persuade them that they should wait until such time as the government was prepared to receive them, with an "adequate [base of] financial support" and in a suitable location. Beteta had remained in California for the express purpose of explaining to the consuls how they should approach the subject of repatriation. The drop in the price of silver had created a very difficult situation for Beteta personally, since he had to continue with any ongoing preparations for the repatriation project but "in a way that did not occasion any immediate or insoluble problems." He also proposed to speak personally with those groups of Mexican nationals wishing to return to the homeland "to accomplish the impossible task" of not deflating their spirits yet, at the same time, convincing them that they should definitely not try to go back to Mexico, "but, instead, ought to wait until the government is prepared to take them in."[6] The fundamental idea was that Beteta's compatriots should remain in the United States.

In his brief pass through California, Beteta met with the state's governor, Culbert L. Olson, to whom he made clear the new twist that his government had put on the repatriation of its migrant citizens. The undersecretary informed Olson that the first stage of the planned return had been completed and that it consisted in bringing Mexican nationals, in a "scientific and orderly" way, to an agricultural colony near Matamoros. He further elaborated the reasons that stood in the way of carrying out a repatriation campaign in California, pointing out that he did not expect very many Mexicans to be repatriated, since, despite their sizeable population in the state, relatively few wanted to return.[7]

The way the Mexican government oversaw the return of its nationals from California contrasted sharply with its actions in Texas. Moreover, Cárdenas was supported by the members of the Congress of Spanish-Speaking People of the United States. This group underscored the dangers that an open, public campaign on behalf of repatriation would pose in California. For example, such a campaign could unintentionally "strengthen the enemies of our compatriots," who wanted to expel them from U.S. soil.[8] Cárdenas agreed, which was why a month before Beteta's arrival in California the president had stated that there were to be no repatriations of Mexican nationals from that state. Likewise, during a visit to Tijuana at the beginning of July, Cárdenas had met with Ellis Patterson, a California state government official, to conclude an agreement that California authorities would not carry out mass deportations.[9] Just as he had done during the first months of his presidency, Cárdenas continued to negotiate with U.S. officials in an attempt to ward off the deportation of his compatriots.

For *La Opinión*, the decision to defer repatriations from California exposed the truth that "appealing" conditions "in our Homeland" were still wanting. Before embarking upon a major colonization scheme, the government—cognizant of what was possible in the country—chose the pragmatic course, opting to reorient the lives of only a small number of Mexican families. In announcing the shrinking of its "vast projects," the government simply adjusted its actions to Mexican reality. Before promoting more repatriations with problematic results, it preferred to conduct a small-scale trial.[10]

As a way of justifying the nonimplementation of the repatriation project in California, it was important for Beteta to stress that his compatriots in that state were by and large in a good situation. He insisted that few of them entertained any desire to return to Mexico, and he publicly thanked the California governor for his attitude toward Beteta's compatriots, whose general circumstances were better than those of Mexicans in other parts of the United States.[11] In short, the purpose of Beteta's visit to California was threefold: to cease promoting repatriation, to urge his compatriots to remain where they were, and to convince Los Angeles city and county officials not to carry out further deportations. Governor Olson's reaction to Beteta's opposition to pushing repatriation in his state was one of condescension. Nonetheless, his position differed from that of other state and local officials who remained interested in deporting Mexican nationals. Some people expressed opposition to the measures Cárdenas had taken.

## The U.S. Reaction to Beteta's Mission

In addressing issues surrounding the presence of Mexicans in his state, Governor Olson argued that they were good citizens and a positive factor within the U.S. workforce. While he said that he had no desire to see them leave, he added that if Mexico could offer them better living conditions, then he was prepared to cooperate in arranging transportation back to Mexico for any of Mexicans in California who were unemployed. Moreover, he vetoed a bill passed by the legislature aimed at removing foreigners, and Mexicans in particular, from public relief rolls.[12]

The law was known as the "Ralph Swing Law" (after the powerful state senator who sponsored it). It stipulated that anyone who had resided in the state for more than five years but had not yet petitioned for naturalization should be ineligible for government-funded public assistance. Olson recognized that the state needed to set some limit on its public welfare budget, but to exclude those who had been brought into the state precisely because they were a cheap labor source (i.e., Mexicans), and who then produced the very wealth that formed the basis of such public funding, seemed fundamentally wrong to him.[13] The more tolerant and fair-minded attitude of the governor, who acknowledged the critical contribution of Mexican manpower to the California economy, contrasted with the thinking of some officials in the state who wanted to continue pursuing deportations.

For example, Helen Murray, an official in the state relief administration, made a direct request to the Mexican government that it furnish her information regarding the repatriation project, information that she and others would then exploit as propaganda to induce Mexicans to return to their own country. Murray was linked to a series of local groups and organizations that had undertaken a broad campaign to get Mexican migrants to repatriate, and she took every opportunity to encourage Mexicans' expulsion (Balderrama and Rodríguez 1995, 180–81). Similarly, at the beginning of June, another California official, Frank Gigliotti, then serving as vice president of the state welfare board, arrived in Mexico City to work out a plan with the Mexican government that would lead to the repatriation of its citizens.

Gigliotti sought to enlist the Mexican government's support in removing more than 40,000 Mexicans from California. In Gigliotti's account, California state authorities hoped that Mexico would carry out a large-scale repatriation, since hundreds of its citizens occupied jobs sought by U.S. workers. He also tried to get Mexico's cooperation in organizing the expulsion of Mexican migrants who were indigent, chronically ill, or elderly.[14] Whether Gigliotti managed to conclude any agreements is not known, but the Mexican officials with whom he met clearly did not carry out any such expulsion. In addition, they would doubtless have explained to him that the repatriation project had been completed and that any future repatriations arranged by the Mexican government would necessarily be limited and selective. It seems fair to say that Gigliotti's mission achieved few, if any, measurable results.

The interest that some state and local-level officials in California took in continuing to expel Mexican nationals was accompanied by the criticisms of still others for whom Mexico's way of promoting the repatriation project did not sit well. Although Beteta's visit did not provoke an outcry in the anglophone U.S. press, some commentators opposed the repatriation plan. A New York Times article highlighted Beteta's statement that only agricultural workers would be chosen for repatriation; the rest of the Mexican population in the United States—and the journalist claimed that Beteta had singled out beneficiaries of public and private assistance—would be excluded. The article also attributed to the Mexican envoy a statement that "if anybody should prop up these people, it was a rich nation." Given Beteta's diplomatic skills, however, it is unlikely that he ever made such an assertion.[15]

The article had a particular resonance because it appeared in the New York Times, from which other U.S. newspapers and magazines often took their cue. The nation's most influential daily, it had forcefully opposed some of President Roosevelt's policy initiatives, just as it had supported the broadsides unleashed by U.S. oil companies, Standard Oil in particular, following the expropriations of 18 March 1938 (Meyer 1981, 436–37). In this context, the opinion expressed in the article echoed the opposition of certain groups in the United States to "maintaining" unemployed Mexicans. Viewing them as a financial burden, a drag on the national economy, these groups argued that such migrants should be expelled, and they criticized the campaign that Beteta carried out.

In another New York Times article, Howard T. Oliver wrote that the Mexican government's posture, in restricting repatriation to a certain class of person, called into question the bilateral relations between the two countries. Beteta's comments, Oliver wrote, laid to rest any doubts regarding the need to reexamine relations between Mexico and the United States. In Oliver's view, not taking nonagricultural workers and Mexicans supported by U.S. relief and social welfare agencies amounted to an "extraordinary and cynical" proposition on the part of Beteta, who over a period of several months had been trying to induce some of his "1,400,000 nationals" (residing in the United States) to return to their native land.[16]

Oliver argued that with Beteta's declarations, on the one hand, and the campaign headed up by Cárdenas, on the other, the Good Neighbor policy had been cast in doubt; since—with all due respect to the Mexicans who had ventured onto U.S. soil in search of a way to earn the living denied to them in their own country—"what kind of neighbor is it who makes a mockery in this fashion of our charity?" What sort of joke, he went on to ask, inspired Mexican authorities to name a colony near Brownsville, Texas, the 18 March, in "pertinacious glorification of the date on which the American oil fields [were] expropriated?"[17]

The colony's name grated on Oliver, as it must have on other people in the United States, because with it Cárdenas had given his colonization project a distinctly nationalistic overtone. But the name did not mock the United States. Rather, it represented Cárdenas's attempt to build internal consensus for his campaign by using the date on which the oil expropriation was carried out. As for the question about how this action squared with the spirit of the Good Neighbor policy, the Cárdenas administration had indeed pursued a unilateral interest, one with two purposes: first, to repatriate hundreds of Mexicans who possessed the experience and skills needed for a special, de-fined project; and second, to leave the responsibility for supporting indigent Mexicans in the United States where it currently lay—in the hands of U.S. charitable and welfare agencies and organizations. At this juncture, Cárdenas had definitely halted the campaign in favor of repatriation, a step that had not caught Oliver's attention, because if it had, his critique would likely have been even more severe.

## The Government's Stance in Ending the Project

After the government closed the book on the formal repatriation plan and chose not to promote the return of Mexican nationals from California, it nevertheless continued supporting repatriation in a limited way and gave the 18 March colony similarly minor assistance. As we have seen, Beteta was wary about drawing a hard-and-fast line under the repatriation project. Its termination, he felt, could have political consequences because of the neg-ative publicity and criticisms it would elicit. Even worse, however, it could undermine the president's prestige, as well as the respect and "affection" he enjoyed.[18] The assistant foreign relations minister thus suggested that the government continue promoting its citizens' return in a limited fashion and, above all, give greater financial support to returnees in the 18 March colony so that the latter might flourish and grow. At the same time, the campaign in favor of repatriation had to be toned down to avoid fomenting interest on the part of Mexican nationals in the United States in returning to the homeland.[19]

To operationalize his ideas, Beteta asked Cárdenas, first, to maintain the repatriation, "regardless of the difficulties that emerge, and even if doing so entails extraordinary sacrifice." Second, if repatriation—as Beteta advised—should become limited primarily (if not entirely) to the 18 March colony, then the colony would have to expand to take in new groups of returnees. The colony, however, depended primarily on the resources directed to it, and these would have to go beyond the 4 or 5 million pesos ostensibly spent over the course of one year to resolve its problems and directed toward transportation, food, gasoline, and the resettlement of the repatriated within the colony itself.[20]

In Beteta's reckoning, of the 3 million Mexicans (an unreliable and grossly exaggerated figure)[21] who, according to U.S. sources, were living north of the Rio Grande, very few would return—a fact that worked in favor of his argument. At the same time, it was important, he felt, not to turn a blind eye to the situation of Mexican nationals in the United States, since those who lacked work there, and some who received welfare, clearly wanted to return to Mexico but were leery of the risks that such a move would entail. Given their doubts and hesitation, and especially because many of them remembered the failure of the Pinotepa colony, Beteta thought it would be wrong to facilitate their repatriation. Cárdenas favored avoiding any significant wave of returnees while still supporting repatriation to a limited degree. Hence he resolved that, beginning in September 1939 and continuing to the end of his term, a total of 1,000 people, or 200 families, would be repatriated per month.[22] This policy was partially observed, in that the government only facilitated the return of some families whose principal destination was the 18 March agricultural colony.

In June 1939, Beteta officially reduced to 100 the number of new families to be incorporated each month into the colony. Nevertheless, at the beginning of August, 140 families coming from the Texas communities of Raymondville, Sebastian, San Benito, Harlingen, Los Fresnos, and La Feria were transported to the 18 March settlement. In addition, Beteta signed an agreement with the engineer Eduardo Chávez that called for 145 families to be transported, in stages, to the colony between September and October 1939. The record shows that, by 17 October, Carlos A. Calderón, Mexico's consul in Brownsville, Texas, had registered the passage not only of these 145 families, who totaled 638 people, but also of 36 additional families whose destination was not the 18 March colony but various other places in the country.[23] Later, there was still more movement in the direction of the colony, as 35 families from Kenedy and Kyle, Texas, were sent there at the beginning of November.[24]

## Colonization Studies and Plans

During the months when the government was actively promoting the 18 March colony and transporting returnees to it, it was also evaluating the suitability of other locations in the country to resettle Mexican nationals coming back from the United States. In some cases, this evaluation had direct practical results, with the Cárdenas administration helping repatriate and resettle small groups by giving them both land and financial assistance. Its interest in conducting these studies had to do with maintaining a kind of equilibrium. On the one hand, the government brought the repatriation project, as a formal, self-contained project, to an end; on the other it wanted to continue operating as it had before: by undertaking studies and supporting in a rather veiled way the repatriation of selected Mexican nationals to places such as Baja California.

## The Studies

In April and May 1939, the Agriculture and Development Ministry carried out studies in a series of Mexican states, such as Tamaulipas, Sonora, Chihuahua, and Baja California, with a view toward resettling groups of returnees. Accordingly, at the end of April, the agriculture minister announced a major project to repatriate 15,000 families, all of whom would be directed into agricultural work. He apprised the president of various places in the country whose conditions made them candidates for colonization. It was a long list and included parcels of greater than 8,000 hectares capable of absorbing no fewer than 400 settlers.[25] At around this same time, the director of the BNCE informed Cárdenas that the bank found it possible to "immediately" accommodate and resettle 246 repatriated families who would be incorporated into the bank's affiliated local communal land credit associations in the states of Colima, Guanajuato, Morelos, Chihuahua, Jalisco, Nuevo León, Sonora, and Nayarit.[26]

The BNCE director enumerated a number of additional possible sites: in Chihuahua, irrigated pasture lands sufficient for 2,000 to 3,000 families; in Baja California, irrigated, uncolonized land belonging to the Colorado River Land Company, as well as land in the Mexicali Valley, where 100 families could settle and grow cotton; in Durango, an 11,000 hectare site known as Llanos de Cabrera with a capacity for 250 settlers; in Oaxaca, a site called San Juan de las Peñas that likewise covered 11,000 hectares and could accommodate 500 settlers; and in Jalisco's Banderas Valley, an even larger piece of land, extending over 20,000 hectares, on which 250 people could settle. The director went on to name areas in Veracruz (Montepío), San Luis Potosí

(Salto, El Trigo, Tambaca), Sonora (Valle del Mayo, Altar, Ocuca, Municipio de Santa Ana, Santa Bárbara), Nuevo León, and, again, Chihuahua. For his part, Manuel Flores, then the chief municipal official of Nuevo León's capital city, Monterrey, facilitated the settlement of 13 repatriated nationals who arrived from Houston, as well as a group of 11 families who totaled 43 individuals.[27]

At the beginning of May 1939, the agriculture minister announced that his department was analyzing which locations in the country were likely to prove most successful for the resettlement of repatriated nationals. With the same purpose in mind, both the Agriculture and Interior Ministries were also examining the programs sketched out by the BNCE to ensure that workers repatriated from the United States would not pose a problem for agricultural areas in Mexico that were already functioning normally. Hence the territory they preferred in which to resettle these people fell within the border states of Chihuahua, Sonora, Tamaulipas, Nuevo León, and Baja California.[28]

The projects announced by the agriculture minister and the regional directors of the BNCE never materialized, and the studies they undertook never bore fruit. The government disseminated wildly inflated figures about the number of Mexican nationals it had tried to repatriate from the United States. Consistent with its action throughout the sexenio, the administration did not want either to organize repatriations in the numbers suggested by these studies or to give the repatriated large expanses of land. While Cárdenas and his circle wanted to be prepared in the event the United States suddenly reverted to large-scale deportations, the Mexican government's own course of action would entail supporting the return and resettlement of only small groups of Mexican migrants. In line with this policy, various government officials continued to carry out studies and offer suggestions regarding places in the country where the repatriated could be resettled.

One of the more energetic efforts in this respect came from Antonio E. Florencia, a senior official in the Agriculture Ministry. The report that he submitted in June 1939, listing and profiling the areas in Mexico best suited for colonization by returnees from the United States, was nothing if not impressive on paper. In Sinaloa, there were projects on the drawing board to irrigate 182,000 hectares, on which some 10,000 families could be established. Sonora had territory contiguous with the Colorado River that could absorb 400 families as well as pasturage belonging to Whisler Land Company where 300 cattle ranching families could be placed. Baja California had terrain belonging to the Colorado River Land Company, and while difficulties in securing it a steady supply of water made it unsuitable for growing crops (at least for the time being), it nonetheless could serve as a site on which to establish 2,000 families.

Repatriated workers could farm lands in northern Coahuila if wells were drilled and installed there. Tamaulipas already had cattle ranching outposts, such as La Sauteña and Río Bravo, with the capacity to take in 1,000 families. Similarly, the Santa Clara hacienda in Chihuahua, where seasonal crops were grown, could absorb 2,000 families. Florencia calculated that, collectively, there were several places in Veracruz—principally in the region of Los Tuxtlas and Santa Ana Rodríguez—with the capacity to accommodate 5,000 families. Nine hundred families could be placed on land in the Valle del Naranjo, in San Luis Potosí; and in this same state, 1,000 additional families could be resettled in the areas of El Salto and Tambaca. Michoacán had areas of land near the Marqués and Tepalcatepec Rivers where still more people could be placed. Finally, authorities in Puebla were disposed to cede some land that adjoined the state of Veracruz.[29]

In the event that sizeable groups of Mexican nationals continued to flow back into the country, Florencia believed it would be necessary to have identified and targeted additional places in the country where they could be settled. Under this scenario, an excellent location for new settlements, he suggested, would be along the coasts of Guerrero and Oaxaca. He believed that this region offered multiple advantages: it would open up new sources of agricultural production and accommodate 25,000 families, which would solve its problem of underpopulation. Similarly, Florencia proposed that coastal areas of Jalisco, near the Barra de Navidad highway, likewise come under development. The region was thinly populated, so introducing new settler families would not cause unrest by putting pressure on lands already communally farmed; its climate was superior to that of the Guerrero coast, and it abounded in natural resources. According to his calculations, 10,000 families could be established in the Jalisco area. Colonization projects mounted in any or all of these three states, argued Florencia, would bring development to regions that were "practically unexplored" but possessed enormous potential wealth. The associated transportation, communication, and public health links and initiatives would constitute permanent structural benefits for the country.[30]

Another state Florencia thought ripe for development was Tabasco, where, he reported, five zones were suitable for colonization, each covering extensive tracts of land. Settlement in this area, he added, would also boost development of the region lying close to the tracks of the Southeast Railway line. In his judgment, an interministerial commission needed to complete studies of areas of land that were available for colonization, after first satisfying the needs of existing local ejidos to avoid confrontations between their communal owners and groups of newly arrived families. Various studies of this nature were indeed being carried out by different agencies with respect to establishing colonization projects in Dublán, Chihuahua; on the Acatlán Hacienda in Michoacán, and near the small communities of El Narano and La Estrella, located in Colima and Jalisco, respectively. In the report that he sent to the president, Florencia noted that the agriculture minister and his top assistant had a still more detailed and complete picture of other places in the country where settlement schemes had been carried out.[31]

If Florencia's report brimmed with optimism, its suggestion that the Guerrero and Oaxaca coasts were crying out for colonization projects revealed his ignorance of the failures of the earlier tropical zone repatriations (El Coloso and Pinotepa), an oversight which became even more obvious in his proposal of various sites that were totally cut off from the rest of the country. Florencia was simply unaware of the kind of problem he was courting.[32]

In mid-1939, there was also discussion about readying some of the land on the La Sauteña property, in Tamaulipas, for resettling Mexican nationals coming from the United States. Earlier, at the beginning of March, measures designed for this purpose were in fact taken by the agriculture minister, who reached an agreement with the La Sauteña Agricultural Company whereby the latter would release 400,000 hectares of land. The minister also promoted another plan to settle some people on irrigated lands located in the Tamaulipas municipalities of Aldama, González, and Padilla. He envisioned investing 2,700,000 pesos to prepare an expanse of 10,000 hectares on which 1,000 families would be resettled. The plan involved repatriating 200 families per month starting in 1940. In addition, he authorized General Napoleón Cabrera, the commanding officer of the army garrison in Nogales, Sonora, to expedite passage for repatriated nationals who had turned up in the town so they could make their way to wherever in the country suited them.[33] As with other studies carried out by Mexican government officials, this one exaggerated both the amount of land to be given over to colonization and the number of repatriated migrants who were to be settled on it. Moreover, the plans never materialized, but the studies directed at establishing other colonies kept rolling off the government press, just as small groups of returnees continued to arrive back in Mexico.

## Settlement Projects and the Repatriated

Following instructions issued by the executive branch, the Agriculture Ministry dispatched a team of ten engineers from its Department of Colonization to the Naranjo Valley, in San Luis Potosí, for the purpose of readying 50,000 hectares of exceptionally rich land for colonization. The idea was to begin the project with a 10,000 hectare carve out, on which fifty repatriated Mexican families, scheduled to arrive on 1 August 1939, would be established. Members of the group would be immediately employed in clearing the land, for which they would receive compensation from the Ministry of Finance and Public Credit (SHCP).[34] A report from this ministry affirmed that there was no shortage of will or effort to comply with Cárdenas's wishes. Indeed, "all directives were duly fulfilled as concerned moving various families of refugees and repatriated [nationals] and getting them settled."[35]

Following the establishment of the 18 March settlement, a second colony designed for repatriated Mexicans—called the 6 October colony in honor of the day, in 1936, when Cárdenas formalized the accord that launched the granting of ejidos in the Lagunera region—also came under development. Its intended location was near the El Salto River, in San Luis Potosí's Naranjo Valley. A complete evaluation of the project, to assess its importance or simply to confirm how many people eventually joined it, is not possible because of the paucity of documentation. Such information as does exist, however, seems to suggest that the colony barely got off the ground. Although the official records, as well as the recollections of some settlers whose experience extends back to that time, provide no direct verification that any repatriated nationals actually reached the spot,[36] it appears that two things did occur in June 1938: first, property deeds were issued for ninety settlers and second, the Naranjo Valley Settlement Commission began initial infrastructural work. In September, the government acquired a power plant and directed that potable water and medical services be supplied for the incoming settlers.[37] Apparently, however, their arrival was only planned and never came about.

At the beginning of September the government also announced that preparations were under way to open a third settlement for repatriated nationals. This colony, to be called the 8 August—to memorialize the 1937 land reforms affecting the henequen-producing estates in Yucatán—was to be situated south of Ciudad Juárez and north of Casas Grandes, in Chihuahua, on high-quality land. According to plans, the government would expend a total of 8 million pesos to organize the return of 3,200 families. This sum, intended to cover the costs of transportation and housing as well as the expenses incurred in getting the first crops planted, translated into an outlay of 2,500 pesos per family.[38] Not surprisingly, the project—perhaps owing to this steep investment cost—never materialized. It likewise failed to attract large contingents of potential settlers, since for them the way the government acted in practice—versus the generous future it pictured in its plans—posed an obstacle. The regime propagandized about repatriating substantial numbers of its citizens but ultimately did no more than sporadically help bring back small groups of Mexican nationals, some of whom wound up in Baja California.

Since May 1939, both Baja California's governor, Rodolfo Sánchez Taboada, and Cárdenas had given some attention to furthering repatriation in this part of the country. As a first effort, Sánchez Taboada helped two groups, composed of thirty and twenty-two families who had been living in Santa Ana and Gardena, California, get established in Mexicali. At the end of July, repatriated nationals began to arrive at the state's Guadalupe ejido. It was decided that Baja California's state government and the BNCE would help these returnees begin agricultural work. To solve the problem of finding housing for the group, Sánchez Taboada requested that the federal government provide 30,000 pesos on an emergency basis to help a total of twenty families.[39] At the beginning of August, the governor and the Agriculture Ministry signed an agreement to open an office that would deal with matters relating to the resettlement of Mexican families in the state.[40]

Some days later, General Ramón B. Arnáiz, president of the Pro-Magaña Committee in California, was able to secure land on behalf of members of the Veterans of the Republic group in Los Angeles.[41] Arnáiz was enthusiastic about the results of his effort, since it enabled fifty families to move to Baja California, where the state government gave them assistance and land. The conditions that Arnáiz set for those who wished to repatriate under this scheme were that they have experience in agricultural work, qualify as campesino families, and have sufficient means to maintain themselves until they could bring in the first harvest. In addition, Arnáiz appealed to Cárdenas to order that 75,000 pesos be remitted for the project, in monthly installments of 15,000 pesos, out of which 30,000 pesos would be taken to establish another twenty families coming from Gardena as well as a second group of twenty families, each of whom would receive a thirty-hectare parcel of land.[42]

Not everything ran as smoothly as Arnáiz wanted. In September he announced that the repatriation program from California had been suspended until such time as the government granted new parcels of land. Still, he stated that requests from people who wished to repatriate and join colonization projects would continue to be accepted.[43] For its part, the Agriculture Ministry had some of its technical specialists visit different parts of the country to study the possibility of placing repatriated families in areas that had been abandoned and now required only "a bit of dedicated effort" to be turned into "veritable gardens [of production]."[44]

Toward the end of 1939, both the agriculture minister and the head of the Demographics Department stated yet again that the government was attempting to reintegrate into the Mexican polity discreet groups of its citizens in the United States who were unemployed, channeling them—as the end point of the process—into agricultural work. For this purpose, it had prepared "extensive tracts of land" in the north of the country and—going beyond the planning phase—had founded the 18 March colony. In addition, new areas of land continued to be set aside and prepared—among them a vast parcel of 300,000 hectares in Mazapil, Zacatecas—on which to resettle "all those Mexicans who still remain abroad, principally in the United States."[45]

The numerous feasibility studies ordered and conducted by government agencies regarding the possibility of establishing colonies for hundreds of its repatriated citizens pointed up the interest at the top level of government in being prepared to reabsorb a great number of individuals in the event of a massive deportation from the United States. The Cárdenas administration, however, did not wish to foster the repatriation and resettlement of people nearly to the extent that its studies proposed; rather, it was responding to the fear that a possible mass return engendered and to pressures from its own citizens. In the absence of some untoward contingency, the objectives underlying official government support for an organized return of Mexican nationals were considerably more modest: to extend help for repatriation only to those with the most extreme need or, in other instances, to small groups. The much-vaunted studies therefore did not usher in a movement for repatriation, but they had their uses nonetheless. They yielded data and information about geographic, environmental, and economic conditions in different regions of Mexico, thereby raising the level of knowledge about the country as a whole. What is more, the names that were given to other colonies (6 October and 8 August) revealed Cárdenas's interest in continuing to use the subject of repatriation as a tool for stoking nationalist sentiment.

## The Limits of Official Help

Both the various studies that analyzed the task of resettling returnees and the few actions actually taken to support a systematic return exposed the limits of official efforts on behalf of repatriation in general, just as they did the lack of support given to many Mexicans in the United States, who—inspired by the Cardenista propaganda in favor of the return of Mexican nationals—took concrete steps to prepare their departure from the host country.[46]

The support that many people in Texas received, through Beteta and the consulates, to leave their U.S. homes and join the 18 March colony was a strong influence in kindling other Mexicans' interest in returning to the homeland. These latter families, however, were denied the same support, so they remained behind, disillusioned, waiting in vain for assistance. For many, the situation was indeed trying. In Corpus Christi, for example, families anxious to be repatriated installed themselves in the offices of the Mexican consulate, from where they stated that they would not move until achieving their objective, since—having sold their homes and furniture—they no longer had a roof over their heads. A similar scene played out in the community of Robstown. Brownsville, too, counted a number of families that were ready for repatriation; many of them were in dreadful straits, bereft of aid, without any hope forthcoming from the consulate that their return to Mexico would be arranged in the near future. A. Calderón, the consul in Brownsville, reported that many fathers told him to his face that they had been deceived by the government's assurance "that the homeland had its arms open to receive them at any time."[47]

Communications in August between Beteta and Cárdenas revealed just how difficult and problematic it had become for the government to manage the repatriation process. On this score, Beteta remarked that he had been correct to think that once people witnessed the "tangible efforts of our government" to take in its citizens and get them resettled, officials would face an avalanche of requests. In the undersecretary's words, "I must confess to you that the results have exceeded all expectations and I don't exaggerate in saying that the latent problem of the return of our compatriots has generated a crisis. We are now facing a serious and urgent situation that we ourselves have provoked."[48] Beteta confirmed that the number of requests submitted to Mexico's consuls by families wishing to repatriate to the 18 March colony already came to "several thousand." Six hundred families from Kenedy, Karnes City, and González, in the jurisdiction of San Antonio's consulate, were prepared to leave the United States; in Houston, 300 families were ready to be transported; in Dallas and Austin, similar numbers were reported; and the jurisdiction of the Corpus Christi consulate had thus far produced 500 requests.[49]

Beteta argued that the relatively small number of requests he had received at the outset of his mission had not been a reliable predictor of the total that would later be submitted. The genuine interest in returning to Mexico, into which he had tapped, was sufficient in itself to cause the scope of the repatriation project to balloon. Beteta recalled a meeting with Cárdenas in which the president voiced to him his satisfaction over the prospect of such a development, since repatriation went to the heart of one of the country's fundamental problems. The resources required for the project thus would be well spent. "The moment had arrived," Beteta urged, "to attack the problem in the way you've foreseen since that time." All the more so, as he saw it, because the difficult situation faced by more than 100 families in the Brownsville jurisdiction, whose repatriation he was endeavoring to arrange, was not a case isolated to that particular region but, rather, one that typified the situation throughout the whole of Texas.[50] For better or worse, Beteta had taken seriously the campaign for an organized return of Mexican nationals that now slipped from the control of its erstwhile promoter: Lázaro Cárdenas.

Thus, in Corpus Christi, Houston, Karnes City, and other places hundreds of requests for repatriation began to accumulate, and, as crops came in and their work cycle was completed, many Mexican field hands and agricultural workers, confidant that the government would deliver on its promises, elected not to sign new contracts. Moreover, the owners of farming properties and agricultural enterprises in Texas, for whom having to switch from one sharecropper to another was an unwanted nuisance, wanted no part of those who had submitted requests for repatriation and refused to renew their contracts. They justified their hard line by their fear that Mexican laborers would leave without paying their debts.[51]

The petitions for repatriation submitted by so many Mexicans in the United States overran the limited boundaries imposed by the Cardenista plans. Mariano S. Moreno, president of the Mexican Honorary Commission of San Benito, Texas, complained about the hollowness of the promises Beteta made to Mexicans living in the United States when he assured them that they would be received with open arms, gifts of land, and financial aid. Nothing of the sort had happened, yet "countless numbers" of Mexican nationals had sold their belongings and were now in a precarious situation for having put their faith in the call issued by the Mexican government.[52] The families of workers in the Bloque de Mineros Mexicanos (Mexican Mining Workers Syndicate) in San Antonio found themselves in such circumstances, as did various individuals in Los Angeles, among them Pedro Fregoso, who requested his repatriation in keeping with the government's well-advertised intentions.[53] His tenuous situation had become untenable due to the Mexican government's lack of attention to supporting his return.[54]

Many men like Fregoso, who believed in Cárdenas's promises, foundered in disillusionment and total destitution. The Cardenista project for a scaled-up return of Mexican nationals had ended and, as we have seen, such support as the government continued to provide was strictly limited. This situation had negative consequences both for those who, hopeful of returning, remained on U.S. soil awaiting official support and for those who were repatriated and had made their way to the 18 March colony.

## The Coup de Grace for Repatriation

During the final year of the Cárdenas administration, 1940, the community of repatriated Mexicans in the 18 March agricultural colony, like the government itself, fell into deep crisis. Several factors, among them the scant official support, led to serious difficulties. As the year began, the colony's representatives requested that the executive branch intervene and allow the colony to bypass its dependency on the BNCA, whose supervision had not alleviated its unhappy conditions. They maintained that all of Eduardo Chávez's assertions were "inaccurate" when he claimed that the settlers enjoyed a "perfect" situation "with all the comforts." In January the emergence of so many problems led Cárdenas to order that the colony cease accepting newly repatriated nationals.[55]

## The Desperate Situation of the 18 March Colony

For the settlers, the year 1940 brought hunger and despair; governmental assistance was all but absent; living conditions deteriorated and sharpened divisions among the settlers themselves. At the beginning of February, Manuel Saldívar Gallegos, general secretary of the 18 March Settlers League, which comprised 25 sections and an overall membership of 930, wrote Cárdenas requesting that the government resume suspended payments to settlers for the work they did clearing the land, and that it not cancel the monthly advances to settlers for this same work. Saldívar Gallegos also asked that the government treat and prepare the lands to be cultivated so that settlers could seed their crops on them, since they had no means with which to support their families. A month later the settlers began "hunger" protests, since the general secretary's appeals for help had not produced positive results.[56] The league's president said that while settlers did not regret having returned to the homeland, the fact remained that in their own country they were suffering privations that they had not experienced while living outside of it.

Another member of the colony, Feliciano Sóstenez, asserted that many of his comrades had been plunged into a serious crisis because they had no way to feed their children, no matter how hard they toiled. Furthermore, other problems had arisen due to the general inattentiveness of the colony's administrators. These could be overcome, he added, if the president would exercise his authority and issue appropriate directives.[57] Agustín Leñero, Cárdenas's private secretary, informed the president that the future of the colony was compromised by the imbalance between the limited aid it received and the excessive number of families it had absorbed. To rectify the situation, Efraín

Buenrostro, national economy minister, estimated that a sum of 400,000 pesos should be invested either by his ministry or by Communications. For now, however—to alleviate the situation for all of a week—the government acquired a supply of corn and beans.[58]

The lengthy list of problems facing the colony continued as before: a lack of potable water and of money to purchase seeds and agricultural tools; insufficient compensation paid to settlers for the work they did clearing the land (payment presently insufficient to cover basic necessities); irrigation canals whose construction had not begun; financing promised but not delivered to ensure that families who had planted their crops could support themselves until harvest time; groundwork for the creation of new cooperatives that required support from above; incomplete work needed to make settlers' houses fully equipped and livable (none yet had doors or windows, and many remained only half built); a critical shortage of providers of medical services; and, finally, a plan to establish schools was still just that—a plan.[59] On a visit to the colony in mid-August 1941, Andrew Weiss, a civil engineer and head of the Advisory Department of the National Irrigation Commission (CNI), corroborated the extent of the problems. Not only did Weiss urge that no more land be opened for settlement, but he also recommended that the 18 March colony be relocated onto higher ground because its current location, Valle Hermosa, could easily flood. Another of Weiss's core recommendations was that all the parcels of land be left fallow for the time being, until the colony's irrigation system was fully able to meet the needs of its resident farmers.[60]

The conditions in the colony and the obvious failures of the planning that went into it had left many of the settlers agitated. Unsurprisingly, some now openly expressed remorse for having returned. Saldívar Gallegos, secretary of the Settlers League, noted that hundreds of migrants had rejoined the homeland out of a desire to make themselves useful to it, and, by doing so, had sacrificed "much of the little" that they had achieved through hard work and privations; now they lacked the most essential items one needed to survive, all as the result of having believed the promises that Beteta made in the government's name. The colony's settlers professed to be convinced that the distress and destitution they were experiencing was altogether at variance with the project that the president had promoted; that they were living through a situation that none had imagined possible and that had spun out of control. A number of the settlers were reduced to tears at their inability to bring anything home to eat. In the face of this grim reality, they sent a commission, headed up by Indalecio Esquivel and Jerónimo Guajardo, to meet with President Cárdenas.[61]

## The President's Position

Cárdenas believed that for the 18 March colony to succeed "small sacrifices" would be required, given the lack of resources with which to attend to unforeseen needs. He informed its Settlers League that such needs "have to be resolved, as in the cases that the colony faces today, by marshalling your full, collaborative spirit, since the government's problems are known to everyone." These problems included a lack of private investment resulting from the uncertain political climate; the flight of foreign capital caused by the oil companies' withdrawal of funds; a fall in state revenue resulting from the drop in oil and silver exports; and an increase in food imports.

Cárdenas asked for understanding on the part of those who had repatriated and, to inoculate himself from bearing the fault, invoked the government's strained budget, although ever since assuming the presidency he had elected to furnish no more than small sums toward assisting his repatriated compatriots. In this case, too, Cárdenas bent only slightly, by authorizing the immediate expenditure of 251,000 pesos to deal with the problems of greatest urgency.[62] He also ordered that payments for clearing the land be increased to 90 pesos per hectare.

The subsidy that he authorized was to be used to stabilize the operations of the colony's cooperatives to relieve them of the danger posed by members' unpaid bills. The president also requested that medical services be expanded, that the construction of settlers' houses be completed, and that 70 heads of household who had set themselves up on open parcels of land be provided a subsidy. He intervened to see that aid was given to another 110 heads of household so they could set themselves up on land that was available. Cárdenas also promised to see that work continued on irrigation canals.[63] Finally, he instructed the Public Education Ministry to provide as many teachers as were needed to educate the community's children, since the six educators then on site were plainly not enough. In late November 1940, José G. Parres, the secretary of agriculture, visited the area, on orders of the president, with the purpose of "easing" the settlers' troubles. Among other things, Parres delivered deeds of ownership to them for their parcels of land.[64] Nevertheless, despite all of these initiatives, the colony's problems persisted and took on new dimensions.

In mid-1940, the women of the 18 March colony were prevented from gathering to deal with matters of interest to them.[65] In addition, the very people in charge of administering and carrying out the colonization project abused the authority that had been granted them. Vicente Santibáñez, an officer in the

Mexican Mining and Metalworkers' Union, in Torreón, Coahuila, requested the removal of Eduardo Chávez. Word had come to him that Chávez had been extorting the colony's campesinos. In addition, as other campesino and workers' organizations in the region had learned, he had also been maneuvering to factionalize the colony, promoting the formation of groups of provocateurs.[66] The situation was made worse by infighting among the colonists themselves, brought on by a struggle between the local organizations backed by Chávez and the National Peasants' Federation.

Chávez was supported by various organizations, among them the Society of Socialist Agricultural Workers. José María Treviño, then president of the agricultural credit associations that operated in the Anáhuac community, asked Cárdenas's successor, Manuel Ávila Camacho (1940–46), to officially confirm Chávez as director of government projects in the Lower Rio Grande Valley, work that he had performed "to widespread approval." Demonstrating his considerable sympathy for Chávez, Treviño maintained that the state of "progress on display in the region" was due to the engineer's efforts.[67] The secretary of the 18 March Settlers League, however, as well as many others he represented, did not agree with this glowing assessment. The conflict between the groups reached such an extreme that some of Chávez's sympathizers murdered Saldívar Gallegos, further polarizing the two camps. Added to the dismal conditions prevailing in the colony, the open confrontation among its residents created a situation that can only be described as chaotic.[68]

## The Results of Getting the Repatriated Settled and Established

Despite the notable troubles and difficulties that afflicted the settlers over the first two years, the 18 March colony managed to survive. Partly as the result of a visit that César Martino, director of the BNCA, made to the settlement in 1940, some of its most pressing problems were finally resolved. For their part, the settlers vowed to be "useful citizens to Mexico" and to match the president's efforts on their behalf and turn their colony into an important center of agricultural production. Subsequently, Ávila Camacho agreed to contribute 326,000 pesos for a program including drainage, a water purification plant, the construction of 100 houses, the clearing of a further 400 hectares of land, and the diversion of water from one of the valley's irrigation systems (Control Number Three as it was technically known) onto farmland in the colony.[69]

Although these government interventions only partially solved the colony's most grinding problems, they were enough to permit it to go on, creating an opening so that settlers' living conditions gradually improved and agricultural production could go forward. By the mid-1940s, some clear progress was evident, as seen, for example, in the applications for credit made by some residents seeking to establish industrial-scale businesses (the mechanized handling of fruits, vegetables, seed removal, etc.). The success of the 1946 harvest enabled the colony to contribute 50 percent toward the cost of constructing a school. By this time, too, its residents enjoyed the services of a modest medical unit, with an x-ray machine, and commercial activity in general began to grow.[70]

From May 1939 to the end of 1940, the government provided some assistance to those who settled in the colony. When conditions deteriorated and pressures on the settlers increased to the point that they could no longer be ignored, the administration allocated additional small sums of money. Before the colonists arrived, however, little was done to prepare or equip the area where they would live. Still, despite the initial deficiencies, the majority of settlers dug in and stayed put, while a smaller number chose to reemigrate to the United States. In the early 1940s, the parcels deserted by those who returned to the United States were declared free of ownership and reallocated.[71] Despite the colony's various setbacks, a repatriation project led and executed by the government had at last managed to endure. The repatriated who put down roots in the 18 March settlement displayed three characteristics unprecedented in the history of Mexican migration to the United States: (1) they constituted a sizeable number of people, (2) they returned and resettled on the basis of government overtures and persuasion, and (3) in contrast to earlier projects, they managed to remain on a permanent basis.

## From the End of the Cardenista Government to Mass Emigration

As the 1940s began, the flow of Mexicans returning to the homeland from the United States increasingly diminished. The government took few measures to support it, its actions limited to promoting the repatriation of the destitute and—faithful to its longtime practice—to conducting studies of different areas of land with the purported aim of settling the repatriated on them. Likewise, official attention began to focus on the migration of Mexican workers spurred by economic conditions in the United States, as those started to change with the advent of the Second World War.

The outbreak of the conflict in Europe converted the peacetime economy of the United States into a war economy, one that soon reached its peak. Government outlays and expenditures increased. In turn, people's purchasing power was strengthened and resources that had been little used during the preceding decade were now being employed with greater intensity. Demand from abroad also strengthened, stimulating higher levels of U.S. production. Between 1939 and 1940, exports rose to $1 billion. Thus, starting in 1940, production indices began to shoot up and the high joblessness that had set in as of 1929 began slowly to reverse itself (Suárez and Parra 1991, 206).

The foreign relations and interior ministers recognized that, in broad terms, the issue of repatriation was not "so important" in 1940 as it had been in previous years, and it had a different cast to it (SRE 1941). As a consequence of the war in Europe, Mexican labor was now actively sought for a variety of services. Many Mexican nationals who lived in the United States proceeded to find work, while others among their compatriots still in Mexico began to migrate north. Moreover, some who had requested assistance from the government so they could return now canceled their petition because they had received offers from the U.S. government to work in the larger weapons factories.[72]

Still, while the work situation of many Mexicans began to improve, the requests for assistance did not cease, and a significant number of Mexican nationals continued to voice a desire to return to their native country. Some within the latter population condemned the fact that Spanish refugees occupied good positions within the administration even as Mexican nationals were reduced to asking for help to leave the United States. Some requested grants of land so they could repatriate; others, such as the Mexican migrants living in Mesa Valley, Arizona, simply wanted to return home and asked for nothing else beyond that. Still others specified that they wanted to return with their wives and children.[73] At the beginning of 1940, at a joint meeting in El Paso, Mexican consuls from New Mexico, Texas, Arizona, Colorado, and Wyoming, discussed a program to repatriate thousands of Mexicans who were living in very bad conditions in the southern and southeastern United States. Colonel Manuel Esparza, the consul based in El Paso, explained the program, whose objective was to place their compatriots in places where they could earn a living while at the same time cooperating with U.S. immigration authorities to reduce Mexican migration to the United States.[74]

During the presidential campaign, Ávila Camacho promised that if elected he would fully support bolstering the development of the 18 March agricultural colony and, more broadly, assist efforts to repatriate Mexicans living in the United States. During the first mass meeting of his campaign for the presidency, he stated, "On the other side of the border there are many fellow Mexicans who wish to return to the land of our elders and shelter themselves under our flag; here, on our soil, they should find a place favorable to their aspirations" (González 1979, 241).

Striking a more restrictive note, the interior minister declared that he would sanction the repatriation only of Mexican nationals who were in ill health, to whom he would provide aid by setting up medical teams in Ciudad Juárez.[75] He softened this position, however, by also furnishing assistance to some destitute Mexican migrants who, as he put it, represented a "truly sorrowful spectacle." In addition, U.S. authorities continued on a regular basis to deport people who had violated the country's immigration laws and to threaten the revival of mass expulsions of foreign nationals. At the beginning of June 1940, as rumors circulated of a possible departure of 12,000 Mexicans from Texas, the State Department—in light of the international political situation—announced that it intended to revise its rules and regulations governing migration. The department proposed a new system of control, to ensure that Mexicans who wished to come to the United States for a limited time might do so, on the condition that their presence on U.S. soil was required for some "legitimate purpose" or to satisfy some "reasonable need," and that they would leave the country once their allotted time had expired (SRE 1940, 437–38).

Following its well-worn path, the Mexican government continued to weigh in on and confront the issue of repatriation by adopting time-honored measures. With the aim of remaining alert to the return of its migrant citizens and to seeing to their reintegration and resettlement, the Interior Ministry's Agrarian Department—still in the period of Cárdenas's rule—assembled a list of available lands on which either foreign immigrants or repatriated nationals could be established, or to which people who had not left the country might be moved to help realize internal colonization schemes. The list contained such detailed information as the name by which the various lands were known, their location (state, district, and municipality), the existence of road and other transportation networks, the surface area and quality of the lands and whether these were irrigated, or remained wilderness, or allowed seasonal cultivation. The different crops that these lands could produce were also specified, as were their climate, altitude above sea level, and the conditions that would affect the housing and health of incoming settlers.

The calls for greater official intervention in favor of repatriation also took on a new coloration with assertions, beginning in November 1940, that Mexicans should not be drafted into the U.S. Army. On this point, the Mexico City newspaper *El Mexicano* declared that the country needed to support the return of "all Mexicans currently living in the United States," before they found themselves obligated to enlist in the U.S. Army. The newspaper's proposal, which it urged the Mexican Senate to consider, called upon the government to appoint a group of civil servants knowledgeable about the circumstances and forces governing the lives of their compatriots in the United States, especially given the state of war that was overcoming that country and in which some European powers were already embroiled. The proposal for a new repatriation program would be mounted so as "to avoid, by whatever means are available to the people and the government of Mexico, the packing off of our compatriots to defend foreign interests."[76]

Within the framework of the Defense Program adopted by the U.S. government in June 1940, that country's industry not only equipped the 4 million soldiers directly engaged in armed conflict outside the country and the more than 11 million people—in the army, volunteer forces, and different social services—involved in the war effort inside the country; it also produced consumables, logistical equipment, and war matériel to support the Allies in their fight against Nazism and fascism. The need for Mexican labor, which began to be felt as soon as the country recovered from the economic crisis of the 1930s, intensified as U.S. citizens left the agricultural sector to take jobs in the defense industries or enlist in the armed forces.[77]

## The United States at War and the Bracero Program

In January 1941, the U.S. Congress approved a proposal by the newly reelected President Roosevelt permitting the country to lend or lease all types of items or articles of war to any nation whose defense was considered vital to the security of the United States. Beginning with the country's declaration of war against Germany, the productive capacity of U.S. industry, focused on turning out the equipment, arms, and matériel needed to prosecute the war, rocketed up. Its output was staggering. One year after Pearl Harbor, the United States produced more war matériel than all the Axis nations combined; around 40 percent of the world's armaments came from its factories.

The needs imposed by war and the restrictions exacted by a state of emergency demanded a more intensive utilization of available resources, their redirection toward industrial output, and higher levels of productivity. The number of people employed, across the civilian and military sectors, increased by some 20 million between 1940 and 1944. Much of this expanded labor force was deployed in work traditionally found in urban areas: armament factories, industrial enterprises, transport, and services of every type. In turn, the country's agricultural production was quickly affected. To cite only one example, in September 1941, 1 million workers moved out of the rural economy and into industrial areas. As a result, sugar producers and cotton planters in Arizona, New Mexico, and Texas requested official permission to import Mexican manpower. In California alone, farm interests calculated that they needed 30,000 agricultural workers in 1942 (Godínez 1991, 311, 313–14).

In April 1942, under pressure from these California sugar producers, the U.S. Immigration and Naturalization Service established a commission to study the problems created by the shortage of farm labor as well as the feasibility of resolving them through a program of importing workers. The commission concluded that the United States had a clear need for Mexican laborers. In addition, it stressed that the Mexican government would need to be a direct participant, given the magnitude of any potential program. On 1 June, some ten days after Mexico's declaration of war against the Axis powers, the U.S. attorney general, Francis Biddle, asked the State Department to approach the Mexican government and take the first formal step toward laying the groundwork for a possible agreement between the two countries over the importation of Mexican labor.

To this end, discussions between the members of a U.S. delegation, headed by agriculture secretary Claude Wickard, and a Mexican delegation, led by E. Hidalgo, representing the Foreign Relations Ministry, began in July. Initially, citing the abuses to which Mexican migrants had been subjected during the period of the First World War (1917–20), when the United States instituted a unilateral program to promote the inflow of braceros from its southern neighbor, Hidalgo took a position against the importation of workers (Alanís Enciso 1999). For the United States to win approval from his side, Hidalgo laid down certain conditions. Every Mexican worker would need to be under formal contract, accorded basic respect, and granted the same advantages that were enjoyed by their U.S. counterparts. Furthermore, the contracting party needed to be the U.S. government, not private individuals, who could easily victimize the workers who signed on with them. In addition, there was to be no repetition of mass deportations, like those that occurred during the 1930s, a decade and more after the war had come to an end. Besides payment of their trip costs to and from the country, braceros were to receive a travel allowance, decent housing, wages consistent with those currently earned in the area where they would be based, protection against discrimination, and so on (García y Griego 1981, 15).

After a mere ten days of discussion, the first diplomatic accord for the importation of Mexican labor to the United States, better known as the Bracero Agreement, was devised. The agreement, amplified by various amendments and additional material, entered into force on 4 August 1942. It lasted for twenty-two years. Under the auspices of the program, more than 400,000 Mexican laborers entered the United States to work for specified periods both in planting and harvesting crops and in maintaining the country's rail lines.

As the 1940s began, the cycle of the world economy turned, reversing the depressed conditions that had prevailed during the previous decade. At the same time, Lázaro Cárdenas's term as president came to an end along with the reforms that his government had promoted. These had met with a tenacious resistance that stymied the implementation of many of Cárdenas's proposals. Those that had taken effect still had little history behind them, which diluted their ability to transform Mexican state and society in any meaningful way (Knight 1993, 51; Knight 1994a, 106–7; Hamilton 1983, 258–61). The economic prosperity taking hold in the United States propelled the migration of thousands of Mexican workers. As a result, just as it had during the First World War and the 1920s, this latest migratory flow became a matter of internal concern and discussion for the governments of Mexico and the United States. Similarly, the north to south movement, the repatriation, of Mexicans living above the Rio Grande continued to be of secondary importance for the Mexican government. Nonetheless, the memory of mass deportations that took place during the first years of the 1930s, the restrictive laws on migration that were subsequently enacted, and the routine expulsions carried out by U.S. immigration authorities kept Mexico's government in a state of constant fear that a mass return of its nationals might be repeated, with all the negative consequences such an event would have for the country. At the same time, however, official interest in preserving the image of a body politic united in support of the return of the country's migrant citizens had not waned. All the same, the successive administrations took, in general, little action during periods, like that of the Cárdenas presidency, when large-scale deportations did not loom on the horizon.

## Conclusions

The historiography of the repatriation of Mexicans from the United States has argued that the government of Lázaro Cárdenas took an aggressive stance on this front, implementing its policy with a vigor analogous to its promotion of agrarian reform. It has similarly claimed that the Cardenista repatriation policy was different from that of previous administrations. My work demonstrates the opposite: the commitment that Cárdenas made and the energies that he dedicated to repatriating his compatriots were not comparable to his efforts on agrarian reform. The Cardenista repatriation policy was characterized by its modest scale and scant funding—never more than the bare minimum. Ultimately, then, this study shows that the Cardenista "project" yielded few positive results with respect to an organized, systematic return of Mexico's migrant workers. Bracketing this fact is that Cárdenas was not an innovator when it came to formulating Mexican migration policy. On the contrary, he maintained the initiatives that had been put forward since the beginning of the twentieth century, whose accomplishments—with few exceptions—had been limited.

On the matter of repatriating migrant nationals who were living in the United States, my study, I believe, firmly establishes that the actions taken by the Mexican government from 1934 to 1940 offered few novel aspects but, instead, were similar to those taken by earlier governments that did not have to confront the specter of mass returns. More specifically, what the Cárdenas administration manifested, and what persisted from earlier times, was a tendency—idealistic in spirit and expressed in speeches and discourse—to promote a return of Mexican nationals according to an exclusive criterion, one that aimed at the settlement of certain lands in the north of Mexico, primarily by people experienced in agricultural work and with some capital to support themselves. As the government construed it, the purpose of this movement was to populate the countryside, increase agricultural output, and create new wealth for the nation, a purpose made explicit in legislation bearing on migration and the agrarian sector. A yawning gap, however, existed between the declarations in favor of an organized return, on the one hand, and the measures taken by Cardenista officials, on the other, a gap that this work brings to light and documents. In their rhetoric and public pronouncements, as well as in the legislation they passed on migration and agrarian affairs, politicians and government officials expressed support for the return of Mexican migrants from the United States, constantly underlining the government's commitment to help bring its citizens back to the homeland. While the declarations of the Cárdenas administration with regard to this commitment left the impression that the government was striving actively to fulfill it, official efforts on the ground fell far short of this goal. Of course, if the circumstances of 1934-40 had been different, and had produced another mass return, there is no doubt that the Cárdenas government would have accepted its returned nationals and taken the necessary action to reintegrate them. But such circumstances never came to pass, which meant that—in terms of concrete action—the measures adopted to institute and carry out an organized return could remain tightly circumscribed.

A more committed intervention by the federal government on behalf of a systematic repatriation did not spark much interest in official circles. Indeed, on various occasions the subject was met with indifference. Likewise, across diverse sectors of Mexican society a consensus emerged in support of the way representatives of the political class responded to the repatriation of Mexican nationals. Leaders of the working class (among them Lombardo Toledano), the press (*Excelsior*, *El Universal*, etc.), and some state governors showed themselves to be in favor of this approach.

Fear at the possible effects of a mass return of Mexican migrants from the United States predominated among officials in the Cárdenas administration. This fear prompted the government to take an interest in comprehending the size, distribution, and living conditions of the Mexican population in the United States and, through studies and analysis, to estimate the number of people who could return at a given time and to determine how it should confront a situation of urgency. These initiatives demonstrated that, in its own way, the Cárdenas government pursued a preventive policy in the face of fears of any mass return similar to what had occurred between 1929 and 1933. In addition, they denoted the degree of official interest in staying ahead of the issue and anticipating any actions that might be needed.

This book sheds light on an aspect of Mexican migration policy that has been little studied to date by specialists on migration between Mexico and the United States, namely, how the Mexican government positioned itself relative to the return of its nationals at times when neither large-scale returns nor heavy emigration took place. As we have seen, such periods were marked by great fear within the political class, and some other sectors of Mexican society, that an inopportune, mass return of migrant workers from abroad would impact the country negatively.

One of the principal justifications for this fear, one that also helps explain the reluctance to support the repatriation project, lay in the belief that conditions within the country would be adversely affected, as would the national treasury. Similarly, some state governors—the governor of Baja California being a prime example—took the view that groups of nationals newly arrived in their territory would constitute a burden on the local population. Tensions would surface and clashes could erupt, it was thought, if returnees were given land and work, since they would compete with the local labor force. This would in turn provoke a backlash against the government. In the main, then, fears persisted that the country's economy and the welfare of local workers would be strongly affected by the repatriation of migrant nationals from the

United States. In this sense, there was a recognition that in the sphere of government little could be done to rechannel a large-scale migratory return.

The alarm over the prospect of such a return was to a certain degree justified, but it was also exaggerated. It was justified by the disruptions that Mexico faced during the first three years of the 1930s, when thousands of its deported citizens flooded into its northern border cities. The cost to these communities, and to the country at large, in coming to the aid of the deportees so they could return to their homes was still fresh in the minds of people. The alarm was exaggerated in the sense that this mass return had not been catastrophic for the country. While no in-depth study on the matter has been carried out, it is nonetheless known that many returned migrants soon resettled in their old towns. They quickly readapted to their former way of life, were the source of few conflicts, and—many years later—returned to the United States. Nor were there any notices or reports during the second half of the 1930s that those who had returned during the depths of the Depression had caused any difficulties or brought on any social or economic dislocation to the places where they resettled. Over the course of the Cárdenas sexenio, furthermore, the repatriation of Mexicans did not generate any significant debate either in the press or in other spheres of Mexican society. In general, the subject aroused little interest because the number of people who wished to return was small, as was the total of those who did in fact return, whether on their own initiative or with official support.

On occasion, weighed down by such fears, the Cárdenas government tried actively to hinder the return of its citizens, principally by assigning this task to some of its officials in the United States. Julián Velarde, a personal representative of Cárdenas, negotiated with U.S. authorities to dissuade them from carrying out further deportations of his compatriots. On other occasions, Mexico's consuls suggested to, or sought to convince, their compatriots in the United States that they should remain in that country, especially if they had jobs or owned land or businesses. Similarly, in late 1938, José Castrejón Pérez, chief of the Interior Ministry's Department of Population, suggested to some Mexican nationals that if they could manage to renew their sharecropping contracts with Texas ranchers, they should by all means do so.[78] It will also be recalled that in mid-1939, Ramón Beteta—only a short while after promoting the repatriation of Mexican agricultural workers in Texas—sought to convince his compatriots in California not to return to their native country.

Still another fundamental element of Cardenista repatriation policy was its hard line against enlarging the scope of any program to return Mexican nationals to the homeland. The main reason for this adamancy lay in the recognition that repatriation was not urgently needed. With the exception of the deportations that took place in 1938, no contingency arose during the second half of the 1930s that required the Mexican government to intervene. In contrast to other works, this study demonstrates that, beginning in 1935, the social position and work conditions of the Mexican community in the United States—while far from ideal—began to change in comparison to the situation that prevailed during the first years of the decade, when U.S. immigration authorities and public welfare officials carried out mass deportations. Over the second half of the 1930s, the U.S. government's economic recovery program helped lessen the pressures for maintaining large-scale deportations. Moreover, the employment situation, strengthened organization, and demographic composition (predominance of second-generation Mexican children) of the Mexican American community played a vital role in shrinking the number of Mexican nationals who returned to Mexico and in building opposition within this same community to the idea of leaving the United States.

Another factor that helped explain the government's limited commitment to promoting and supporting the return of its citizens was its strong focus on problems affecting the country's campesinos and urban workers. The policies directed toward agrarian matters, employment, and colonization privileged the interests of workers who had remained in the country versus those who had left it. In practice, the most important colonization and agrarian projects undertaken during the Cárdenas sexenio, with Baja California as a leading example, primarily involved moving and resettling people already inside the country.

On some occasions, national agrarian policy did make room for Mexican agricultural workers coming from the United States, since they were viewed as able to stimulate agricultural development in different regions of the country. At the same time, however, the government did not view them as beneficiaries of its agrarian reform program, nor did it parcel out much land to them. Only a few returnees became prominent members of the ejidos. For their part, while workers' and union leaders may have announced their support for aiding the return of their compatriots who languished in difficult conditions, they also made it clear, by word and action, that their primary duty was to attend to local labor and worker needs. For all these reasons, then, the official government policy on repatriation did not entail promoting it outside the country's borders. In like fashion, the government opposed earmarking public funds for a matter that lacked urgency and—unlike the oil field expropriations and the situation of campesinos and urban workers—did not rank as a high national priority.

In addition, on those occasions when it was extended, official support for an organized return had very definite limits. For example, although the government promoted the return of a small group to establish the colony of La Esperanza and took ameliorative measures with regard to the deportations that occurred at the end of 1938, its involvement implied neither significant funding for the first nor a major commitment to the latter. When it supported the return of twenty families to La Esperanza, it took no major actions to ensure their successful resettlement or their maintenance. Indeed, so grossly did the government fail on this score that the small settler population had disappeared near the end of the Cárdenas sexenio. Similarly, in the face of the exigencies created by the late 1938 deportations, rather than commit to financing repatriations, the government requested financial assistance from the country's unions and workers' organizations.

By the same token, the reincorporation of Mexican nationals coming from the United States was not a core part of the Cárdenas regime's international policy. Rather, the controversies stemming from the country's agrarian reform, insofar as it affected U.S. interests, and more critically, from the expropriation of the oil companies, were the axis on which relations between the two countries turned. Furthermore, with respect to migration, the government's greatest concern was to stem the outflow of Mexican workers and to promote the inflow of particular foreigners (Spanish refugees, above all). These two interests outweighed that of bringing back Mexican nationals from across the Rio Grande. For Cárdenas, the repatriated, and the fate of Mexican migrants in the United States, occupied a place of secondary importance in both his foreign and domestic policy. In this sense, this book compels a reconsideration of the traditional, and romanticized, idea about the nationalist-inspired commitment of the Mexican government to repatriating its nationals who had left for the United States in search of better prospects.[79]

Until now, historians and others interested in repatriation have parroted the government's rhetoric in favor of such a movement and trained their analysis on periods in which official action with respect to repatriation was most significant (1920–23 and 1929–33). Thus it is not surprising that they highlight the government's commitment and the numerous measures taken to support a return of the country's nationals. That interpretation, however, lacks other elements that would enable a fuller understanding of the Mexican government's repatriation policy. In particular, previous studies have not examined either the actions that the government took during times when it did not have to confront mass returns or the continuity of its policy toward the return of migrant workers as such policy played out over a longer period. In contrast to other studies, my analysis shows that, on the subject of migration, the Mexican government followed a repatriation policy that was characterized by fear and relative disinterest.

In addition, this book also makes clear that the most salient action taken by the Cárdenas government on the question of repatriation was the implementation of an agricultural colonization project, the plans for which began to be outlined and developed on the heels of a late 1937 executive order. Cárdenas's personal interest and involvement were essential to setting these plans in motion, as were two factors of international import: an agreement concluded with Los Angeles city and county officials and the criticisms directed against Cárdenas over the arrival in Mexico of Spanish Civil War refugees. The Cardenista initiative was thus influenced in part by something that had nothing to do with the United States but instead drew on events in Spain and reflected a pillar of Mexican foreign policy in which offering support to the refugees was front and center.

The main objective of the repatriation plan was to found an agricultural settlement in northern Mexico by resettling agricultural workers who had learned how to cultivate and grow cotton during their time in the United States. The plan was designed and implemented on the basis of suggestions made by Manuel Gamio, who summed up a trend that had predominated since early in the century: the promotion of a gradual and modest repatriation of agricultural workers, and their settlement in new farming colonies. Seen from this perspective, the proposed plan was not new; its only innovation lay in the government's decision that it would put these ideas into practice through a pilot colonization scheme that rested on selecting and mobilizing a group of individuals.

The promotional campaign in the United States on behalf of a government-supported return of Mexican nationals lasted only three months (from April through June 1939), since the government's intention was to organize the repatriation of a few hundred of its citizens who lived in Texas. The undertaking was unprecedented both in the manner it went forward and in its results: it was promoted by the executive branch and revolved around the difficult challenge of convincing a skeptical audience. Initially, few migrants displayed much interest in returning to Mexico because they were doubtful about and distrustful of the Cardenista plan. Ultimately, however, the government managed to convince a group totaling some 4,000 to return voluntarily, mobilizing and collecting them in Texas, transporting them to Mexico, and regrouping them into a new settlement. The government's success was notable in another respect as well. From a regional perspective, the large inflow of people helped build up the population of the Lower Rio Grande Valley. Moreover, unlike pre-1934 settlements founded by the government to resettle Mexican nationals coming from the United States, this one has survived to the present day. The plan was thus successful in realizing its objectives.

Cárdenas used the repatriation campaign and the founding of the 18 March colony to advance his interests both domestically and abroad. Domestically, the government employed the colony's establishment as a nationalist symbol to celebrate its repatriation policy. Abroad, the colony helped contain and deflect the pressures constantly exerted by immigration authorities and public welfare officials in Los Angeles, as well as by a range of forces in the United States generally, to carry out more deportations of Mexican nationals.

Together with agrarian reform and the oil expropriation, repatriation became, little by little during the sexenio, an element of Cárdenas's nationalist rhetoric. Workers' leaders and other politicians close to the seat of power acted similarly. For each of these parties, repatriation served to demonstrate their interest in the Mexican community living in the United States. The high-water mark in this process was the founding of the 18 March agricultural colony (a name that memorialized the oil expropriation, a key symbol of Cardenista nationalism). The wide publicity that Cárdenas gave to this event and the tone in which he cast it were, perhaps, his final attempt at forging a national consensus around an executive branch decision at a moment when Mexican society was deeply polarized. In a context of slowdown and retreat in the areas of labor, agrarian, and educational reform, Cárdenas undertook a project that had little or no effect on Mexican society in terms of the total resources devoted to it, the location to which the repatriated were sent, or the number of people who arrived in the new settlement. At the same time, the president used repatriation and the founding of the colony as devices with which to divert public attention from the serious economic and political situation in which the country found itself at the end of the 1930s.

The evidence seems clear that this colony was the only one to which Cárdenas personally paid attention during his time as president. Although other settlements were founded with migrants who returned from the United States (such as La Esperanza) and still others that were already established also received returning nationals, in none of these cases did the government extend help with enthusiasm. No other colonization project received the publicity and the backing given to the 18 March.

The Cardenista project was a singular and dramatic experiment that brought no pointed change in government repatriation policy. Such official measures as were taken to support the repatriated continued to be limited.

Those living in the 18 March agricultural colony had to overcome considerable difficulties to survive and put down roots. The arrival of people in the colony and the process of settlement were disorganized and rushed. The newly arrived—women, men, and children—were forced to live in dreadful conditions. Sickness stalked the colony. It was overpopulated, with shortages of potable water, housing, food, medical services, and little land yet under irrigation. These same problems afflicted people who arrived to settle in other agricultural communities in northern Mexico. The situation facing other groups of Mexicans in need of assistance, whether they lived in various parts of the United States or in Mexico itself, was equally serious.

The government's support for repatriation continued to be limited and directed only at solving the most urgent problems of a select number of nationals and to helping, in a veiled way, some families who made their way to Baja California. Likewise, during the period in which it developed and implemented the repatriation project, and again later, the government continued acting as it had from the time Cárdenas ascended to the presidency, that is, by undertaking numerous studies aimed at identifying places where more returnees could be established; by furnishing support, outside the public eye, for the repatriation and resettlement of small groups of people; by attending to the most urgent cases; and by trying to hold repatriations in check. In the north of the United States it insisted that Mexicans (especially working-class Mexicans) who had jobs or business interests in that country should remain there. In California, home to the second-largest Mexican community in the United States after Texas (California, 134,312; Texas, 159,266), the government sought to persuade its citizens not to return to Mexico. It also negotiated with U.S. authorities to dissuade them from deporting Mexican nationals. The stream of studies conducted ostensibly to determine the best locations in which to resettle returnees and the few concrete actions that were taken to spur and aid their return proved the limits of official support for repatriation in general. They underscored both the government's reluctance to go beyond what was absolutely necessary and its recognition that stemming its workers' continuing migration to the United States was not a challenge that was easily met.

The reasons why the Cárdenas government elected not to take more forceful measures to support a return movement suggest three fundamental impulses guiding and permeating its approach to the issue. The first was fear of the social, economic, and demographic consequences of repatriation, a fear present among officials in the Cárdenas administration at the very moment proposals were put forward to deal with the return of their compatriots. It led them on occasion to try to block the return of Mexican nationals, some of whom the government encouraged to stay in the United States, or to carefully avoid displaying any support for their return. The second impulse was bound up with a policy that might be characterized as reacting to and following the course of external events. So long as economic conditions in the United States did not give rise to a mass return, the Mexican government did no more than develop plans for future contingencies while channeling its energies toward preventing such an occurrence. Indeed, some officials at the time believed that governmental intervention to promote the return of Mexican nationals was altogether unnecessary. The government, in their view, should concentrate on improving conditions within the country such that its citizens abroad, after witnessing their country's peace and prosperity, would come back to the homeland—gradually—of their own volition. Finally, the government's domestic priorities, its focus on policies that affected rural and urban workers within the country, led it to see repatriation as of secondary importance, a luxury not meriting great investment.

This study examines only one period in the history of Mexican governmental action in respect to the repatriation of its nationals from the United States. More historical work needs to be done on the initiatives and actions taken by Mexican officials in other eras (the Porfiriato, the period of the Revolution, and even the 1950s, when hundreds of Mexicans were deported under the program known as Operation Wetback) and their implications for the country. To this point, the output of research—especially the work done by Mexicans—on the phenomenon of migration has tended to focus on the migration of Mexicans to the United States in the contemporary period. An especially key issue meriting greater study and analysis is the question of what effect mass deportations of Mexican nationals had on the social, economic, and demographic realities of Mexican border communities, of returning migrants' hometowns and villages, and of Mexico's largest cities. Such studies would help explain the degree to which successive Mexican governments' fear of the return of their nationals was justified or whether it was merely a perception based on assumptions that lacked substance.

Finally, this study brings back to light at least two aspects of Mexican migration policy that began to appear during the first decades of the nineteenth century and that continue to appear in initiatives with respect to the return of the country's nationals from the United States. The first is a reactive policy that responds to circumstances surrounding return flows of migrants. In other words, when such flows are moderated, the initiatives pursued by Mexico in support of repatriation are likewise modest in scope. The second pertains to

the political class's ever-present fear of a mass return and its possible consequences for the country. This fear was palpable with the 1986 passage of the
Simpson-Rodino Law by the U.S. Congress and, more recently, by reactions
to the 11 September 2001, terrorist attacks in New York City and Washington,
D.C. In both cases, the strict application of U.S. migration laws on hundreds of
Mexicans residing illegally in the country alarmed some Mexican government
officials, conjuring up a mass return of many hundreds (if not thousands) of
their compatriots, something that did not occur. As in the second half of the
1930s, however, neither did the Mexican government, in the face of this fear,
devise any special measures to deal with such an eventuality. Fundamentally,
the prevailing idea remained that "they should stay there," both to shield the
country from difficulties and for their own good.

# NOTES

ABBREVIATIONS

| | |
|---|---|
| AC | Fondo Presidente Ávila Camacho |
| ACERMLC | Archivo del Centro de Estudios de la Revolución Mexicana, Lázaro Cárdenas, A.C. (Jiquilpan, Michoacán) |
| AGN | Archivo General de la Nación (Mexico City) |
| AHA | Archivo Histórico del Agua (Comisión Nacional del Agua (Mexico City) |
| AHSRE | Archivo Histórico de la Secretaría de Relaciones Exteriores (Mexico City) |
| APLC | Fondo Archivo Particular de Lázaro Cárdenas |
| APRB | Archivo Particular de Ramón Beteta |
| ASRA | Archivo de la Secretaría de la Reforma Agraria (Mexico City) |
| CAG | Colonias Agrícolas y Ganaderas |
| DGG | Fondo Dirección General de Gobierno |
| DT | Fondo Departamento del Trabajo |
| FAS | Fondo Aprovechamiento Superficiales |
| FC | Fondo Presidente Cárdenas |
| FJM | Fondo Francisco J. Múgica |
| LC | Fondo Lázaro Cárdenas |
| NARA | National Archives and Records Administration, College Park, Maryland |
| O/C | Fondo Presidente Obregón-Calles |
| SRE | Fondo Secretaría de Relaciones Exteriores |
| USDS | U.S. Department of State, Records of the Immigration and Naturalization Service, Series A, Part 2, Mexican Immigration, 1906–30 |

FOREWORD TO THE ENGLISH-LANGUAGE EDITION

1. Francisco E. Balderrama and Raymond Rodriguez, *Decade of Betrayal: Mexican Repatriation in the 1930s* (Albuquerque: University of New Mexico Press, 1995).

2. Marc R. Rosenblum and Doris Meissner, "The Deportation Dilemma: Reconciling Tough and Humane Enforcement," *Migration Policy Institute*, April 2014, http://www.migrationpolicy.org/research/deportation-dilemma-reconciling-tough-humane-enforcement.

3. Douglas Massey, "The Past and Future of Mexico-U.S. Migration," in *Beyond la Frontera: The History of Mexico-US Migration*, edited by Mark Overmyer-Velázquez (New York: Oxford University Press, 2011).

4. Daniel Kanstroom, *Deportation Nation: Outsiders in American History* (Cambridge, Mass.: Harvard University Press, 2007), x.

5. Ben Vinson III and Bobby Vaughn, *Afroméxico: Herramientas para la historia* (Mexico City: Fondo de Cultura Económica, 2004), 38–42.

6. Bobby Vaughn and Ben Vinson III, "Unfinished Migrations: From the Mexican South to the American South: Impressions on Afro-Mexican Migration to North Carolina," in *Beyond Slavery: The Multilayered Legacy of Africans in Latin America and the Caribbean*, edited by Darién J. Davis (New York: Rowman & Littlefield, 2007), 226. See also Gonzalo Aguirre Beltrán, *La población negra de México: Estudio etnohistórico* (Mexico City: Fuente Cultural, 1989).

7. In his work, Elliot Young examines Chinese exclusion legislation in Mexico as part of a larger transnational deportation regime that included the United States and Caribbean countries such as Cuba. Young, *Alien Nation: Chinese Migration in the Americas from the Coolie Era through World War II* (Chapel Hill: University of North Carolina Press, 2014).

8. Grace Peña Delgado, "At Exclusion's Southern Gate: Changing Categories of Race and Class among Chinese Fronterizos," in *Continental Crossroads: Remapping US-Mexico Borderlands History*, edited by Samuel Truett and Elliott Young (Durham, N.C.: Duke University Press, 2004); Evelyn Hu-DeHart, "Racism and Anti-Chinese Persecution in Sonora, Mexico, 1876–1932," *Amerasia* 9, no. 2 (1982): 1–28; Robert Chau Romero, *The Chinese in Mexico, 1882–1940* (Tucson: University of Arizona Press, 2010); Julia Maria Schiavone Camacho, *Chinese Mexicans: Transpacific Migration and the Search for a Homeland, 1910–1960* (Chapel Hill: University of North Carolina Press, 2012).

9. José Jorge Gómez Izquierdo, *El movimiento antichino en México (1871–1934): Problemas del racismo y del nacionalismo durante la Revolución Mexicana* (Mexico City: Instituto Nacional de Antropología e Historia, 1991); Gerardo Rénique, "Race, Region, and Nation: Sonora's Anti-Chinese Racism and Mexico's Postrevolutionary Nationalism, 1920s–1930s," in *Race and Nation in Modern Latin America*, edited by Nancy P. Appelbaum, Anne S. Macpherson, and Karin Alejandra Rosemblatt (Chapel Hill: University of North Carolina Press, 2003), 219–26; Jason Oliver Chang. "Racial Alterity in the Mestizo Nation," *Journal of Asian American Studies* 14, no. 3 (2011): 331–59.

10. Mark Overmyer-Velázquez, "Good Neighbors and White Mexicans: Constructing Race and Nation on the Mexico-US Border," *Journal of American Ethnic History* 33, no. 1 (2013): 5–34.

11. Examples include Jorge Durand et al., "The Changing Geography of Mexican Immigration to the United States: 1910–1996," *Social Science Quarterly* 81 (March 2000): 1; Jorge A. Bustamante, *Cruzar la línea: La migración de México a los Estados Unidos* (Mexico City: Fondo de Cultura Económica, 1997); Wayne A. Cornelius, David FitzGerald, Jorge Hernández Díaz, and Scott Borger, eds., *Migration from the Mexican Mixteca* (Boulder, Colo.: CCIS and Lynne Rienner, 2009).

12. Some recent publications include Julie Weise, *Corazón de Dixie: Mexicanos in the U.S. South since 1910* (Chapel Hill: University of North Carolina Press, 2015); Deborah Cohen, *Braceros: Migrant Citizens and Transnational Subjects in the Postwar United States and Mexico* (Chapel Hill: University of North Carolina Press, 2011); Ana Elizabeth Rosas, *Abrazando el Espíritu: Bracero Families Confront the US-Mexico Border* (Berkeley: University of California Press, 2014); and Gilbert G. Gonzalez, *Guest Workers or Colonized Labor? Mexican Labor Migration to the United States* (New York: Routledge, 2015).

13. Fernando Saúl Alanís Enciso, *El primer Programa Bracero y el gobierno de México, 1917–1918* (San Luis Potosí: Colegio de San Luis, 1999).

14. David FitzGerald, "Inside the Sending State: The Politics of Mexican Emigration Control," *International Migration Review* 40, no. 2 (2006): 259–93.

15. Other works by Fernando Saúl Alanís Enciso include *El Primer Programa Bracero y el gobierno de México*; "No cuenten conmigo: La política de repatriación del gobierno mexicano y sus nacionales en Estados Unidos, 1910–1928," *Estudios Mexicanos* 19 (2003): 401–61; "Manuel Gamio: El inicio de las investigaciones sobre la inmigración mexicana a Estados Unidos," *Historia Mexicana* 52, no. 4 (April–June 2003): 979–1020; "De factores de inestabilidad nacional a elementos de consolidación del Estado posrevolucionario: Los exiliados mexicanos en Estados Unidos, 1929–1933," *Historia Mexicana* 54, no. 4 (April–June 2005): 1155–205; and "¿Cuántos fueron? La repatriación de mexicanos de Estados Unidos durante la Gran Depresión: Una interpretación cuantitativa, 1930–1934," *Aztlán: A Journal of Chicano Studies* 32, no. 2 (Fall 2007): 65–91.

16. Alanís Enciso, *El Primer Programa Bracero y el gobierno de México*; David FitzGerald, "Mexican Migration and the Law," in Overmyer-Velázquez, *Beyond la Frontera*.

17. Deirdre M. Moloney, *National Insecurities: Immigrants and U.S. Deportation Policy since 1882* (Chapel Hill: University of North Carolina Press, 2012).

18. Nicholas De Genova, "The Legal Production of Mexican/Migrant 'Illegality,'" *Latino Studies* 2, no. 2 (2004): 160–85.

19. Adriana Kemp and Rebeca Raijman, "The Making and Unmaking of a Community of Latino Labor Migrants in Israel," in "Global Latin(o) Americanos: Transoceanic Diasporas and Regional Migrations," edited by Mark Overmyer-Velázquez and Enrique Sepúlveda, special issue of *LASA Forum* 46, no. 4 (Fall 2015): 11.

20. James D. Cockcroft, *Outlaws in the Promised Land: Mexican Immigrant Workers and America's Future* (New York: Grove, 1986), cited in De Genova, "The Legal Production of Mexican/Migrant 'Illegality,'" 165.

21. Jorge Bustamante, *Report of the Special Rapporteur on the Human Rights of Migrants: Mission to the United States of America* (Geneva: United Nations, 5 March 2008). See also Mark Overmyer-Velázquez, "Histories and Historiographies of Greater Mexico," in Overmyer-Velázquez, *Beyond la Frontera*.

22. Seth Freed Wessler writes about the deplorable medical conditions in the prisons and notes that, "as of June 2015, these facilities—which are distinct from immigration detention centers, where people are held pending deportation—housed nearly 23,000 people." The three companies operating the eleven immigrant-only contract prisons received $625 million in 2013 from the Federal Bureau of Prisons. Wessler, "This Man Will Almost Certainly Die," *The Nation*, 28 January 2016.

23. See the collection of related articles in Migration Policy Institute, "Rising Child Migration to the United States," http://www.migrationpolicy.org/programs/us-immigration-policy-program/rising-child-migration-united-states (accessed 7 March 2016).

24. Tanya Golash-Boza and Pierrette Hondagneu-Sotelo, "Latino Immigrant Men and the Deportation Crisis: A Gendered Racial Removal Program," *Latino Studies* 11, no. 3 (2013): 271–92.

25. California State Bill SB 670, "Apology Act for the 1930s Mexican Repatriation Program," 22 February 2005, http://www.leginfo.ca.gov/pub/05-06/bill/sen/sb_0651-0700/sb_670_bill_20051007_chaptered.html.

# INTRODUCTION

1. In this case, the term refers to the return of Mexicans and their children who were residing in the United States.

2. The number of persons repatriated between 1929 and 1933 was officially reported as 399,092 (Hoffman 1974, 175).

3. In 1934, 23,934 Mexicans were repatriated from the United States; in 1935, 15,368; in 1936, 11,599; in 1937, 8,037; in 1938, 12,024; in 1939, 15,925; and in 1940, 12,536; for a total of 99,423 (Hoffman 1974, 175; Mexico 1940, 23; Mexico 1941, 20).

4. In this case, the term repatriated (*repatriado*) refers to persons who returned under the umbrella of official government support. At the same time, cases existed in which persons returned by their own means, because they were expelled or deported, and these people, too, were also classified by Mexican authorities as repatriated persons. As a rule, both the different stances and actions of the Mexican government and the sources I have consulted make no distinction between these categories of persons who repatriated. The designation was applied loosely, generalized to cover all those who returned to the country, whatever the cause or reason.

# CHAPTER ONE

1. *El Nacional*, 24 January 1936; *El Universal*, 24 January 1936.

2. Work contracts were called *enganches* or "hooks," and the contractors, *enganchadores*. These contracts were in most cases purely verbal.

3. *El Imparcial*, 17 November 1910; González Navarro 1954, 277.

4. Alanís Enciso 1999:65–75. AHSRE, exp. 17-10-163, General Cándido Aguilar (minister of foreign relations) to Manuel Aguirre Berlanda (minister of the interior), Mexico City, 21 May 1918; *Evolución*, 2 May 1918.

5. Mexico 1883; Carreras de Velasco 1974, 44.

6. Alanís Enciso, 2001a, 45–56; *El Demócrata Fronterizo*, 15 January and 24 August 1918.

7. Cardoso 1977, 576–95; AGN, O/C, exp. 429-A-2, Eduardo Ruiz (Mexican consul in Los Angeles) to Álvaro Obregón (president of Mexico), 30 April 1921.

8. Carreras de Velasco 1974, 46; AGN, SRE, c. 48, exp. 183, Juan B. Vega (chief of the consular department) to Miguel A. Limón (official in charge of the Mexican consulate in Clifton, Arizona), 16 May 1919. See in particular containers 48 and 49, Sección de Gobernación, of the SRE archive.

9. Secretaría de Agricultura y Fomento n.d., 576; de la Peña 1950, 157.

10. Secretaría de Agricultura y Fomento 1928; AGN, SRE, c. 90, exp. 7805.

11. *Excelsior*, 8 February 1934; *Diario de los Debates de la Cámara de Diputados*, 1 September 1934.

# CHAPTER TWO

1. *Excelsior*, 8 April 1935; McKay 1982, 242, 254–56, 294; *El Universal*, 15 July, 1 December, 26 December, and 30 December 1936; *La Opinión*, 26 November 1936.

2. Sánchez 1993, 222; *El Universal*, 28 July and 11 August 1937.

3. *La Opinión*, 9 February 1938; *El Universal*, 11 February and 2 November 1938.

4. Sánchez 1993, 224; *Diario de los Debates de la Cámara de Diputados*, 6 December 1935.

5. Balderrama and Rodríguez 1995, 81; *El Universal*, 15 November 1937 and 20 August 1938; AGN, FC, exp. 503.11/3, "Estudio sobre la situación económica actual de los trabajadores mexicanos en Estados Unidos," Jesús M. González, Mexico City, 18 January 1936.

6. McKay 1982, 233–38; AGN, FC, exp. 503.11/3, Siegfried Goetza (executive director of the Mexican Community Association) to the supervisors of Los Angeles County, 8 February 1935.

7. *El Universal*, 29 March 1935; Balderrama and Rodríguez 1995, 81; AGN, FC, exp. 503.11/3, "Estudio sobre la situación económica actual de los trabajadores mexicanos en Estados Unidos," Mexico City, 18 January 1936.

8. *Diario de los Debates de la Cámara de Diputados*, 6 December 1935.

9. *Excelsior*, 12 April 1937; *El Universal*, 4 January 1939.

10. McKay 1982, 233, 238; AGN, FC, exp. 503.11/3, Siegfried Goetza to the supervisors of Los Angeles County, 8 February 1935.

11. ACERMLC, FJM, c. 1, exp. 21, doc. 1; AGN, FC, exp. 503.11/3, Telegram from Julián Velarde (president of the Latin American Chamber of Commerce of the Americas) to Lázaro Cárdenas (president of Mexico), Los Angeles, 21 February 1935; AGN, FC, exp. 503.11/3, Julián Velarde to Luis I. Rodríguez (private secretary to the president), Los Angeles, n.d.

12. Hoffman 1974, 175; *El Universal*, 14 August 1936; AGN, FC, exp. 503.11/3, Manuel Portillo (resident of Nuevo Laredo, Tamaulipas) to the president, Nuevo Laredo, 6 August and 23 September 1936.

13. *El Universal*, 23 January, 5 March, 20 May, 25 June, and 31 August 1937; *La Prensa*, 18 May and 13 June 1937.

14. *El Heraldo*, 29 December 1937; *El Universal*, 25 October 1938.

15. *El Universal*, 7 May and 11 June 1938; *El Heraldo*, 20 October 1938.

16. *El Universal*, 15 July 1938; *Excelsior*, 3 November 1938.

17. *El Universal*, 16 December 1936, 27 March 1937; *La Opinión*, 10 April 1937; AGN, DGG, 2.300 (29) 23997, Ramón Beteta (assistant minister of foreign relations) to the secretary of the interior, Mexico City, 14 April 1937; AGN, PC, exp. 503.11/3, Julián Velarde, Los Angeles, 2 February 1936.

18. *El Universal*, 7 June 1937.

19. *La Prensa*, 20 January 1937; *El Universal*, 23 January, 10 May, 7 June, 7 July, 5 August, and 3 November 1937, 21 April 1938; NARA, USDS, r. 21, p. 5, doc. 426, Report by the U.S. consul in Matamoros, Tamaulipas, to the Department of State, Matamoros, Tamaulipas, September 1937.

20. *El Universal*, 18 November 1937 and 11 May 1938.

21. NARA, USDS, r. 20–21, no. 398 and 426, Report by the U.S. consul in Matamoros to the Department of State, Matamoros, Tamaulipas, 30 September 1936 and September 1937.

22. *Diario de los Debates de la Cámara de Diputados*, 6 December 1935; Castillo and Ríos Bustamante 1990, 224–25; ACERMLC, vol. 3, exp. 34, Francisco Urbina to the Chamber of Deputies, Dallas, 11 August 1936; *Excelsior*, 14 August 1936.

23. Valdés 1991, 32, 37; McKay 1982, 275–78; *La Prensa*, 14 August 1936 and 1 August 1937.

24. Calculations by the Los Angeles Department of Statistics and the U.S. Bureau of Statistics, cited in *El Universal*, 23 September and 3 November 1939.

25. Castillo and Ríos Bustamante 1990, 224; AGN, FC, exp. 503.11/3, Silviano Barba González (secretary of the interior) to the president, Mexico City, 28 May 1936.

26. APRB, exp. 308, leg. 8, Economic conditions of workers in Port Arthur (consular office in Beaumont, Texas), Mexico City, 31 March 1939.

27. *El Universal*, 3, 8, 13, 29–31 July, 10 August, and 23 September 1936; *La Opinión*, July 1936.

28. *La Opinión*, April, May, and July 1937; June and September 1938.

29. During the 1930s, the pecan-shelling business was one of the pillars of San Antonio's economy. The industry, which employed some 15,000 persons on a temporary basis, had received a strong boost in this period from improvements in the machinery for shelling, in transporting the product, and in the consolidation of orchards into economic units that augmented the commercialization of pecans.

30. Arroyo 1975, 259–60; *El Universal*, 9 February, 22 March 1938, 13–14 December 1938, 21 February 1939.

31. AGN, FC, 503.11/3; AGN, DGG, exp. 2/382 (24) 24221, c. 52, exp. 41, Ing. Vázquez del Mercado (interior ministry official).

32. AGN, FC, exp. 503.11/3, Chamber of Deputies member Antonio Nava to the president, Mexico City, 15 January 1936; AGN, FC, exp. 503.11/212, Manuel Gamio (chief of the Demography Department of the Ministry of Interior) to the head of the Oficina Pro-Territorios, Mexico City, 26 September 1938.

33. AGN, FC, exp. 503.11/3, Rio Hondo, Texas, 6 January 1936; ACERMLC, FJM, vol. 157, doc. 147, letter from José Landozequi (a Mexican living in the United States) to Francisco J. Múgica (Minister of Communications and Public Works), 22 February and 25 March 1937.

34. ACERMLC, FJM, vol., 157, doc. 147, letter from José Landozequi to Francisco J. Múgica, 22 February 1937.

35. *Excelsior*, 7 August 1935.

36. For a more detailed analysis of the different classifications and the definition of each concept (deportation and repatriation), see Hoffman 1974, 166–69.


CHAPTER THREE

1. Ashby 1963, 99, 286–89; González 1981, 22–26; Knight 1994, 85–86, 91–94; Hamilton 1983, 108–13. One of the most important measures taken was to encourage workers groups to make extensive use of strikes. The mobilization begun in 1935 reached an unprecedented level of organization. In that year, 642 strikes were called, compared to 202 in the preceding year. From this perspective, the labor policy of the Cárdenas regime was genuinely radical.

2. ACERMLC, FJM, c. 1, exp. 21, doc. 1, "Estudio sobre expulsión de mexicanos de los Estados Unidos realizado por Francisco J. Múgica" (finance minister until June 1935, later communications and public works minister), Mexico City, 11 December 1934.

3. AGN, FC, exp. 503.11/3, Emilio Portes Gil (foreign relations minister) to the president of the Colonia Unida de Mexicanos, El Paso, Texas, 18 February 1935.

4. ACERMLC, FJM, c. 1, exp. 21, doc. 1, "Estudio sobre expulsión de mexicanos de los Estados Unidos realizado por Francisco J. Múgica," Mexico City, 11 December 1934.

5. Ibid.

6. Ibid.

7. Ibid.

8. Ibid.

9. Ibid.

10. Ibid.

11. AGN, FC, exp. 503.11/3, "Plan de Trabajo de Julián Velarde (director general de la Comisión Encargada de la Organización, Compilación, Repatriación y Colonización de Mexicanos en la Unión Americana) al general Lázaro Cárdenas (presidente de México)," 6 February 1935.

12. Ibid.

13. AGN, FC, exp. 503.11/3, Communication of the Ministry of Foreign Relations to the president, Mexico City, 16 July 1935; ACERMLC, FJM, c. 1, exp. 21, doc. 1, "Estudio sobre expulsión de mexicanos," Mexico City, 11 November 1934.

14. *Excelsior*, 7 August 1935; AGN, FC, exp. 503.11/3, AGN, FC, exp. 503.11/3, "Estudio sobre la situación económica actual de los trabajadores mexicanos en Estados Unidos," Jesús M. González, Mexico City, 18 January 1936.

15. *Excelsior*, 8 August 1936; *El Universal*, 20 May and 25 June 1937.

16. *Diario de los Debates de la Cámara de Diputados*, 6 December 1935.

17. Ibid.

18. Ibid.

19. AGN, FC, exp. 503.11/3, Study concerning the present economic situation of Mexican workers in the United States, Mexico City, 18 January 1936.

20. Ibid.

21. Ibid.

22. Wilkie 1978, 528–29. Other comparisons can be made to illustrate the unacceptable risks contained in González's proposal: what the government collected during the sexenio from the exploitation of natural resources (oil, mining, salt, water, lumber, fishing, etc.) yielded a total of 197,913,618 pesos. For its part, the Banco Nacional de Crédito Ejidal on average distributed annually a total of 57,854,870 pesos in credit to ejido members for machinery, tools, seeds, and whatever else they needed to work their land.

23. AGN, FC, exp. 503.11/3, Silvano Barba González (head of the Labor Department until June 1935 and later minister of interior) to the president, Mexico City, 28 May 1936; U.S. Bureau of the Census 1940, area, region, or country of birth of the population of foreign origin. See http://www.census.gov/population/www/documentation/twps0029/tab04.html.

24. *El Universal*, 23 June 1936.

25. *El Universal*, 30 October 1936; *El Porvenir*, 14 August 1937.

26. AGN, FC, exp. 503.11/3, Vicente Lombardo Toledano to the president, Mexico City, 15 May 1937; *El Universal*, 12 August 1937.

27. *Excelsior*, 14 June 1937.

28. AGN, FC, exp. 503.11/3, Luis Islas to the president, 2 June 1937; *Excelsior*, 14 June 1937.

29. ACERMLC, FJM, vol. 155, doc. 75, Request from the Unión Nacional de Veteranos de la Revolución to Francisco J. Múgica, February 1937.

30. *Acción*, 25 November 1937.

31. AGN, FC, exp. 503.11/3, Emilio Portes Gil to the president of the Colonia Unida de Mexicanos, El Paso, Texas, 18 February 1935.

32. Loyo 1935, 368; *El Universal*, 8 February 1936; AGN, FC, exp. 503.11/3, Silvano Barba González to Francisco J. Múgica, Mexico City, 7 February 1936.

33. AGN, FC, exp. 503.11/3, Cisneros Canto to Luis I. Rodríguez (private secretary to the president), Mexico City, 18 December 1936; NARA, USDS, r. 21, p. 5, doc. 426, Report by the U.S. consul in Matamoros, Tamaulipas, to the Department of State, Matamoros, Tamaulipas, September 1937.

34. *Excelsior*, 8 April 1935.

35. AGN, FC, exp. 503.11/3, Silvano Barba González to the Department of the Federal District, Mexico City, 15 May 1936.

36. *El Universal*, 23 March 1936; ACERMLC, FJM, vol. 3, exp. 34, Silvano Barba González to Francisco J. Múgica, Mexico City, 20 March 1936.

37. *El Universal*, 6 April and 6 May 1936.

38. AGN, FC, exp. 503.11/3, Memorandum from the president's private secretary, National Palace, 15 June 1936.

39. AGN, FC, exp. 503.11/3, Francisco Castillo Nájera to the president, Washington, D.C., 15 July 1936; González 1981, 107.

40. Correa 1941, 39; Novo 1964, 474; *El Nacional*, 21 February 1936.

41. *El Universal*, 8 February 1936; ACERMLC, FJM, vol. 3, exp. 34, Silvano Barba González to Francisco J. Múgica, Mexico City, 20 March 1936; *El Universal*, 23 March 1936.

42. For more information on this episode, see Alanís Enciso 2001b, 141-63.

43. *Diario Oficial de la Federación* 89, no. 10 (12 March 1935): 122-23; Presidential accord of 14 June 1935.

44. *El Universal*, 15 March 1935.

45. *Excelsior*, 20 February 1935; Hoffman 1974, 76, 102-3.

46. *Excelsior*, 5 March 1935; Anguiano Téllez 1995, 54.

47. *Excelsior*, 13 April 1935; *El Universal*, 6 and 12 April 1935.

48. *El Universal*, 8 November 1935.

49. Piñera 1987, 3, 222-23; *Excelsior*, 11 December 1935; *El Universal*, 11 December 1935 and 3 February 1936.

50. ACERMLC, FJM, c. 4, anexo 3.7, doc. 48, Saturnino Cedillo to Francisco J. Múgica, Mexico City, 6 February 1936.

51. *Excelsior*, 11 December 1935.

52. ACERMLC, FJM, c. 4, anexo 3l7, doc. 48, Saturnino Cedillo a Francisco J. Múgica, Mexico City, 6 February 1936; *El Universal*, 3 February 1936.

53. *Informe rendido el 1ro de septiembre de 1936 por el C. presidente la República General de División Lázaro Cárdenas*, 34; *Agricultura*, July–August 1937, 561.

54. AGN, FC, exp. 503.11/3, Memorandum from the president's private secretary, National Palace, 15 June 1936.

55. ACERMLC, FJM, c. 3, anexo 3.7, doc. 47, Exposition of the president of the republic concerning the comprehensive reconstruction of the territories of Baja California and Quintana Roo, Mexico City, 28 September 1936; ACERMLC, FJM, c. 3, anexo 3.7, doc. 47, Lázaro Cárdenas, Declaration to the nation, 28 September 1936; ACERMLC, FJM, vol. 109, doc. 39.

56. ACERMLC, FJM, c. 3, anexo 3.7, doc. 47, Exposition of the president of the republic concerning the comprehensive reconstruction of the territories of Baja California and Quintana Roo, Mexico City, 28 September 1936.

57. Cummings 1981, 19–23; AGN, FC, exp. 503.11/212, Lázaro Cárdenas to Manuel Orozco M. (representative of the Primo Tapio union), San Pedro, Coahuila, 10 November 1936.

58. ACERMLC, FJM, vol. 148, doc. 54, Manuel Díaz Santana (from the Delegación Agraria of Baja California) to Francisco J. Múgica, 22 March 1937, Mexicali, Baja California; *El Regional*, 20 March 1937.

59. *Colonización en el Valle de Mexicali, B.C.* 1958, 170; SEGOB 1939, 77–78; *Agricultura*, September–October 1938, 85–91.

## CHAPTER FOUR

1. *El Nacional*, 30 July 1936.

2. *Diario Oficial de la Federación*, page 1, chapter 2, article 8vo.; chapter 2, article 6; chapter 2, article 10, 29 August 1936.

3. *Diario Oficial de la Federación*, page 1, chapter 1, article 7; secondary title, "Demografía," article 29, article 36, 29 August 1936; Lombardo Toledano 1934, 10.

4. *Diario Oficial de la Federación*, articles 29, 36, 38, and 39, 29 August 1936.

5. The 1926 migration law did refer to farmworkers who wished to return and devote themselves to agriculture.

6. *Diario de los Debates de la Cámara de Diputados*, 1 September 1934, no. 8, p. 10, vol. 1; 5 November 1936, no. 3, p. 9, vol. 4; 28 December 1936, no. 25, p. 25; Secretaría de Gobernación, *Informe del general Abelardo L. Rodríguez ante el Congreso General*, 1 September 1934. The SEGOB reported that by September 1934 it had spent 135,000 pesos on passage for repatriated Mexicans.

7. *El Universal*, 20 May and 25 June 1937.

8. *El Universal*, 31 August 1937; *El Nacional*, 7 October 1937; *Diario de los Debates de la Cámara de Diputados*, 14 December 1937; SEGOB 1937, 26.

9. Concerned over the rise of fascism in Europe, President Franklin Roosevelt proposed a meeting of the American republics to discuss solidarity and maintaining peace in the Western Hemisphere. The conference, which took place in December 1936, also gave Roosevelt a platform from which to promote his "Good Neighbor Policy" toward Latin America. (Translator's note.)

10. *El Universal*, 10 May and 1 September 1937.

11. SEGOB 1937; NARA, USDS, r. 21, p. 5, doc. 426, Report of the U.S. Consul in Matamoros, Tamaulipas, to the Department of State, Matamoros, Tamaulipas, September 1937; *El Universal*, 4 October 1937, 28 October 1937, 18 November 1937, and 11 May 1938.

12. *El Universal*, 28 October 1937.

13. *El Universal*, 18 November 1937, 11 May 1938.

14. AGN, FC, 503.11/3, José Castrejón Pérez to Ignacio García Téllez (minister of the interior), Piedras Negras, Coahuila, 18 October 1938.

15. ACERMLC, FJM, vol. 157, doc. 233, Francisco J. Múgica to Pedro Sarabia, Mexico City, 4 October 1937.

16. ACERMLC, FJM, vol. 146, doc. 233, Francisco J. Múgica to Ramón Beteta, Mexico City, 16 February 1937.

17. AGN, FC, exp. 524/115, Coronel Gabriel Leyva V. to the president, Culiacán, Sinaloa, 18 June 1936.

18. AGN, FC, exp. 503.11/189, Eleazar del Valle (private citizen) to the president regarding colonization on the Oaxacan coast, 4 April 1936.

19. NARA, USDS, r. 20, no. 398, Report by the U.S. consul in Matamoros to the Department of State, Matamoros, Tamaulipas, 30 September 1936; Hoffman 1974, 116.

20. AGN, FC, exp. 503.11/212, Manuel Díaz Romero (member of the Comité de Pequeños y Medianos Agricultores, organized in the United States), Mexicali, Baja California, 3 December 1936.

21. AGN, FC, exp. 503.11/3, Julián Velarde to Luis I. Rodríguez (private secretary to President Cárdenas), Los Angeles, [n.d.].

22. AGN, FC, 503.11/3, José Castrejón Pérez to Ignacio García Téllez, Piedras Negras, Coahuila, 18 October 1938.

23. AGN, DGG, exp. 2/382(24) 24221, c. 52, exp. 41, Francisco Vázquez del Mercado to the Mexican consul in Laredo, Texas, Mexico City, 10 April 1937.

24. *El Nacional*, 2 March 1937.

25. Official Mexican statistics put the number of returnees in 1935 at 15,368; and in 1936 at 11,599. Hoffman 1974, 175.

26. *El Universal*, 21 April 1936.

27. *El Universal*, 25 August, 25 September, 22 December 1936; and 3 June, 31 August 1937; *La Prensa*, 26–29 August 1936, 3–5 June 1937; García 1979, 32–33.

28. *El Universal*, 11 August 1937.

29. *El Universal*, 29 July 1937.

30. Hoffman 1974, 153; *El Universal*, 21 October 1937.

31. *El Universal*, 16 February 1938.

32. AGN, FC, exp. 503.11/3, Letter from José Zertuche to the president, San Antonio, 22 February 1938; *La Prensa*, 21 February 1938, AGN, FC, exp. 503.11/3.

33. *Excelsior*, 8 and 31 March 1938.

34. *Excelsior*, 8 March 1938.

35. AGN, FC, exp. 503.11/3, José Castrejón Pérez to Ignacio García Téllez, Piedras Negras, Coahuila, 18 October 1938.

36. AGN, FC, exp. 503.11/212, Miguel Vargas Solórzano (chief of the Federal Territories Office, Ministry of the Interior) to Julián Jaques and other signatories, Mexico City, 25 October 1938.

37. AGN, FC, exp. 503.11/3, Silvano Barba González to the president, Mexico City, 27 October 1938.

38. *El Universal*, 11 June 1938.

39. Piñera 1987, 3, 208; *El Universal*, 23 July 1938.

40. AGN, FC, exp. 503.11/3, Coronel Rodolfo Sánchez Taboada to the president, Mexicali, Baja California, 15 and 16 October 1938.

41. AGN, FC, exp. 503.11/3, President to Rodolfo Sánchez Taboada, Mexicali, Baja California, 12 October 1939; AGN, FC, exp. 503.11/3, Rodolfo Sánchez Taboada to the president, Mexicali, Baja California, 18 April 1940.

42. AGN, FC, exp. 503.11/3, Mayer G. Varela (official in the president's office) to Rodolfo Suárez Taboada, Mexico City, 19 April 1940; AGN, FC, exp. 503.11/3, "El presente remite acuerdo al secretario de Hacienda y Crédito Público," National Palace, 19 April 1940.

43. *El Heraldo*, 28 April 1938; *El Universal*, 7 May 1938.

44. *El Universal*, 20 October 1938.

45. *El Universal*, 28 October 1938.

46. AGN, FC, exp. 503.11/3, Letter from Guadalupe Ibarra (president of the Terminal Company Workers Union) to Isaac Olive (official within the Autonomous Labor Department), Veracruz, 28 September 1938; *El Universal*, 10 September 1938.

47. AGN, FC, exp. 503.11/3, Manuel Gamio to the chief of the Administrative Department, Mexico City, 18 October 1938.

48. AGN, FC, exp. 503.11/3, Letter from Alberto Fanghanel (general secretary of the Single Union [*Sindicato Único*] of Government Service Workers of the Territory of Baja California Norte) to the territorial governor, Mexicali, Baja California, 6 October 1938.

49. AGN, FC, exp. 503.11/3, Letter from Guadalupe Ibarra to Isaac Olive, Veracruz, 28 September 1938; AGN, FC, exp. 503.11/3, Letter from Ricardo Castro (representative of the Labor Union for workers in the Sugar and Associated Industries of the Mexican Republic) to the president, Carlos A. Carrillo, Veracruz, 5 October 1938; AGN, FC, exp. 503.11/3, Letter from Anastasia Paredes (general secretary of the Superba Union of Male and Female Workers in the Manufacturing of Socks and Hosiery) to the president, León, Guanajuato, 5 October 1938; AGN, FC, exp. 503.11/3, Juan Montejo (secretary general of the General Wood Cutters Union) to the president, Dzibalchén, Hopelchén, Campeche, 9 January 1939. The Single Union of Government Service Workers of Baja California Norte also joined in, contributing 256 pesos. AGN, FC, exp. 503.11/3, Letter from Alberto Fanghanel to the governor of the territory, Mexicali, Baja California, 6 October 1938. The Industrial Union of Mining, Metallurgical, and Associated Workers of the Republic of Mexico sent a check for 337 pesos to help support the deportees. AGN, FC, exp. 503.11/3, Letter from Raúl Castellano (private secretary to the president) to Antonio Villalobos (head of the Department of Labor), National Palace, Mexico City, 4 November 1938; AGN, FC, exp. 503.11/3, Letter from Luis G. Ortiz (a high level official in the Revolutionary Action Union) to the president, Cuautepec, Hidalgo, 20 October 1938; AGN, FC, exp. 503.11/3, Manuel Gamio to the chief of the Administrative Department, Mexico City, 18 October 1938.

50. *El Universal*, 20 October 1938; Hoffman 1974, 160–61.

51. AGN, FC, exp. 503.11/3, Francisco J. Múgica to the president, Mexico City, 18 November 1938.

52. NARA, USDS, roll 21, doc. 998, Monthly report on political matters by the U.S. consul in Nuevo Laredo, Tamaulipas; Nuevo Laredo, Tamaulipas, 1 December 1938; McKay 1982, 410–11.

CHAPTER FIVE

1. AGN, FC, exp. 549.51/17, message to the Mexican community in San Antonio and environs, 1 January 1939.

2. APRB, exp. 308, leg. 8, Ramón Beteta to the consulates, 23 January 1939.

3. APRB, exp. 308, leg. 8, statistics on Mexicans favorable to repatriating with government assistance; economic conditions of workers in Port Arthur (consular office in Beaumont, Texas) and Mexican consulate in Dallas, Mexico City, 31 March 1939.

4. APRB, exp. 308, leg. 8, economic conditions of Mexican workers living in the jurisdiction of Chicago, 31 March 1939.

5. APRB, exp. 308, leg. 8, summary of repatriations requested by the Mexican consulates in the United States, Houston consulate, Mexico City, 3 April 1939.

6. APRB, exp. 308, leg. 8, statistics on Mexicans favorable to repatriating with government assistance; consular office in Beaumont, Texas; and the Mexican consulate in Dallas, Mexico City, 31 March 1939.

7. APRB, exp. 308, leg. 8, statistics on Mexicans favorable to repatriating with government assistance in the jurisdictions of Chicago, Brownsville, and New Orleans, report sent to Mexico City, 31 March 1939; *La Prensa*, 30 November 1938. *El Mundo*, 1 December 1938.

8. APRB, exp. 308, leg. 8, Alejandro M. Bravo to Eduardo Hay (secretary of foreign relations), Brownsville, Texas, 13 February 1939.

9. Ibid.

10. AGN, FC, exp. 503.11/3, Ramón Beteta to the president, San Antonio, 10 April 1939.

11. Llinás Álvarez 1996, 35; *El Heraldo, Excelsior*, 5 April 1939; *La Prensa*, 9 April 1939.

12. APRB, exp. 306, leg. 5, Ramón Beteta to Antonio Villalobos (Autonomous Department of Labor), New York, 5 May 1938.

13. *El Universal*, 2 May and 22 July 1939.

14. Ibid.

15. Llinás Álvarez 1996, 26–35; AGN, FC, exp. 503.11/3-1, Ramón Beteta to the president, New York, 5 May 1939.

16. Hoffman 1974, 156–57.

17. NARA, USDS, roll 21, exp. 502, Report of the U.S. consul in Matamoros, Tamaulipas, 29 April 1939.

18. AGN, FC, exp. 503.11/3, Ramón Beteta to the president, San Antonio, 14 April 1939.

19. *El Heraldo*, 14 and 18 April 1939; *La Prensa*, 27 April 1939; Llinás Álvarez 1996, 35; APRB, exp. 310, leg. 3, Correspondence with the secretary of foreign relations, dossier on general repatriation to Mexico, Ramón Beteta to Eduardo Hay, Corpus Christi, Texas, 16 April 1939; NARA, USDS, roll 21, exp. 502, Report of the U.S. consul in Matamoros, Tamaulipas, 29 April 1939.

20. APRB, exp. 306, leg. 5, Ignacio García Téllez to Ramón Beteta, Mexico City, 18 April 1939.

21. McKay 1982, 416; *La Prensa*, 16 April 1939; *El Heraldo*, 14 and 18 April 1939.

22. AGN, FC, exp. 503.11/3, Ramón Beteta to the president, San Antonio, 14 April 1939; *La Prensa*, 16 April 1939.

23. APRB, exp. 308, leg. 8, Address given by Ramón Beteta, Houston, 20 April 1939.

24. Ibid.

25. The amount allocated by the foreign relations ministry, at the end of December 1938, to assist Mexicans abroad came to no more than 16,000 pesos; *Diario de los Debates de la Cámara de Diputados*, 21 December 1938, no. 23, p. 55, vol. 3.

26. APRB, exp. 306, leg. 5, Ramón Beteta to Ignacio García Téllez, San Antonio, 19 April 1939.

27. *Excelsior*, 21 and 22 April 1939; AGN, FC, exp. 503.11/3, the president to Agustín Leñero, San Luis Potosí, 19 April 1939; AGN, FC, exp. 503.11/3, Eduardo Hay to the Mexican consul in San Antonio, 22 April 1939.

28. *Excelsior*, 21 April 1939.

29. APRB, exp. 309, leg. 2, Ramón Beteta to the president, San Antonio, 27 April 1939; AGN, FC, exp. 503.11/3-1, Ramón Beteta to the president, San Antonio, 25 April 1939.

30. AHSRE, Repatriaciones, exp. 20–23–52, Report by Ramón Beteta to the president on his trip to the United States, which, together with the work being carried out in the 18 March agricultural settlement in Tamaulipas, is part of the program to repatriate Mexicans working in the United States, Matamoros, Tamaulipas, 27 April 1939; *El Universal*, 2 May 1939.

31. NARA, USDS, roll 21, exp. 502, Report of the U.S. consul in Matamoros, Tamaulipas, 29 April 1939; McKay 1982, 416–17; *La Prensa*, 29 April, 4 May, and 7 June 1939.

32. AGN, FC, exp. 503.11/31, Ramón Beteta to the president, 11 August 1939.

33. *La Prensa*, 9 and 16 April 1939.

34. *La Prensa*, 27 April 1939; Balderrama and Rodríguez 1995, 149.

35. AGN, FC, exp. 503.11/3, Ramón Beteta to the president, San Antonio, 10 April 1939.

36. Conversation with Elena Zúñiga, Valle Hermoso, Tamaulipas, 6 April 1939; AGN, FC, exp. 503.11/3, Ramón Beteta to the president, New York, 10 May 1939.

37. AGN, FC, exp. 503.11/3–1, Ramón Beteta to the president, New York, 10 May 1939.

38. Balderrama and Rodríguez 1995, 149; Llinás Álvarez 1996, 35; AGN, FC, exp. 503.11/3, Ramón Beteta to the president, New York, 10 May 1939.

39. AGN, FC, exp. 503.11/3, Ramón Beteta to the president, New York, 10 May 1939.

40. *El Mundo*, 23 April 1939.

41. *Acción*, 25 April 1939.

42. *El Mundo*, 23 April 1939.

43. *El Heraldo*, 22 April 1939; *Excelsior*, 22 April 1939.

44. *El Popular*, Mexico City, 20 April 1939.

45. AGN, FC, exp. 565.4/1940; Report by Manuel Gamio to the president, Mexico City, 13 February 1939.

46. AGN, FC, exp. 503.11/3, Fernando Foglio M. (assistant minister of agriculture and development) to Agustín Leñero, Mexico City, 21 April 1939; *Excelsior*, 18 April 1939; *El Heraldo*, 5 and 22 April 1939.

47. *El Porvenir*, 16 April 1939.

48. *El Mundo*, 23 April 1939.

49. AGN, FC, exp. 503.11/3, Fernando Foglio M. to Agustín Leñero, Mexico City, 21 April 1939; AGN, FC, exp. 503.11/3, Fernando Foglio M. to the president, 24 April 1939; *El Mundo*, 13 and 23 April 1939; *El Heraldo*, 14 and 22 April 1939.

50. AGN, FC, exp. 503.11/3, the president to the chief engineer of the Irrigation System in Pabellón (Aguascalientes) and Ciudad Juárez (Chihuahua), 18 May 1939.

51. AGN, FC, exp. 503.11/3, President Lázaro Cárdenas to the state governors, National Palace, 12 April 1939; AGN, FC, exp. 503.11/3, the president to Lieutenant Colonel Rafael M. Pedrajo (governor of Baja California Sur), National Palace, 12 April 1939; *El Mundo, El Heraldo, La Opinión*, 14 April 1939.

52. AGN, FC, exp. 503.11/3, Gustavo L. Talamantes to the president, Chihuahua, 25 April 1939.

53. NARA, USDS, RG59, 311.1215/128, Report by Lee R. Blohm to the U.S. embassy, Chihuahua, Mexico, 19 March 1939; *El Mundo*, 23 April 1939. The Northern Agricultural Company offered a million hectares. *El Heraldo*, 16 April 1939.

54. AGN, FC, exp. 503.11/3, Gustavo L. Talamantes to the president, 25 April 1939; NARA, USDS, RG59, 311.1215/128, Report by Lee R. Blohm to the U.S. embassy, Chihuahua, Mexico,

19 March 1939; AGN, FC, exp. 503.11/3, Fernando Foglio to the president's private secretary, Mexico City, 9 May 1939.

55. NARA, USDS, RG59, 311.1215/128, Report by Lee R. Blohm to the U.S. embassy, Chihuahua, Mexico, 19 March 1939.

56. AGN, FC, exp. 503.11/3, Rafael Rangel (governor of Guanajuato) to the president, Guanajuato, 21 April 1939; *El Heraldo*, 22 April 1939; *El Porvenir*, 21 April 1939.

57. *La Opinión*, 24 April 1939; *El Mundo*, 24 April 1939; *Excelsior*, 24 April 1939.

58. AGN, FC, exp. 503.11/3, Marte R. Gómez to the president, Ciudad Victoria, Tamaulipas, 19 April 1939.

59. AGN, FC, exp. 503.11/3, Elpidio Perdomo to the president, May 1940.


CHAPTER SIX

1. On the Spanish Civil War, see Jackson 1985, 183–277; Thomas 1967, 135–229; and Preston 1967.

2. See Matesanz 1995, 445–54; and Fagen 1975, 34–35.

3. Campbell 1976, 83–84, 107–8. For more on the opposition groups, see Márquez Morfi 1988, 138–43; and Matesanz 1995, 363–435.

4. *El Mundo*, 23 June 1939.

5. Ibid.

6. *El Universal*, 14 April 1939.

7. *Excelsior*, 23 January 1939.

8. *La Prensa*, 12 April 1939.

9. AGN, FAC, exp. 549.5/38, newspaper clipping sent by Eliseo Valles Cortés to the president, National Palace, 29 April 1941. This document is located in the Fondo Ávila Camacho, although it refers to events that occurred in 1939.

10. Ibid.

11. *La Prensa*, 28 June 1939; *La Opinión*, 29 June 1939.

12. *La Opinión*, 24 June 1939.

13. *La Opinión*, 29 July 1939.

14. NARA, USDS, RG59, 311.1215/128, Report by Lee R. Blohm to the U.S. embassy, Chihuahua, Mexico, 19 March 1939.

15. APRB, exp. 306, leg. 5, Ramón Beteta to Ignacio García Téllez, San Antonio, 19 April 1939; Pla Brugat 1994, 219. The first vessel carried 1,599 passengers, the second, 994, and the third, 2,065.

16. AGN, FC, exp. 503.11/3, Report by Ramón Beteta to the president, San Antonio, 17 April 1939.

17. ACERMLC, FJM, c. 7, exp. 300, doc. 1, Lázaro Cárdenas, Decree of expropriation by which the Lower Rio Grande Valley flood controls, installed to protect its irrigation system, were declared a public utility.

18. *El Mundo*, 24 April 1939.

19. ASRA, ACAG, exp. 4928-I-C, Observations by Manuel Gamio concerning the possibility of founding settlements in the Lower Rio Grande Valley, 13 February 1939; AGN, FC, exp. 565.4/1940, Manuel Gamio to the president, Mexico City, 13 February 1939.

20. *El Mundo*, 23 and 24 April 1939; NARA, USDS, roll 21, exp. 502, Report by the U.S. consul in Matamoros, Tamaulipas, 29 April 1939. Báez n.d.

21. *Memoria de la Secretaría de Relaciones Exteriores*, September 1939 to August 1940, 423; AGN, FC, exp. 503.11/3-1, the president to Ramón Beteta, C. Valles, San Luis Potosí, 21 April 1939; AGN, APC, r. 4, part 1, 609-16, Reports on government officials' tours through the nation's states.

22. AGN, FC, exp. 503.11/3, the president to Eduardo Hay, Ramírez, Tamaulipas, 23 April 1939; AGN, FC, exp. 503.11/3-1, Ramón Beteta to Agustín Leñero, San Antonio, 25 April 1939; *El Universal*, 14 June 1939; *Excelsior*, 22 April 1939.

23. ACERMLC, FJM, c. 29, carp. 4, doc. 4, presidential agreement on the [Public] Works of the Lower Rio Grande, Camp C1-K19, Tamaulipas, 24 April 1939; *El Mundo*, 27 April 1939.

24. Ibid.

25. Ibid.

26. *El Mundo*, 24 April 1939; AGN, APC, r. 4, part 1, 609-16, Reports on government officials' tours through the nation's states.

27. Chávez Ramírez 1988, 62. The state's population increased from 344,039 in 1930 to 455,849 in 1940. Gobierno del Estado de Tamaulipas 1940, 9.

28. *El Universal*, 27 April and 2 May 1939; *Memoria de la Secretaría de Gobernación*, September 1938 to August 1939, 54.

29. AGN, APC, r. 4, part 1, 609-16, Reports on government officials' tours through the nation's states; *El Mundo*, 24 April 1939.

30. AGN, FC, exp. 565.4/1940, Manuel Gamio to the president, Mexico City, 13 February 1939; ASRA, ACAG, exp. 4928-1-C, Observations by Manuel Gamio on the possibility of founding settlements in the Lower Rio Grande Valley, 13 February 1939.

31. APRB, exp. 309, leg. 2, Ramón Beteta to the president, San Antonio, 10 April 1939. *El Porvenir*, 6 May 1939. *El Mundo*, 13 April 1939.

32. APRB, exp. 309, leg. 2, the president to Ramón Beteta, Mexico City, 13 April 1939. AGN, FC, exp. 565.4/1940, Ignacio García Téllez to Agustín Leñero, Mexico City, 12 April 1939; *El Mundo*, 13 April 1939; APRB, exp. 306, leg. 5, Ramón Beteta to Ignacio García Téllez, San Antonio, 19 April 1939.

33. APRB, exp. 309, leg. 2, the president to Ramón Beteta, Mexico City, 13 April 1939.

34. ASRA, CAG, exp. 4928-1-C, Report by the engineering technician Mario A. Grajales (assistant head of the Office of Population in Matamoros), 28 February 1939; *El Porvenir*, 23 April 1939.

35. AGN, FC, exp. 503.11/3, Ramón Beteta to the president, San Antonio, 10 April 1939; AGN, FC, exp. 503.11/3, Fernando Foglio M. to Agustín Leñero, Mexico City, 21 April 1939.

36. APRB, exp. 309, leg. 2, Ramón Beteta to the president, Brownsville, Texas, 16 April 1939; AGN, FC, exp. 565.4/1940, Ramón Beteta to the president, Matamoros, Tamaulipas, 17 April 1939.

37. *Excelsior*, 25 April 1939.

38. *El Universal*, 5 May 1939, 21 June 1938.

39. APRB, exp. 306, leg. 5, Ignacio García Téllez to Ramón Beteta, San Antonio, 18 April 1939.

1. *Periódico Oficial del Gobierno del Estado de Tamaulipas*, 18 November 1938, 2–3. APRB, exp. 307, leg. 4, Eduardo Chávez (director of [public] works for the Bajo Río Bravo and the official in charge of implementing repatriation inside Mexico and of administering the 18 March colony) to Ramón Beteta, Camp C1-K9, Tamaulipas, 30 April 1939.

2. *Excelsior*, 24 April 1939; AGN, FC, exp. 503.11/3-1, the president of the Republic, concerning the establishment of the 18 March colony for repatriated nationals, Torreón, Coahuila, 8 May 1939; Tamaulipas, 24 April 1939.

3. According to Gilberto Loyo, the type of building seen most frequently in the country "is the detached house, that is, a generally small, one-family house, almost always set at some distance from others, so that in provincial towns it is to all intents and purposes a free-standing house in the strictest sense of the word." Loyo 1948, 89.

4. AGN, FC, exp. 503.11/3-1, the president, concerning the establishment of the 18 March colony for repatriated nationals, Torreón, Coahuila, 8 May 1939; Tamaulipas, 24 April 1939.

5. Ibid.

6. APRB, exp. 307, leg. 4, Eduardo Chávez to Ramón Beteta, Camp C1-K9, Tamaulipas, 30 April 1939; APRB, exp. 309, leg. 2, Ramón Beteta to the president, New York, 10 May 1939.

7. APRB, exp. 309, leg. 2, Ramón Beteta to Lázaro Cárdenas, San Antonio, 26 April 1939; APRB, exp. 306, leg. 5, Ramón Beteta to Ignacio García Téllez, San Antonio, 26 April 1939; *La Opinión*, 24 April 1939; *La Prensa*, 5 May 1939. Jesús Barajas appears in table 5.3, but as wishing to relocate to Ocotlán, Jalisco; he perhaps changed his mind about where he wanted to go after signing on to return.

8. *El Heraldo*, 5 April 1939; AGN, FC, exp. 503.11/3-1, Ramón Beteta to Agustín Leñero, San Antonio, 25 April 1939; NARA, r. 21, no. 513, Herndon W. Goforth (U.S. consul in Matamoros, Tamaulipas), 30 June 1939.

9. McKay 1982, 420; AHSRE, Repatriaciones, exp. 20-23-52, Ramón Beteta to Ernesto Hidalgo (official in the Foreign Relations Ministry), 27 May 1939; *Excelsior*, 16 and 23 May 1939. The group comprised 100 families and approximately 500 individuals.

10. McKay 1982, 420–21; *La Prensa*, 11 May 1939.

11. McKay 1982, 422. Although the precise number of persons who returned to Mexico from this part of Texas is not known, reports submitted at the time indicate that more than 362 families resettled in Mexico.

12. *La Prensa*, 28 May and 7 June 1939; McKay 1982, 425.

13. Morison et al. 1993, 749; interview with Félix Araujo Ramírez, Valle Hermoso, Tamaulipas, 6 April 1997; interview with Bartolo Loera Castillo, Valle Hermoso, Tamaulipas, 6 April 1997.

14. AGN, FC, exp. 503.11/3-1, report from the Ministry of Communications and Public Works to the president, n.d.

15. McKay 1982, 425; *La Prensa*, 19 and 25 June 1939.

16. Interview with Elena Zúñiga Rosales de Araujo, Valle Hermoso, Tamaulipas, 6 April 1997.

17. McKay 1982, 420. A group of sixteen families, totaling sixty persons, made up the first contingent. The number of persons who left San Antonio totaled forty-four. AGN, FC,

exp. 503.11/3-1, Mexican consul in San Antonio to the president, San Antonio, 21 June 1939; *La Prensa*, 7, 20, and 28 June 1939.

18. McKay 1982, 424; *Excelsior*, 21 July 1939; *La Prensa*, 12 July 1939; ACA, SRA, leg. 355, Memorandum from Alberta Munguía de Amador to director of the Department of Colonization and Agrarian Affairs, 15 June 1971.

19. *Diario de los Debates de la Cámara de Diputados*, 1 September 1939; Mexico 1939; Mexico, *Memoria de la Secretaría de Comunicaciones y Obras Públicas presentada al Congreso de la Unión por el C. secretario del ramo Ing. Melquiades Angulo*, September 1939 to August 1940 (Mexico City: 1940), 151.

20. Mexico 1940, 23; APRB, exp. 308, leg. 8, Ignacio H. Sanata (assistant chief of the Population Service), the flow of deportees and repatriated nationals between January 1939 and 16 May of that year.

21. McKay 1982, 429; interview with José Luis Serrano, Valle Hermoso, Tamaulipas, 6 April 1997.

22. AHSRE, Repatriaciones, exp. 20-23-52, Report sent by Ramón Beta to the president from the 18 March colony, San Antonio, 11 August 1939.

23. *La Prensa*, 7, 12, and 14 August 1939; interview with Elena Zúñiga Rosales de Araujo, Valle Hermoso, 6 April 1997.

24. *La Prensa*, 12 July 1939; AGN, FC, exp. 503.11/3-1, undated report on the 18 March colony by Ramón Beta to the president; *Memoria de la Secretaría de Gobernación*, September 1939 to August 1940, 69.

25. AGN, FC, exp. 503.11/3-1, undated report by Ramón Beta to the president on the 18 March colony.

26. Gobierno del Estado de Tamaulipas 1940, 18; SEGOB 1940, 40, 69, 59; NARA, r. 21, no. 513, Herndon W. Goforth. Tamaulipas, 30 June 1939; Aranda 1950, 14.

27. McKay 1982, 431; interviews with Bartolo Loera Castillo, Francisco Villegas Herrera, Miguel Algape Garza, José Dolores Ambriz, Valle Hermoso, Tamaulipas, 6 April 1997.

28. ASRA, CAG, leg. 437, Eduardo Chávez to Adolfo Orive Alba (spokesman for the National Irrigation Commission), Mexico City, undated; ASRA, CAG, leg. 437, Manuel I. Zazaua (general director of the Lower Rio Grande Irrigation District) to the National Bank of Agricultural Credit, Mexico City, 6 February 1943.

29. Interview with Bartolo Loera Castillo, José Luis Serrano, Elena Zúñiga, and Francisco Villegas Herrera, Valle Hermoso, Tamaulipas, 6 April 1997.

30. Interview with Bartolo Loera Castillo, José Luis Serrano, Elena Zuñiga, and Francisco Villegas Herrera, Valle Hermoso, Tamaulipas, 6 April 1997.

31. AGN, APLC, r. 10, part 1, no. 1128, exp. 524.5, Letter from Marcelino Sepúlveda forwarded to the minister of foreign relations by Javier Osorio (Mexican consul in Corpus Christi, Texas), 5 August 1939.

32. AGN, FC, exp. 503.11/3-1, Genaro Mendoza (general secretary of the Regional Federation of Workers of Matamoros) to Lázaro Cárdenas, Matamoros, Tamaulipas, 24 September 1939.

33. AGN, FC, exp. 503.11/3-1, Juan Gallardo Moreno, in a memorandum to the governor of Tamaulipas, Mexico City, 18 August 1939.

34. AGN, FC, exp. 503.11/3-1, Francisco B. Múgica to the president, Matamoros, Tamaulipas, 18 July 1940; AGN, AC, exp. 503.11/1. fol. 3, Telegram from some of the 18 March colony settlers to the president, Mexico City, 24 December 1940.

1. APRB, exp. 312, leg. 6, Ramón Beteta to the president, Los Angeles, 19 July 1939.

2. Ibid.

3. *La Prensa*, 12 June 1939; *La Opinión*, 21 June 1939; AGN, FC, exp. 503.11/3, Coronel Ignacio M. Beteta to Salvador S. Romero, 21 June 1939.

4. AGN, FC, exp. 711/203, Ramón Beteta to the president, 19 July 1939; *Los Angeles Times*, July 1939.

5. APRB, exp. 312, leg. 6, Ramón Beteta to Francisco Castillo Nájera, San Diego, 15 July 1939; APRB, exp. 309, leg. 2, Ramón Beteta to the president, San Francisco, 24 July 1939.

6. APRB, exp. 312, leg. 6, Ramón Beteta to Francisco Castillo Nájera (Mexico's ambassador to the United States), San Diego, 15 July 1939.

7. *La Opinión*, 11 August 1939; AGN, FC, exp. 711/203, Ramón Beteta to the president, San Francisco, 24 July 1939.

8. AGN, FC, exp. 711/203, Ramón Beteta to the president, San Francisco, 24 July 1939.

9. *Excelsior*, 9 and 10 July 1939; *La Opinión*, 8 July 1939.

10. *La Opinión*, 21 June 1939.

11. AGN, FC, exp. 711/203; Ramón Beteta to the president, San Francisco, 19 July 1939; Hoffman 1974, 156-57; *Los Angeles Times*, 20 June 1939; *El Mundo*, 21 July 1939.

12. AGN, FC, exp. 711/203, Ramón Beteta to Lázaro Cárdenas, San Francisco, 19 July 1939; Hoffman 1974, 156-57; *Los Angeles Times*, 20 July 1939; *El Mundo*, 21 July 1939.

13. AGN, FC, exp. 711/203, Ramón Beteta to Lázaro Cárdenas, San Francisco, 19 July 1939; *La Opinión*, 20 and 25 July 1939.

14. *Excelsior*, 6 June 1939; *La Prensa*, 7 June 1939; *El Mundo*, 10 June 1939.

15. AGN, FC, exp. 503.11/3-1, Ramón Beteta to the president, San Antonio, 27 April 1939; *New York Times*, 17 and 19 July 1939.

16. *New York Times*, 17 July 1939. *Mexican Life* 15, no. 3 (March 1939): 9.

17. *New York Times*, 17 July 1939.

18. AHSRE, Repatriaciones, exp. 20-23-52, Report on the 18 March colony sent by Ramón Beteta to the president, San Antonio, 11 August 1939; AHSRE, Repatriaciones, exp. 20-23-52, Ramón Beteta to the president, San Antonio, 11 August 1939.

19. AGN, FC, exp. 503.11/3, Ramón Beteta to the president, San Antonio, 11 August 1939.

20. Ibid.

21. According to Gamio's calculations, the Mexican population in the United States numbered some 500,000. Gamio 1931. Another source indicates that the number of people of Mexican origin distributed across the states where they were most heavily concentrated came only to 377,433. Reisler 1976, 270.

22. *La Prensa*, 9 September 1939; AGN, FC, exp. 503.11/3, Pedro Gragoso (secretary general of the Los Angeles branch of the Committee of the Mexican Revolution) to the president, Los Angeles, 13 September 1939; AGN, FC, exp. 503.11/3, Juan Gallardo Moreno to the secretary of foreign relations, National Palace, 19 September 1939.

23. AGN, FC, exp. 503.11/3-1, Ramón Beteta to the president, Brownsville, Texas, 9 and 10 August 1939; AGN, FC, exp. 503.11/3, Carlos A. Calderón, Mexican consul in Brownsville, Texas, 17 October 1939.

24. AGN, FC, exp. 503.11/3-1, Moisés Reséndez and other returnees to the president, Matamoros, Tamaulipas, 13 November 1939.

25. *El Universal* and *Excelsior*, 23 April 1939.

26. *La Opinión*, 24 April 1939.

27. *Excelsior*, 23 April 1939; *El Porvenir*, 28 April 1939.

28. *El Porvenir*, 6 May 1939.

29. AGN, FC, exp. 503.11/3, Antonio E. Florencia to the president, 1 June 1939.

30. Ibid.

31. Ibid.

32. Ibid.

33. *El Heraldo*, 11 March 1939; *Acción*, 14 January 1939; AGN, FC, exp. 503.11/3, Ignacio M. Beteta (head of the Physical Education Department) to Salvador S. Romero (director of Mexico's National Railways), Huatabampo, Sonora, 21 June 1939.

34. González Navarro 1994, 3, 302–3. González Navarro indicates that the number of repatriated that the government contemplated for resettlement in the Naranjo Valley was 16,000. *El Universal*, in contrast, in its issue of 20 July 1939, cites the figure that I use, which to me seems more convincing. ASRA, CAG, Colonia El Naranjo, exp. 9296-4, May 1939. *El Mundo*, 25 July 1939.

35. ASRA, CAG, Colonia El Naranjo, exp. 9246-2-C, Funds supplied to the Naranjo Valley Colony, 2 November 1942.

36. I am grateful to Professor Miguel Ángel Herrera, of the Colegio de San Luis, for the information provided here. Interview with Santos García Maldonado, resident of El Naranjo. Interview with Miguel Carreón, president of the El Salto agricultural colony, San Luis Potosí, 26 February 1999; Documents and archive of the office of the president of the El Salto colony, File on the Comisión de Colonización Zona Norte, exp. 403-2-071, Inspection report provided to the El Salto and El Naranjo colonies, 1948; *Diario Oficial de la Federación*, 16 July 1941; *La Prensa*, 9 September 1939.

37. *La Prensa*, 13 September 1939; ASRA, CAG, Colonia El Naranjo, exp. 9296-4, May 1936.

38. *La Prensa*, 9 September 1939.

39. AGN, FC, exp. 503.11/3, Colonel Rodolfo Sánchez Taboada to the president, Mexicali, Baja California, 5 May and 28 July 1939; *Diario de los Debates de la Cámara de Diputados*, 1 September 1939.

40. AGN, FC, exp. 503.11/3, Agreement with the Agriculture Ministry regarding the establishment of a colonization office in Baja California, 2 August 1939.

41. "Pro-Magaña" refers to Gildardo Magaña, the then governor of Michoacán. Before his sudden death in 1939, he was suggested as a possible successor to Cárdenas. (Translator's note.)

42. *La Opinión*, 27 August and 13 September 1939; AGN, FC, exp. 503.11/3, Rodolfo Sánchez Taboada to the president, Ensenada, Baja California, 9 August 1939.

43. *La Opinión*, 10 September 1939.

44. AGN, FC, exp. 503.11/3, According to the Agriculture Ministry, 22 August 1939.

45. *La Opinión*, 9 October 1939.

46. AGN, FC, exp. 503.11/3-1, report from the Communications and Public Works Ministry to the president, n.d.

47. *El Universal*, 14 June 1939; AGN, APLC, r. 10, part 1, Castillo Nájera to the president, Washington, D.C., 31 July 1939.

48. AGN, FC, exp. 503.11/3-1, Ramón Beteta to the president, San Antonio, 11 August 1939.

49. AHSRE, Repatriaciones, exp. 20-23-52, Ramón Beteta to the president, San Antonio, 11 August 1939; *Informe presidencial leído ante la XXVII legislatura: Diario de los Debates de la Cámara de Diputados*, 1 September 1939.

50. AGN, FC, exp. 503.11/3, Ramón Beteta to the president, San Antonio, 11 August 1939.

51. Ibid.

52. AGN, FC, exp. 503.11/3, Mariano S. Moreno to the president, San Benito, Texas, 1 January 1940.

53. AGN, FC, exp. 503.11/3, Ignacio Zamora (from the Bloque de Mineros Mexicanos in San Antonio) to the president, San Antonio, 29 February 1940.

54. AGN, FC, exp. 549.5/11, Pedro Fregoso, a resident of Los Angeles, to the president, 4 July 1941, Los Angeles.

55. AGN, FC, exp. 503.11/3, Felipe Gil Cantú (general secretary of the BNCA's Workers Union) to the president, 2 January 1940; AGN, FC, exp. 503.11/3-1, Manuel Gamio forwarding a communication from Eduardo Chávez to the office of the president's private secretary, Mexico City, 16 January 1940.

56. AGN, FC, exp. 503.11/3-1, Juan Gallardo Moreno to Eduardo Chávez, National Palace, 6 February 1940; AGN, FC, exp. 503.11/3-1, Mariano Padilla (secretary for Acción Campesina) to the president, Mexico City, 2 April 1940.

57. AGN, FC, exp. 503.11/3-1, Feliciano Sóstenez to the president, 24 March 1940.

58. AGN, FC, exp. 503.11/3-1, Agustín Leñero to Efraín Buenrostro, Nacional Palace, 10 June 1940.

59. AGN, FC, exp. 503.11/3-1, Indalecio Ezequiel (general secretary of the 18 March Settlers League) to the president, Matamoros, Tamaulipas, 24 June 1940.

60. AHA, FAS, c. 3337, exp. 45736, fols. 71, Report to the executive director, concerning the observations made on the Lower Rio Grande [Valley] Project by engineer Andrew Weiss, Mexico City, 6 September 1941.

61. AGN, FC, exp. 503.11/3-1, Indalecio Esquivel to the president, Matamoros, Tamaulipas, 24 June 1940; AGN, FC, exp. 503.11/3-1, the president to the 18 March Settlers League, Mexico City, 30 June 1940.

62. AGN, FC, exp. 503.11/3-1, the president to Eduardo Suárez (Minister of the Treasury and Public Credit), 30 June 1940.

63. AGN, FC, exp. 503.11/3-1, the president to the 18 March Settlers League, Mexico City, 30 June 1940.

64. AGN, FC, exp. 503.11/3-1, Representation of the Anáhuac and 18 March settlements to the president, Matamoros, Tamaulipas, 28 November 1940.

65. AGN, FC, exp. 503.11/3-1, Indalecio Ezquivel to the president, Matamoros, Tamaulipas, 24 June 1940.

66. AGN, FC, exp. 503.11/3-1, Vicente Santibáñez to the president, Torreón, Coahuila, 11 September 1940.

67. AGN, FC, exp. 503.11/1, fol. 2, José María Treviño to General Manuel Ávila Camacho, Matamoros, Tamaulipas, 4 December 1940.

68. AGN, AC, exp. 503.11/1, fol. 3, telegram from some of the 18 March colony's settlers to the president, Mexico City, 24 December 1940.

69. AHA, FAS, 3337, exp. 45736, fols. 71, Report to the executive director, concerning the observations made on the Lower Rio Grande [Valley] Project by engineer Andrew Weiss, Mexico City, 6 September 1941.

70. AGN, AC, exp. 503.11/1, Vicente Aparicio (Social Delegation of the 18 March colony) to the president, 30 September 1946.

71. ASRA, CAG, leg. 437, Manuel I. Zazaua (general manager of the Rio Bravo Irrigation District) to the Agronomy Department, National Irrigation Commission, Camp C1-K9, Tamaulipas, 21 January 1943.

72. *Excelsior*, 12 October 1939; *El Universal*, 26 June 1940; ASRA, CAG, leg. 437, Manuel I. Zazaua to the National Bank of Agricultural Credit. Mexico City, 6 February 1943.

73. AGN, AC, exp. 549.5/7, Teódulo E. Pérez (Mexican resident of San Francisco) to the president, San Francisco, 16 December 1940; AGN, AC, exp. 549.5/13, Blas Chacón H. (Mexican resident of Brawley, Calif.) to the president, Brawley, Calif., 23 December 1940; AGN, AC, exp. 549.5/14, José Álamo (representative of the Mexican Honorary Society of Mesa, Arizona) to the president, Mesa, Arizona, 1 and 8 January 1941; AGN, AC, exp. 549.5/3, Petition from Los Angeles, 12 March 1940; AGN, AC, exp. 549.5/6, Petition from Decatur, Ind., 12 November 1940; AGN, AC, exp. 549.5/8, Petition from Penryn, Calif., 17 December 1940; AGN, AC, exp. 549.5/27, Petition from Fort Collins, Colo., 25 January 1941; AGN, AC, exp. 549.5/35, Petition from Colton, Calif., 21 March 1941.

74. *El Mundo*, 6 February 1940; *Excelsior*, 6 February 1940.

75. AGN, FC, exp. 503.11/7, the interior minister to the Mexican consul in the United States, Mexico City, 20 June 1940; *El Universal*, 28 June 1940.

76. *El Mexicano*, 14 November 1940.

77. Godínez 1991, 311; *La Opinión*, 28 September 1939.

78. AGN, FC, 503.11/3, José Castrejón Pérez to Ignacio García Téllez, Piedras Negras, Coahuila, 18 October 1938.

79. In large measure, the notion of wide-ranging support for the return of Mexican nationals had its roots in the repatriation promoted by the Mexican government after the 1848 war with the United States, when the government pushed a plan to bring to Mexico those Mexicans who—following the conclusion of the war—had remained on what was now the U.S. side of the border. This idea persisted to the end of the nineteenth century and was revived in the twentieth, when the emphasis became promoting the return of migrant agricultural workers who "had taken advantage of their stay in the United States."

# BIBLIOGRAPHY

PRIMARY SOURCES

*Archives*

Archivo del Centro de Estudios de la Revolución Mexicana, Lázaro Cárdenas, A.C.
(Jiquilpan, Michoacán)
    Fondo Francisco J. Múgica
    Fondo Lázaro Cárdenas
Archivo General de la Nación (Mexico City)
    Fondo Archivo Particular de Lázaro Cárdenas
    Fondo Departamento del Trabajo
    Fondo Dirección General de Gobierno
    Fondo Presidente
        Ávila Camacho
        Cárdenas
        Obregón-Calles
    Fondo Secretaría de Relaciones Exteriores
Archivo Histórico del Agua (Comisión Nacional del Agua, Ciudad de México)
    Fondo Aprovechamiento Superficiales
Archivo Histórico de la Secretaría de Relaciones Exteriores (Mexico City)
Archivo Particular de Ramón Beteta
Archivo de la Secretaría de la Reforma Agraria (Mexico City)
    Colonias Agrícolas y Ganaderas
National Archives and Records Administration, College Park, Maryland
    U.S. Department of State
        Records of the Immigration and Naturalization Service, Series A, Part 2, Mexican
            Immigration 1906–1930 (Microfilm)


*Newspapers and Magazines*

*Acción* (Nogales, Sonora)
*El Agricultor Mexicano*
*Agricultura*
*Agricultura y Ganadería*
*El Demócrata Fronterizo* (Laredo, Texas)

*Diario de los Debates de la Cámara
    de Diputados* (Mexico City)
*Diario Oficial de la Federación* (Mexico City)
*Evolución* (Laredo, Texas)
*Excelsior* (Mexico City)

*El Heraldo* (Chihuahua, Chihuahua)
*El Imparcial* (Mexico City)
*Los Angeles Times*
*Mexican Life*
*El Mexicano* (Ciudad Juárez, Chihuahua)
*El Mundo* (Tampico, Tamaulipas)
*El Nacional* (Mexico City)
*New York Times*
*La Opinión* (Los Angeles)

*Periódico Oficial del Gobierno del Estado de Tamaulipas* (Tamaulipas)
*Popular* (Mexico City)
*El Porvenir, El Periódico de la Frontera* (Monterrey, Nuevo León)
*La Prensa* (San Antonio)
*El Regional* (Baja California)
*El Universal* (Mexico City)

## Interviews

José Dolores Ambriz, son of repatriated national. Arrived at the age eleven from Violeta, Texas. Valle Hermoso, Tamaulipas, 6 April 1997.

Elena Zúñiga Rosales de Araujo, repatriated from Houston. Valle Hermoso, Tamaulipas, 6 April 1997.

Miguel Carreón, president of the El Salto Agricultural Colony, San Luis Potosí. El Salto, San Luis Potosí, 26 February 1999.

Bartolo Loera Castillo, repatriated from Hop, Texas. Valle Hermoso, Tamaulipas, 6 April 1997.

Renato Vázquez Farias, town historian of Valle Hermoso. Valle Hermoso, Tamaulipas, 6 April 1997.

Miguel Aldape Garza, son of Porfirio Aldape Treviño, who repatriated from Harlingen, Texas. Valle Hermoso, Tamaulipas, 6 April 1997.

Francisco Villegas Herrera, repatriated in 1932 to Ciudad Anáhuac, Nuevo León. Arrived from Brady, Texas. Valle Hermoso, Tamaulipas, 6 April 1997.

Santos García Maldonado, resident of Naranjo, San Luis Potosí since 1937. Born in 1921 in Rascón, San Luis Potosí. El Salto, San Luis Potosí, 26 February 1999.

Pedro Martínez Méndez, son of repatriated national. Born 22 November 1939. His family arrived from Roseboy, Texas. Valle Hermosa, Tamaulipas, 6 April 1997.

José Luis Serrano Navarro, repatriated from Baytown, Texas. Valle Hermoso, Tamaulipas, 6 April 1997.

Félix Araujo Ramírez, flood barrier worker on the Rio Grande River and resident of the municipality of Matamoros since 1935. Valle Hermoso, Tamaulipas, 6 April 1997.

## SECONDARY SOURCES

Acuña, Rodolfo. *América ocupada: Los chicanos y su lucha de liberación*. Mexico City: Era, 1976.

Alanís Enciso, Fernando Saúl. "La Constitución de 1917 y la emigración de trabajadores mexicanos en Estados Unidos." *Relaciones: Estudios de Historia y Sociedad* 22 (Summer 2001a).

———. "La colonización de Baja California con mexicanos provenientes de Estados Unidos (1935-1939)." *Frontera Norte* 13, no. 26 (July–December 2001b).

———. "El gobierno de México y la repatriación de mexicanos de Estados Unidos, 1934-1940." PhD diss., Colegio de México, 2000a.

———. "Los primeros pasos hacia la construcción de la política de emigración de mexicanos a Estados Unidos: El caso de la Secretaría de Gobernación." In *La Secretaría de Gobernación: Acción política del gobierno mexicano: Población y movimientos migratorios*, vol. 4, coordinated by Luz María Valdés. Mexico City: Secretaría de Gobernación/Instituto Nacional de Estudios Históricos de la Revolución Mexicana, 2000a.

———. *El primer programa bracero y el gobierno de México, 1917–1918*. Mexico City: Colegio de San Luis, 1999.

Anguiano, Arturo. *El Estado y la política obrera del cardenismo*. Mexico City: Era, 1986.

Anguiano Téllez, María Eugenia. *Agricultura y migración en el valle de Mexicali*. Mexico City: Colegio de la Frontera Norte, 1995.

Ankerson, Dudley. *El caudillo agrarista: Saturnino Cedillo y la revolución mexicana en San Luis Potosí*. Mexico City: Gobierno del Estado de San Luis Potosí/INEHRM/Secretaría de Gobernación, 1994.

Aranda Apellaniz, Javier. "Exploración sanitaria del río Bravo, Tamaulipas, parasitosis intestinal." Thesis, UNAM, 1950.

Arroyo, Luis Lombardo. "Chicano Participation in Organized Labor: The COI in Los Angeles, 1938–1950. An Extended Research Note." *Aztlán: International Journal of Chicano Studies Research* 6, no. 2 (1975).

Ashby, Joe C. *Organized Labor and the Mexican Revolution under Lázaro Cárdenas*. Chapel Hill: University of North Carolina Press, 1963.

Báez, Eugenio A. "Visita del C. Presidente de la República Lázaro Cárdenas a la Colonia Agrícola Anáhuac." Unpublished, n.d.

Balderrama, Francisco E., and Raymond Rodríguez. *Decade of Betrayal: Mexican Repatriation in the 1930s*. Albuquerque: University of New Mexico Press, 1995.

Becker, Marjorie. *Setting the Virgin on Fire: Lázaro Cárdenas, Michoacán Peasants, and the Redemption of the Mexican Revolution*. Berkeley: University of California Press, 1995.

———. "Torching La Purísima, Dancing at the Altar: The Construction of Revolutionary Hegemony in Michoacán, 1934–1940." In *Every Form of State Formation: Revolution and Negotiation of Rule in Modern Mexico*, edited by Gilbert M. Joseph and Daniel Nugent. Durham, N.C.: Duke University Press, 1994.

———. "El cardenismo y la búsqueda de una ideología campesina." *Relaciones: Estudios de Historia y Sociedad*, no. 20 (Winter 1987).

Benítez, Fernando. *Lázaro Cárdenas y la Revolución Mexicana*. Vol. 3 of *El Cardenismo*. Mexico City: Fondo de Cultura Económica, 1978.

Betten, Neil, and Raymond A. Mohl. "From Discrimination to Repatriation: Mexican Life in Gary, Indiana, during the Great Depression." *Pacific Historical Review*, no. 42 (1973): 370–88.

Bogardus, Emory S. *The Mexican in the United States*. Los Angeles: University of Southern California Press, 1934.

Brinkley, Alan. *Historia de Estados Unidos*. Mexico City: McGraw Hill, 1996.

———. "El Nuevo Trato y la idea del Estado." In *Estados Unidos visto por sus historiadores*, compiled by Arriaga Weiss et al., vol. 2. Mexico City: Instituto Mora, 1991.

Buve, Raymond. "Los gobernadores de estado y las movilizaciones de los campesinos en Tlaxcala." In *Caudillos y campesinos en la Revolución Mexicana*, edited by D. A. Brading. Mexico City: Fondo de Cultura Económica, 1993.

——. "Ni Carranza ni Zapata: Acenso y caía de un movimiento campesino que intentó enfrentarse a ambos: Tlaxcala, 1910–1919." In *Revuelta, rebelión y revolución: La lucha rural en México del siglo XVI al siglo XX*, compiled by Friedrich Katz, vol. 1. Mexico City: Era, 1990.

Cabrera, Luis. *Veinte años después, el balance de la Revolución: La campaña presidencial de 1934. Las dos revoluciones*. Mexico City: Botas, 1938.

Campbell, Hugh G. *La derecha radical en México, 1919–1949*. Mexico City: Secretaría de Educación Pública, 1976.

Cárdenas, Lázaro. *Palabras y documentos públicos de Lázaro Cárdenas, 1928–1970*. 2 vols. Mexico City: Siglo Veintiuno, 1978a.

——. *Informes de gobierno y mensajes presidenciales de año nuevo, 1928–1940*. Mexico City: Siglo Veintiuno, 1978b.

——. *Apuntes*. Vols. 1–4. Mexico City: UNAM, 1972–74.

Cardoso, Lawrence A. *Mexican Emigration to the United States, 1897–1931*. Tucson: University of Arizona Press, 1980.

——. "La repatriación de braceros en la época de Obregón, 1920–1923." *Historia Mexicana* 26 (April–June 1977): 576–95.

Carr, Barry. "The Mexican Communist Party and Agrarian Mobilization in the Laguna, 1920–1940: A Worker-Peasant Alliance." *Hispanic American Historical Review* 67, no. 1 (February 1987).

Carreras de Velasco, Mercedes. *Los mexicanos que devolvió la crisis, 1929–1932*. Archivo Histórico Diplomático Mexicano. Mexico City: Secretaría de Relaciones Exteriores, 1974.

Castillo, G. Pedro, and Antonio Ríos Bustamante. *México en Los Ángeles: Una historia social y cultural, 1781–1985*. Mexico City: Alianza Editorial Mexicana, 1990.

Chávez Ramírez, Eduardo. *Ingeniería y humanismo*. Mexico City: Gobierno del Edo. de Tabasco/Instituto de Cultura de Tabasco, 1988.

Clark, Victor S. "Mexican Labor in the United States." *Bulletin*, no. 78 (1908). Washington, D.C.: Department of Commerce and Labor.

Coatsworth, John H. *El impacto económico en los ferrocarriles en el porfiriato: Crecimiento y desarrollo*. 2 vols. Mexico City: Secretaría de Educación Pública, 1976.

Comisión Nacional de Irrigación. *Comisión Nacional de Irrigación durante el régimen del general de división Lázaro Cárdenas, 1934–1940*. Mexico City: CNI, 1940a.

Consulado de México, Dallas. *Estadística de los mexicanos dispuesto a repatriarse con ayuda gubernmental: Condiciones económicas de los trabajadores de Port Arthur (agencia consular en Beaumont, Tex.) y Consulado de México en Dallas, Texas*. Mexico City, n.p.: 1939.

Contreras, Ariel José. *México, 1940: Industrialización y crisis política*. Mexico City: Siglo Veintiuno, 1977.

Córdova, Arnaldo. *La Revolución en crisis: La aventura del maximato*. Mexico City: Cal y Arena, 1996.

——. *La política de masas del cardenismo*. Mexico City: Era, 1974.

Correa, Eduardo J. *El balance del cardenismo*. Mexico City: Talleres Linotipográficos Acción, 1941.

Cosío Villegas, Daniel. *Historia moderna de México: El porfirato, vida económica.* Vol. 1. Mexico City: Hermes, 1989.

Cummings, Laura. *Don Zeferino: Villista, bracero y repatriado.* Mexico City: Centro de Investigaciones Históricas, UNAM-UABC, 1981.

de la Peña, T. Moisés. "Problemas demográficos y agrarios." *Problemas Agrícolas e Industriales de México* 2, nos. 3–4 (July–December 1950): 9–327.

Dirección de Agricultura y Ganadería. *Memoria de los trabajos ejecutados por las direcciones de Agricultura y Ganadería e Instituto Biotécnico, mayo 1934 a mayo 1940.* Mexico City: Dirección de Agricultura y Ganadería, 1940.

Divine, Robert. *American Immigration Policy, 1924–1952.* New Haven, Conn.: Yale University Press, 1957.

Dulles, John W. F. *Ayer en México.* Mexico City: Fondo de Cultura Económica, 1989.

Durón González, Gustavo. "Repatriación de mexicanos." In *Problemas migratorios de México: Apuntamientos para su solución,* 143–44. Mexico City: Talleres de la Cámara de Diputados, 1925.

Eckstein, Salomón. *El ejido colectivo en México.* Mexico City: Fondo de Cultura Económica, 1966.

*El exilio español en México, 1939–1982.* Mexico City: Fondo de Cultura Económica/ Salvat, 1984.

Fabila, Alfonso. *El problema de la emigración de obreros y campesinos mexicanos.* Mexico City: Talleres Gráficos de la Nación, 1929.

Fagen, Patricia Weiss. *Transterrados y ciudadanos: Los republicanos españoles en México.* Mexico City: Fondo de Cultura Económica, 1973.

Falcón, Romana. *Revolución y caciquismo: San Luis Potosí, 1910–1938.* Mexico City: Colegio de México/Centro de Estudios Históricos, 1984.

Freidel, Frank. *America in the Twentieth Century.* New York: Alfred A. Knopf, 1960.

———. *Franklin D. Roosevelt: The Apprenticeship.* Boston: Little, Brown, 1952.

Gamio, Manuel. *Hacia un México nuevo: Problemas sociales.* Mexico City: Instituto Nacional Indigenista, 1935.

———. *The Mexican Immigrant: His Life Story.* Chicago: University of Chicago Press, 1931.

———. *Mexican Immigration to the United States: A Study of Human Migration and Adjustment.* Chicago: University of Chicago Press, 1930a.

———. *Número, procedencia y distribución geográfica de los inmigrantes mexicanos en los Estados Unidos.* Mexico City: Talleres Gráficas Editoriales, Diario oficial, 1930b.

García, Mario T. *Desert Immigrants: The Mexicans of El Paso, 1880–1920.* New Haven, Conn: Yale University Press, 1981.

García, Richard A. "Class, Consciousness, and Ideology: The Mexican Community of San Antonio, Texas, 1930–1940." *Aztlán: International Journal of Chicano Studies Research* 9 (1979).

Garcíadiego Dantan, Javier, coord. *Evolución del Estado mexicano: Reestructuración, 1910–1940.* Vol. 2. Mexico City: Caballito, 1986.

García y Griego, Manuel. *The Importation of Mexican Contract Laborers to the United States, 1942–1964.* Working Papers in U.S.-Mexican Studies, 11. La Jolla: University of California, San Diego, 1981.

Gilbert, James A. "A Field Study in Mexico of Mexican Repatriation Movement." Thesis, University of Southern California, 1934.

Gilly, Adolfo. *El cardenismo, una utopía mexicana*. Mexico City: Cal y Arena, 1994.

Glantz, Susana. *El ejido colectivo de Nueva Italia*. Mexico City: Centro de Investigaciones Superiores, INAH, 1974.

Gobierno del Estado de Tamaulipas. *Informe de las labores realizadas por el Gobierno del Estado de Tamaulipas durante el ejercicio de 1940, que rinde ante el H. Congreso el ciudadano Ingeniero Marte R. Gómez, gobernador constitucional del estado*. Ciudad Victoria, Tamaulipas: Talleres Tipográficos del Gobierno, 1940.

Godínez, Víctor. "El impacto económico de la Segunda Guerra Mundial." In *EUA: Síntesis de su historia III*, vol. 10. Mexico City: Instituto Mora, 1991.

Gómez-Quiñones, Juan, and David Maciel. *Al norte del río Bravo (pasado lejano) (1600-1930)*. Mexico City: Siglo Veintiuno/Instituto de Investigaciones Sociales, UNAM, 1991.

González de la Vara, Martín. "El traslado de familias de Nuevo México al norte de Chihuahua y la formación de una región fronteriza, 1848-1854." *Frontera Norte* 6, no. 11 (January-June 1994).

González, Luis. *Historia de la Revolución Mexicana, 1934-1940: Los días del presidente Cárdenas*. Mexico City: Colmex, 1981.

———. "El *match* Cárdenas-Calles o la afirmación del presidencialismo mexicano." *Relaciones: Estudios de Historia y Sociedad* 1, no. 1 (Winter 1980).

———. *Historia de la Revolución Mexicana, período 1934-1940: Los artífices del Cardenismo*. Mexico City: Colegio de México, 1979.

González Félix, Maricela. *El proceso de aculturación de la población de origen chino en la ciudad de Mexicali*. Mexico City: UABC, Instituto de Investigaciones Sociales, 1989.

González Navarro, Moisés. *Los extranjeros en México y los mexicanos en el extranjero, 1821-1970*. Vols. 1-3. Mexico City: Colegio de México, 1994.

———. *La colonización en México*. Mexico City: Talleres de Impresión de Estampillas y Valores, 1960.

———. "Los braceros en el porfiriato." In *Estudios sociológicos: Sociología económica*, vol. 2. Mexico City: Instituto de Investigaciones Sociales, UNAM, 1954.

Guerín-Gonzáles, Camille. *Mexican Workers and American Dreams: Immigration, Repatriation, and California Farm Labor, 1900-1939*. New Brunswick, N.J.: Rutgers University Press, 1994.

———. "Repatriación de familias inmigrantes mexicanas durante la Gran Depresión." *Historia Mexicana* 35, no. 2 (1985).

Guerra, Françoise-Xavier. *México: Del antiguo régimen a la Revolución*. Vol. 1. Mexico City: Fondo de Cultura Económica, 1993.

Gullet, Gayle. "Women Progressives and the Politics of Americanization in California, 1915-1920." *Pacific Historical Review* 44, no. 1 (February 1995).

Haber, Stephen H. *Industria y subdesarrollo: La industrialización en México, 1890-1940*. Mexico City: Alianza, 1992.

Hall, Linda B. "El refugio: Migración mexicana a los Estados Unidos, 1910-1920." *Históricas* (January-April 1982).

Hamilton, Nora. *México: Los límites de la autonomía del Estado*. Mexico City: Era, 1983.

Harvey, Neil, ed. *Mexico: Dilemmas of Transition*. London: Institute of Latin American Studies, University of London/British Academic Press, 1993.

Hawley, Ellis. *The New Deal and the Problem of Monopoly*. Princeton, N.J.: Princeton University Press, 1966.

Hernández Acosta, Teodoro. *Nacimiento y fracaso del Algodón-Matamoros (1938–1965)*. Reynosa: Universidad Autónoma de Tamaulipas, Instituto de Investigaciones Históricas, 1980.

Hernández Chávez, Alicia. *Historia de la Revolución Mexicana, 1934–1940: La mecánica cardenista*. Mexico City: Colegio de México, 1979.

Hoffman, Abraham. *Unwanted Mexican Americans in the Great Depression: Repatriation Pressures, 1929–1939*. Tucson: University of Arizona Press, 1974.

Humphrey, Norman D. "Mexican Repatriation from Michigan: Public Assistance in Historical Perspective." *Social Service Review*, no. 15 (September 1941).

Instituto Mora. *Estados Unidos de América*. Vols. 1–10. Mexico City: Instituto Mora, 1988.

Instituto Nacional de Estadística, Geografía e Informática. *Estadísticas históricas de México*. 2 vols. Mexico City: INEGI, 1990.

Jackson, Gabriel. *La república española y la Guerra Civil, 1931–1939*. Barcelona: Orbis, 1985.

Joseph, Gilbert M. *Revolution from Without: Yucatan, Mexico, and the United States, 1880–1924*. Cambridge: Cambridge University Press, 1982.

Joseph, Gilbert M., and Daniel Nugent, eds. *Every Form of State Formation: Revolution and Negotiation of Rule in Modern Mexico*. Durham, N.C.: Duke University Press, 1994.

Katz, Friedrich. "Las rebeliones rurales a partir de 1810." In *Revuelta, rebelión y revolución: La lucha rural en México del siglo XVI al siglo XX*, compiled by Friedrich Katz, vol. 1. Mexico City: Era, 1990.

———, coord. *Porfirio Díaz frente al descontento popular regional, 1891–1893*. Mexico City: Universidad Iberoamericana, 1986.

———. *La servidumbre agraria en México en la época porfiriana*. Mexico City: Era, 1984.

Kenny, Michel, et al. *Inmigrantes y refugiados españoles en México (siglo XX)*. Mexico City: Casa Chata, 1979.

Kerin, Dorothy P. *El valle de Mexicali y la Colorado River Land Company, 1902–1946*. Mexicali: UABC, 2001.

Kiser, George, and Martha Woody, comps. *Mexican Workers in the United States: Historical and Political Perspectives*. Albuquerque: University of New Mexico Press, 1979.

Knight, Alan. *La Revolución Mexicana: Del porfiriato al nuevo régimen constitucional*. 2 vols. Mexico City: Grijalbo, 1996.

———. "Cardenismo: Juggernaut or Jalopy?" *Journal of Latin American Studies* 26, no. 1 (1994a).

———. "Popular Culture and the Revolutionary State in Mexico, 1910–1940." *Hispanic American Historical Review* 3, no. 74 (1994b).

———. State Power and Political Stability in Mexico." In *Mexico: Dilemmas of Transition*. London: Institute of Latin American Studies, University of London/British Academic Press, 1993.

———. "The Mexican Petroleum Nationalization, 1938–1988." Paper presented at a conference in Austin, Texas. Austin: Institute of Latin American Studies, University of Texas at Austin, 1988.

————. *U.S.-Mexican Relations 1910–1940: An Interpretation.* Monograph Series 28. San Diego: Center for U.S.-Mexican Studies, UCSD, 1987.

————. "La Revolución Mexicana: Burguesa, nacionalista o simplemente una gran rebelión?" *Cuadernos Políticos*, no. 48 (October–December 1986).

Landa y Piña, Andrés. *Política demográfica estatuida en el Plan sexenal.* Mexico City: Talleres Gráficos de la Nación, 1935.

————. *El servicio de migración en México.* Mexico City: Talleres Gráficos de la Nación, 1930.

Legislatura de la Cámara de Diputados (XLVI). *Los presidentes de México ante la nación. Informes, manifiestos y documentos. De 1821 a 1966.* Vols. 1–6. Mexico City: Imprenta de la Cámara de Diputados, 1966.

Lerner, Victoria. *Historia de la Revolución Mexicana: La educación socialista.* Mexico City: Colegio de México, 1979.

León, Samuel. "Cárdenas en el poder (1)." In *Evolución del Estado mexicano: Reestructuración, 1910–1940,* edited by Javier Garcíadiego Dantan, vol. 2. Mexico City: Caballito, 1986.

Leuchtenburg, William Edward. *Franklin D. Roosevelt and the New Deal, 1932–1940.* San Francisco: Harper and Row, 1963.

Levenstein, Harvey A. "The AFL and Mexican Immigration in the 1920s." *Hispanic American Historical Review*, May 1968.

Lida, Clara E. *Inmigración y exilio: Reflexiones sobre el caso español.* Mexico City: Siglo Veintiuno, 1997.

Lida, Clara E., comp. *Una inmigración privilegiada: Comerciantes, empresarios y profesionales españoles en México en los siglos XIX y XX.* Madrid: Alianza, 1994.

Lida, Clara E., and Pilar Pacheco Zamudio. "El perfil de una inmigración: 1821–1939." In *Una inmigración privilegiada: Comerciantes, empresarios y profesionales españoles en México en los siglos XIX y XX,* compiled by Clara E. Lida. Madrid: Alianza, 1994.

Llinás Álvarez, Edgar. *Vida y obra de Ramón Beteta.* Mexico City: Libros del Umbral, 1996.

Lombardo Toledano, Vicente. *El plan sexenal de gobierno del Partido Nacional Revolucionario.* Mexico City: n.p., 1934.

López, Ronald W. "The El Monte Berry Strike of 1933." *Aztlán: International Journal of Chicano Studies Research* 1, no. 1 (Spring 1970).

Lorey, David E., ed. *United States-Mexico Border Statistics. Since 1900.* Latin American Center Publications. Los Angeles: UCLA, 1993.

Loyo, Gilberto. *Gilberto Loyo: Obras.* Vols. 1–2. Mexico City: Libros de México, 1974.

————. *La política demográfica de México.* Mexico City: S. Turranzas del Valle, 1935.

————. *Emigración de mexicanos a los Estados Unidos.* Rome: Instituto Poligráfico dello Stato, 1931.

Márquez Morfí, Lourdes. "Los republicanos españoles en 1939: Política, inmigración y hostilidad." *Cuadernos Hispanoamericanos*, no. 458 (August 1988): 128–50.

Martínez, John. *Mexican Emigration to the U.S., 1910–1930.* Berkeley, Calif.: R. and E. Associates, 1950.

Martínez Assad, Carlos. *Los rebeldes vencidos: Cedillo contra el Estado cardenista.* Mexico City: UNAM, Instituto de Investigaciones Sociales/Fondo de Cultura Económica, 1990.

Matesanz, José Antonio. "México ante la Guerra Civil española, 1936-1939." PhD diss., Centro de Estudios Históricos, Colegio de México, 1995.

———. "La dinámica del exilio." In *El exilio español en México, 1939-1982*. Mexico City: Fondo de Cultura Económica/Salvat, 1982.

May, Dean L. *From New Deal to New Economics: The American Liberal Response to the Recession of 1937*. New York: Garland, 1981.

McKay, Reynolds. "Texas Mexican Repatriation during the Great Depression." PhD diss., University of Oklahoma, 1982.

McWilliams, Carey. *Al norte de México: El conflicto entre "anglos" e "hispanos."* Mexico City: Siglo Veintiuno, 1972.

Medina, Luis. *Historia de la Revolución Mexicana, 1940-1952: Del cardenismo al avilacamachismo*. Mexico City: Colegio de México, 1978.

Meneffe, Salden. "Los trabajadores migratorios mexicanos al sur de Texas." In *Problemas agrícolas e industriales de México*. Mexico City: n.p., 1958.

Mexico. *Seis años de gobierno, 1934-1940*. Mexico City: Talleres Tipográficos de la Nación, 1940.

———. *Informe presidencial a la XXXVII Legislatura*. Mexico City: Talleres Tipográficos de la Nación, 1939.

———. *Informe rendido el 1ro de septiembre de 1936 por el C. Presidente de la República General de División Lázaro Cárdenas*. Mexico City: Depto. Aut. de Publicidad y Propaganda, 1936.

———. *Ley de colonización*. Mexico City: n.p., 1883.

Meyer, Jean. *La Cristiada*. 3 vols. Mexico City: Siglo Veintiuno, 1994.

———. *El sinarquismo: Un fascismo mexicano? 1937-1947*. Mexico City: Cuadernos de Joaquín Mortiz, 1979.

Meyer, Lorenzo, et al. *Historia de la Revolución Mexicana,1928-1934: Los inicios de la institucionalización*. Mexico City: Colegio de México, 1995.

———. *México y los Estados Unidos en el conflicto petrolero (1917-1942)*. Mexico City: Colegio de México, 1981.

———. *Historia de la Revolución Mexicana, 1928-1934: El conflicto social y los gobiernos del maximato*. Mexico City: Colegio de México, 1978.

———. "La etapa formativa del Estado mexicano contemporáneo, 1928-1940." In *La crisis en el sistema político mexicano, 1928-1977*. Mexico City: Centro de Estudios Internacionales, Colegio de México, 1977.

Michels, Albert L. "Las elecciones de 1940." *Historia Mexicana* 21, no. 1 (1971).

———. "The Crisis of Cardenismo." *Journal of Latin American Studies* 2 (May 1970).

———. "Cárdenas y la lucha por la independencia económica de México." *Historia Mexicana* 18, no. 1 (July–September 1968).

Miller Puckett, Fidelia. "Ramón Ortiz: Priest and Patriot." *New Mexico Historical Review* 20, no. 4 (October 1950).

Milton, David. *The Politics of US Labor from the Great Depression to the New Deal*. New York: Monthly Review, 1982.

Mirón Lince, Rosa María. "Cárdenas en el poder (II)." In *Evolución del Estado mexicano. Reestructuración, 1910-1940*. Vol. 2, coordinated by Javier Garcíadiego Dantan. Mexico City: Caballito, 1986.

Monsely, Edward H., and Edward D. Terry. *Yucatán: A World Apart*. Tuscaloosa: University of Alabama Press, 1980.

Montejano, David. *Anglos y mexicanos en la formación de Texas, 1836-1986*. Mexico City: Consejo Nacional para la Cultura y las Artes/Alianza, 1987.

Morett S., Jesús. *Alternativas de modernización del ejido*. Mexico City: Diana, 1992.

Morison, Samuel Eliot, et al. *Breve historia de los Estados Unidos*. Mexico City: Fondo de Cultura Económica, 1993.

Nathan, Paul. *México en la época de Cárdenas*. Mexico City: Problemas Agrícolas e Industriales de México, 1955.

Nelson Cisneros, Víctor. "UCAPAWA and Chicanos in California: The Farm Worker Period, 1937-1940." *Aztlán: International Journal of Chicano Studies Research* 7, no. 3 (1978).

———. "La clase trabajadora en Texas, 1920-1940." *Aztlán: International Journal of Chicano Studies Research* 6, no. 2 (1975).

Nevins, Allan, and Henry Steele Commager. *Breve historia de los Estados Unidos*. Mexico City: Fondo de Cultura Económica, 1994.

Novo, Salvador. *La vida en México en el período presidencial de Lázaro Cárdenas*. Mexico City: Empresas Editoriales, 1964.

Parra, Ricardo, et al. "Chicano Organizations in the Midwest: Past, Present and Possibilities." *Aztlán: International Journal of Chicano Studies Research* 7, no. 2 (1976).

Partido Nacional Revolucionario (PNR). *Plan sexenal: Texto oficial*. Mexico City: S. Turranzas del Valle, 1934.

———. *Proyecto de Plan sexenal*. Mexico City: Talleres Gráficos de la Nación, 1933.

Pérez Montfort, Ricardo. *Estampas de nacionalismo popular mexicano: Ensayos sobre cultura popular y nacionalismo*. Mexico City: Centro de Investigaciones y Estudios Superiores en Antropología Social, Casa Chata, 1994.

———. *Hispanismo y falange: Los sueños imperiales de la derecha española y México*. Mexico City: Fondo de Cultura Económica, 1992.

Piñera Ramírez, David, coord. *Visión histórica de la frontera norte de México*. Vols. 1-3. Mexico City: Centro de Investigaciones Históricas UNAM-UABC, 1987.

———, coord. *Panorama histórico de Baja California*. Mexico City: Centro de Investigaciones Históricas UNAM-UABC, 1983.

Pla Brugat, Dolores. "Características del exilio en México en 1939." In *Una inmigración privilegiada: Comerciantes, empresarios y profesionales españoles en México en los siglos XIX y XX*, compiled by Clara E. Lida. Madrid: Alianza, 1994.

———. "Españoles en México (1895-1980): Un recuento." *Secuencia*, no. 24 (September-December 1992): 107-20.

Preston, Paul. *The Coming of the Spanish Civil War: Reform, Reaction and Revolution in the Second Republic*. London: Methuen, 1967.

Raby, David L. *Educación y revolución social en México*. Mexico City: Secretaría de Educación Pública, 1974.

Reisler, Mark. *By the Sweat of Their Brow: Mexican Immigrant Labor in the United States, 1900-1940*. Westport, Conn.: Greenwood, 1976.

Reyes Nevares, Salvador. "México en 1939." In *El exilio español en México, 1939-1982*. Mexico City: Salvat, 1982.

Reyes Osorio, Sergio, et al. *Estructura agraria y desarrollo agrícola de México*. Mexico City: Fondo de Cultura Económica, 1974.

Rincón Serrano, Romeo. *El ejido mexicano*. Mexico City: Centro Nacional de Investigaciones Agrarias, 1980.

Romo, Ricardo. *History of a Barrio. East of Los Angeles*. Austin: University of Texas Press, 1983.

Rouaix, Pastor. *Génesis de los artículos 27 y 123 de la Constitución política de 1917*. Mexico City: Instituto Nacional de Estudios Históricos de la Revolución Mexicana, 1992.

Sánchez, J. George. *Becoming Mexican American: Ethnicity, Culture, and Identity in Chicano Los Angeles, 1900–1945*. New York: Oxford University Press, 1993.

Santibáñez, Enrique. *Ensayo acerca de la inmigración mexicana en los Estados Unidos*. San Antonio: Clegg, 1930.

Secretaría de Agricultura y Fomento. *Memoria de los trabajos ejecutados por las Direcciones de Agricultura y Ganadería e Instituto Biotécnico de 1934 a 1949 del período presidencial del Gral. Lázaro Cárdenas*. Mexico City: Secretaría de Agricultura y Fomento, 1940.

———. *Memoria de la Secretaría de Agricultura y Fomento*. Mexico City: Secretaría de Agricultura y Fomento, 1928.

———. *Recopilación de las principales leyes*. Mexico City: Secretaría de Agricultura y Fomento, n.d.

Secretaría de Comunicaciones y Obras Públicas. *Memoria de la Secretaría de Comunicaciones y Obras Públicas presentada al Congreso de la Unión por el C. secretario del ramo Ing. Melquiades Angulo*. Mexico City: Secretaría de Comunicaciones y Obras Públicas, 1940.

Secretaría de Economía Nacional. *Compendio estadístico*. Mexico City: SEN, Dirección General de Estadística, 1941.

Secretaría de Gobernación (SEGOB). *Memoria de la Secretaría de Gobernación, 1939–1940*. Mexico City: Talleres Tipográficos de la Nación, 1940.

———. *Memoria de la Secretaría de Gobernación, 1938–1939*. Mexico City: DAPP, 1939.

———. *Memoria de la Secretaría de Gobernación, 1937–1938*. Mexico City: DAPP, 1938.

———. *Memoria de la Secretaría de Gobernación, 1936–1937*. Mexico City: DAPP, 1937.

———. *Informe del General Abelardo L. Rodríguez ante el Congreso General*. Mexico City: SEGOB, 1934.

Secretaría de Relaciones Exteriores (SRE). *Memoria de la Secretaría de Relaciones Exteriores, 1940–41*. Mexico City: Secretaría de Relaciones Exteriores, 1941.

———. *Memoria de la Secretaría de Relaciones Exteriores, 1934–1940*. Mexico City: Talleres Tipográficos de la Nación, 1940.

———. *Memoria de la Secretaría de Relaciones Exteriores, 1938–1939*. Mexico City: Secretaría de Relaciones Exteriores, 1939.

———. *Memoria de la Secretaría de Relaciones Exteriores, 1936–1937*. Mexico City: Secretaría de Relaciones Exteriores, 1937.

———. *La migración y protección*. Mexico City: Secretaría de Relaciones Exteriores, 1928a.

———. *Memoria, 1927–1928*. Mexico City: Secretaría de Relaciones Exteriores, 1928b.

———. *Memoria, 1926–1927*. Mexico City: Secretaría de Relaciones Exteriores, 1927.

———. *Memoria, 1925–1926*. Mexico City: Secretaría de Relaciones Exteriores, 1926.

Shulgovski, Anatol. *México en la encrucijada de su historia*. Mexico City: Fondo de Cultura Popular, 1968.

Silva Herzog, Jesús. *Lázaro Cárdenas: Su pensamiento económico, social y político*. Mexico City: Nuestro Tiempo, 1975.

Simon, Daniel. "Mexican Repatriation in East Chicago, Indiana." *Journal of Ethnic Studies*, no. 2 (1974): 11–23.

Smith, Lois Elwin. *Mexico and the Spanish Republicans*. Berkeley: University of California Press, 1955.

Smith, Robert Freeman. *The United States and Revolutionary Nationalism in Mexico, 1916–1932*. Chicago: University of Chicago Press, 1972.

Solís, Leopoldo. *Planes de desarrollo económico y social en México*. Mexico City: Secretaría de Educación Pública, 1975.

Soule, George. *Prosperity Decade: From War to Depression, 1917–1929*. 3 vols. New York: Rinehart, 1947.

Suárez, Ana Rosa, and Alma Parra. "El Estado y la economía." In *EUA 10: Síntesis de su historia III*. Mexico City: Instituto Mora, 1991.

Taft, Philip. *Organized Labor in American History*. New York: Harper and Row, 1964.

Taracena, Alfonso. *La Revolución desvirtuada*. Vols. 1–7. Mexico City: Costa Amic, 1936.

Terán Carbajal, Manuel. *Agua, tierra y hombre: Semblanza de Eduardo Chávez*. Mexico City: Desfiladero, 1985.

Thomas, Hugh. *La Guerra Civil española*. Paris: Ruedo Ibérico, 1967.

Tirado, Miguel David. "Mexican American Community Political Organization: The Key to Chicano Political Power." *Aztlán: International Journal of Chicano Studies Research* 1, no. 1 (1970).

Townsend, William. *Lázaro Cárdenas, demócrata mexicano*. Mexico City: Biografías Gandesa, 1959.

Tzvi, Medin. *Ideología y praxis política de Lázaro Cárdenas*. Mexico City: Siglo Veintiuno, 1972.

U.S. Bureau of the Census. "Region and Country or Area of Birth of the Foreign-Born Population," 1940. http://www.census.gov/population/www/documentation/twps0029/tab04.html.

Valdés, Dennis Nodín. *Al Norte: Agricultural Workers in the Great Lakes Region, 1917–1970*. Austin: University of Texas Press, 1991.

Vaughan, Mary Kay. "The Implementation of National Policy in the Countryside: Socialist Education in Puebla in [the] Cárdenas Period." In *La ciudad y el campo en la historia de México: Memoria de la VII Reunión de Historiadores Mexicanos y Norteamericanos*, 893–904. Mexico City: UNAM, 1992.

———. "Ideological Changes in Mexican Educational Policy, Programs, and Texts (1920–1940)." In *Los intelectuales y el poder en México: Memoria de la VI Reunión de Historiadores Mexicanos y Estadunidenses*, 507–26. Mexico City: Colegio de México; Los Angeles: UCLA Latin American Center, 1991.

Vera Estañol, Jorge. *La Revolución Mexicana: Orígenes y resultados*. Mexico City: Porrúa, 1957.

Weber, Devra Anne. "The Organizing of Mexicano Agricultural Workers: Imperial Valley and Los Angeles, 1928–34, an Oral History Approach." *Aztlán: International Journal of Chicano Studies Research* 3, no. 2 (Fall 1972).

Weyl, Nathaniel. *La reconquista de México: Los días de Lázaro Cárdenas*. Mexico City: Problemas Agrícolas e Industriales de México, 1955.

Wilkie, James W. *La Revolución Mexicana (1910–1976): Gasto federal y cambio social*. Mexico City: Fondo de Cultura Económica, 1978.

Zorrilla, Luis. *Historia de las relaciones entre México y Estados Unidos de América*. Mexico City: Porrúa, 1965.

# INDEX

188, 191; relationship with Cárdenas, 105–6, 114, 137, 153, 160, 166, 174, 175; implementation of repatriation plan of 1939, 105–14, 120–21, 122, 131, 137, 158; on La Esperanza, 141; and 18 March agricultural colony, 147, 148, 153–54, 155, 158, 159–60, 165–66, 174, 179; on suspension of repatriation project, 159–60, 165–66; and repatriation in California, 160–65, 188, 193

Biddle, Francis, 184

Big Spring, Calif., 41, 58

Blacks, xii

Bloque de Mineros Mexicanos (Mexican Mining Workers Syndicate), 175, 179

Bojórquez, Juan de Dios, 57

Border Patrol, xi, 14, 39

Box, John C., 14

Bracero program (1942–64), xiv, 183–85

Brady, Tex., 148

Brandford, Marvin T., 35, 37

Bravo, Alejandro M., 104

Bridgeport, Tex., 4

Brooks, Emma Tenayuca, 47

Brownsville, Tex.: deportation of Mexicans in, 39; employment of Mexicans born in United States, 41, 154; Mexican community in, 102–3; Beteta's implementation of repatriation project in, 109, 148, 174, 175

Buenaventura, Chihuahua, 125–26

Buenrostro, Efraín, 176–77

Bustamante, Jorge, xv–xvi

Cabrera, Napoleón, 170

Calderón, A., 174

Calderón, Carlos A., 166

Calexico, Calif., 102

California: subnational engagement with Mexico, xv; Mexican American communities in, xvii, 102, 107; repatriation of Mexicans in, 4, 19, 25, 48, 90, 105; Mexican labor in, 11, 12, 13, 34, 184; and U.S. labor policy,

33, 34; and U.S. welfare policy, 35, 78, 163; deportation of Mexicans in, 36, 37, 38, 55, 97–98, 106, 107, 162, 163, 164; and U.S. immigration policy, 39; employment of Mexicans born in United States, 41; Mexican population of, 57; Beteta's nonimplementation of repatriation project in, 160–65, 188, 193

California Federation of Mexican Laborers and Farmworkers Unions, 46

California Relief Administration, 34

Calles, Plutarco Elías, xiii, 27, 51, 57, 74, 100

Caminaguato, Sinaloa, 81

Cannery and Agricultural Workers Industrial Union, 45

Cárdenas del Río, Lázaro: assistance for Spanish Civil War refugees, xii, xiii, xxi, 3, 4, 5, 9, 79, 86, 125, 126, 127–36, 191, 210n15; agrarian reform of, xiii, 5, 6, 7, 75, 86, 100, 107, 123, 137, 139, 182, 185–86, 189, 190, 192; and nationalization of oil industry, xiii, 92, 98, 100, 108, 121, 123, 144, 165, 189, 190, 192; nationalist discourse of, xix, xx, xxi, 75, 82, 93, 99, 100, 123, 165, 173, 190, 192; repatriation policy of, xix–xxi, 2, 3, 5–8, 26, 27–28, 53, 55–56, 57, 58, 60, 63, 64, 65, 67, 68–71, 73, 75, 76–77, 86–89, 92–99, 173–75, 185–86, 188–90, 193–94; presidential term of (sexenio), xxi, 63, 73, 82, 92, 99–100, 105, 139, 168, 185, 188, 189, 203n22; historiography of government, 2–6; repatriation project, 1939, 3, 5–6, 8, 9, 101–2, 105–14, 120–26, 130–43, 151–52, 159, 173–75, 192; settlement initiatives of, 5, 6, 7, 123–26; demographic policies of, 7; Mexican opposition to, 8; assumption of presidency, 51, 52; consolidation of power base, 74–75; labor policy of, 75, 80, 202n1; repatriation project ending, 159–60, 164–66, 168; position on 18 March agricultural colony, 178–79, 192–93

Carranza, Venustiano, xiv, 17, 20

Flores Villar, Miguel, 154–55
France, 128
Franco, Francisco, xii, 127
Fregoso, Pedro, 175
Frente Constitucional Democrático
    (Constitutional Democratic Front), 129
Frente Socialista de Abogados, 129
Furniture Workers Union, 45

*Gachupines*, 129
Galeana, Chihuahua, 126
Galindo, Juan, 153
Galván, Telésforo, 149
Galveston, Tex., 102
Gamio, Manuel: on repatriation policy,
    xiv, 23–24, 83–84, 89–93, 106, 109, 123,
    136, 138, 139, 142–43, 191; survey of
    Mexican community in United States,
    57, 89, 214n21; and Demographics
    Department, 89, 123, 136
García Téllez, Ignacio, 88–89, 92, 97, 106,
    112, 134, 139, 142
Gardena, Calif., 172
Garrido Canabal, Tomás, 68
Gary, Ind., 46, 106
Garza, Ambrosio, 94
General Confederation of Workers, 96
General Population Records, 75
Gigliotti, Frank, 163–64
Golash-Boza, Tanya, xvi
Gómez, Adolfo, 134
Gómez, Marte R., 126, 136–37, 147, 157
Gonzales, Tex., 4, 174
González, Jesús M., 34–35, 57, 59–60, 65,
    203n22
González, Manuel C., 109
González Navarro, Moisés, 4–5, 215n34
Good Neighbor policy, 165
Grajales, Mario A., 124, 140
Great Depression: and subordination of
    Afro-Mexican population, xii; U.S.
    deportation of Mexicans during,
    xiii, 1, 2, 3–5, 15, 24–29, 188; Mexican
    repatriation during, xiii, 15, 16, 24–29,
    36, 51, 53, 107, 188, 200n3; and Mexican

migration to United States, xiii, 15,
    24–29, 36, 200n3; Mexican repatriation
    policy during, 3–4, 5, 6, 15, 24–29; and
    New Deal, 30–33
Gregory, Tex., 157
Guadalajara, Jalisco, 13, 148
Guajardo, Jerónimo, 177
Guanajuato, 51, 126, 167
Guerin-Gonzales, Camille, 4
Guerra Aceves, Salvador, 68
Guerrero, 25, 169, 170

Harlingen, Tex., 41, 44, 104, 151, 166
Hay, Eduardo, 79, 106, 112
Hearst, William Randolph, 125
Hebbronville, Tex., 113
Hernández Cházaro, Eduardo, 104–5
Hidalgo, E., 184
Hidalgo Mutual Aid Society, 44
Hispanophilia, 130
Hitler, Adolph, 149
Hoffman, Abraham, 2–3, 5
Hondagneu-Sotelo, Pierrette, xvi
Hop, Tex., 149
Houston, Tex.: Mexican community in,
    42–43, 103; repatriation of Mexicans in,
    48, 168, 174; Beteta's implementation of
    repatriation project in, 110–11, 112–13,
    148, 150, 175

Illegal Immigration Reform and
    Responsibility Act (IIRIRA), xi, xii
Illinois, 15, 25, 35, 48, 106, 141–42
Immigration Act (1924), 14
Immigration and Customs Enforcement
    (ICE), xi, xii
Immigration Reform and Control Act
    (1986), 9, 195
Immigration Tolerance Table for 1937, 75
Imperial Valley Workers Union (Unión de
    Trabajadores del Valle Imperial), 44
Indiana, 41, 96
Industrial Union of Mining, Metallurgical,
    and Associated Workers of the Republic
    of Mexico, 207n49

Los Fresnos, Tex., 104, 166
Louisiana, 33, 41
Lower Rio Grande Commission, 139, 144
Lower Rio Grande Valley: employment
of Mexicans born in United States,
41; Cárdenas's tour of, 65–66; Beteta's
implementation of repatriation project
in, 109–10; and colonization projects,
123, 134, 136–40, 144–45, 179; population
of, 151, 192. *See also* 18 March
agricultural colony, Tamaulipas
Loyo, Gilberto, 27, 92, 212n3
Lozano, Ignacio, 87, 133
Lugo, José Inocente, 20

Madero, Francisco I., 17, 19, 23
Magaña, Gildardo, 87–88
Magueyes colony, Nuevo León, 151–52
Malakoff, Tex., 151
Martino, César, 179
Matamoros, Tamaulipas: and colonization
projects, 26, 80–81, 132, 136–43, 144, 149,
161; and U.S. immigration policy, 40;
and repatriation of Mexicans, 62, 65–66,
80–81, 95; and Mexican migration to
United States, 80; population of, 138
Maximato (1928–34), 74
Mazapil, Zacatecas, 173
McAllen, Tex., 102, 113, 148
McDonough, Gordon L., 35, 38, 97
McKay, Reynolds, 3–4, 5
Mesa, Manuel, 136
*Mestizaje*, xii
Mexicali, Baja California, 67–68, 69,
71, 72, 81
Mexican American Movement, 43
Mexican Americans, 4, 34, 43, 44–48
Mexican Chamber of Deputies, 60
Mexican Community Association, 46
Mexican community in United States:
remittances of, xiv, xix, 107; living
conditions of, 1, 9, 16, 17, 18, 21, 29,
41, 42–44, 58–59, 60, 61, 63, 103, 121,
133, 162, 181, 189; organizing activities
of, 1, 44–46; treatment by U.S. and

Mexican authorities, 4; skepticism
and opposition to leaving United
States, 4, 9, 48, 50, 61, 102–5, 113–14,
162, 166, 189, 191; repatriation's impact
on, 4, 42; and U.S. welfare groups
and organizations, 22, 30, 35, 36, 78;
and U.S. economy, 33; as naturalized
citizens, 33, 34, 114; citizenship of,
33, 34, 114, 120; U.S. welfare policy
toward, 33, 34–36, 50, 102; U.S. labor
policy towards, 33–34, 50; decline in
population of, 36, 37; population of, 36,
37, 57–58, 60, 86, 88, 166, 214n21; and
threats of deportations, 36–38; labor
and employment situation of, 40–42,
57, 103, 181; social situation of, 42–44,
189; strike participation of, 46–48;
Mexican government's relationship
to, 51; interest in repatriation, 57; and
illegal status, 58; Mexican consuls'
census of, 58, 88, 102; proposals for
repatriation of, 58–62; studies on,
58–62, 64, 65; xenophobic reception of,
64; data on those seeking repatriation,
114, 115–19; on Mexican repatriation
project, 132–36; on Spanish Civil War
refugees, 132–36, 181. *See also* Mexican
migrant workers; Mexicans born in
United States
Mexican Confederation of Workers
(Confederación de Trabajadores de
México, CTM), 61, 83, 134
Mexican consuls in United States: and
repatriation policy, 19, 20–21, 22, 24,
25, 59, 62, 77, 102, 109, 112, 113, 120, 137,
161, 188; census of Mexican returnees,
53–55; census of Mexican community in
United States, 58, 88, 102; repatriations
requested, 102, 103, 104, 159–60, 173,
174, 181; and 18 March agricultural
colony, 154, 166
Mexican economy: and Mexican returnees,
xiv, 2, 7, 18, 19, 23, 27, 28, 29, 72, 101–2,
120, 186; and social problems, 11, 12–13;
and Mexican Revolution, 13

Mexican Federation of Laborers and Farmworkers, 46

Mexican government: and anti-immigrant political discourse, xii; and Chinese exclusion, xii, xiii, 198n7; deportation of Central American migrants, xvi; migration policy of, xxi, 15–17, 18, 21, 27, 63, 75, 76–80, 82, 97, 181; labor policy of, 1, 2, 75, 202n1; agrarian policy of, 2, 107, 182, 189. *See also* Cárdenas del Río, Lázaro; Mexican repatriation policy

Mexican Honorary Commission, 82, 149–50, 175

Mexican labor: interrelationship with U.S. capital, xv–xvi, 11–12; and repatriation policy, 8, 52, 96, 97, 190, 207n49; and railroad construction, 11, 13; internal migration of, 12; effect of Mexican returnees on, 53, 83; Cárdenas's policies on, 75, 80, 202n1; and World War II, 181, 183–84; and Bracero Program, 183–85. *See also specific unions*

Mexican migrant workers: racial profiling of, xv; undocumented migrants, xvi, 9; repatriation requests of, 48–49; Mexican government's policies on, 59, 61, 62, 63–64, 66–73

Mexican Migration Service, 49

Mexican migration to United States: and development of migratory trends, xiii, xvii, 6, 9–10; during Great Depression, xiii, 15, 24–29, 36, 200n3; and allegiance to Mexico, xiv; human rights of, xv–xvi; perceptions of, xix, 6; first stage, 1880–1917, 11–13, 18–20; second stage, 1917–1928, 13–14, 20–24; and political and religious violence, 14, 51; Mexican press on, 16, 17; Mexican government's prevention of, 63, 75, 76–80, 82, 97, 181; and labor contracts, 79–80, 184; and promotion of illegal migration, 80; and World War II, 185

Mexican National Railways, 95–96

Mexican political class: attitudes toward Mexican returnees, xx, xxi, 9, 53, 187, 194–95; Calles as leader of, 51, 57, 74

Mexican press: on Mexican migration to United States, 16, 17; on repatriation policy, 64, 69, 84–85, 87, 88, 93–94, 98–99, 113, 121–23, 130–31, 182–83, 187; on Spanish Civil War refugees, 129

Mexican repatriation policy: continuity of, xiii–xiv, xx, 8, 63, 185–86; and disposition for preference of migrants remaining in United States, xiv, xx, xxi, 9, 107, 188, 193–94, 195; and nationalism, xix, xx, xxi, 62, 66, 82, 83–85, 99, 100, 173, 190, 192; and rail passage back to Mexico, 2, 7, 25, 29, 49, 62, 63, 95–96, 100; repatriation project, 1939, 3, 5–6, 8, 9, 101–2, 105–14, 120–26, 130–43; during Great Depression, 3–4, 5, 6, 15, 24–29; proposals versus actions taken, 7, 21, 23, 29, 56, 66, 67, 69, 73, 89, 126, 186; and effect of mass repatriation, 9, 52–55, 64–65, 89, 187–88, 190, 194–95; and U.S. deportation policy, 18, 20–21, 182; and designation of repatriated persons, 18, 200n4; and nineteenth-century territorial losses, 18, 217n79; and land grants, 18–20, 28, 48, 61, 65–68, 71–73, 81, 93–94, 97, 109–10, 186; and Mexican consuls in United States, 19, 20–21, 22, 24, 25, 59, 62, 77, 102, 109, 112, 113, 120, 137, 161, 188; and U.S. welfare groups and organizations, 22; and colonization projects, 22, 24, 25–27, 28, 29, 48, 53–54, 61, 62, 68, 69–73, 78, 80–81, 89–94, 109–10, 123–26, 136–43, 144, 145–58, 162, 167–75, 182, 189, 191–92, 193; and food relief, 25; and U.S./Mexican border, 29, 53, 54, 56, 59, 62–64, 71, 95–96, 107; budget for, 52, 53, 54–55, 58, 59, 60, 64–65, 73, 77, 94–95, 112, 124, 137, 142, 178, 208n25; proposals for repatriation, 58–62, 65–66, 86–89; Mexican press on, 64, 69, 84–85, 87, 88, 93–94, 98–99, 113, 121–23, 130–31,

182–83, 187; and Demographic Studies and Repatriation section, 75–76, 78, 95; and general population law of 1936, 76–77; and limits of official assistance, 82–85, 140, 173–75, 176; commission on, 90–91, 93; bilateral negotiations for repatriation, 97–100, 127, 190; repatriation project ending, 159–60, 164–66; historiography of, 185–86

Mexican returnees: during Great Depression, xiii, 1, 2, 3–5, 24–29, 58; reduction following Great Depression, xiii, 1, 6, 7, 57; Mexican government's policies toward, xiii–xiv, xix–xxi, 6–9, 53–54, 56, 99–100; ties to Mexico questioned, xiv, xx, 1, 24, 83–85, 122; and economic growth, xiv, 2, 7, 18, 19, 23, 27, 28, 29, 72, 101–2, 120, 186; social and economic reintegration of, xx, 1, 2, 7, 23–24; resettlement of, 1, 2, 3, 4–5, 7–8, 21, 25, 26, 53–54, 56, 84, 123–26, 140–43, 179–80, 188; reassimilation of, 5, 25, 26–27, 83–84; land grants for, 18–19, 28, 61, 65–68, 71–73, 81, 93–94, 97, 109–10, 181; and social class, 23–24, 28; figures for flow of (1933–49), 49–50; reasons for returning, 49–50, 147, 181; effect on Mexican demographics, 52, 53, 188, 193, 194; effect on Mexican labor, 53, 83; and U.S./Mexican border, 63; and limits of official assistance, 82–85, 140, 173–75, 176, 181; and nationalism, 83–84; population of, 84, 180, 194, 206n25; prison records of, 84–85; health of, 85, 97, 122, 147, 155, 182; and tradition-bound way of life, 91, 188; and repatriation project ending, 161

Mexican Revolution (1910–20): anti-immigrant political discourse following, xii; and Mexican migration to United States, 13, 16–17; and Mexican repatriation policy, 19, 29, 194; anniversary commemoration of, 101; indigenist principles of, 130

Mexican Revolutionary Party, 87

Mexicans born in United States: citizenship of, 9, 15, 43, 114, 120; living conditions of, 27, 30, 40, 41, 43–44, 103, 122, 189; and U.S. welfare policies, 33, 35–36; and U.S. labor policies, 34; as second-generation, 36, 42, 43, 44; deportation of, 38, 43; organizing activities of, 44–46; strike participation of, 46–48; repatriation requests of, 48–49, 102, 103, 104, 159–60, 173, 174, 181; as Mexican returnees, 81, 83, 156. *See also* Mexican Americans

Mexican states: prohibition of *enganchadores*, xv, 16, 17; and resettlement locations, 8, 54–55; and Mexican migration to United States, 15–16; and repatriation policy, 70–71, 87, 97, 125, 126, 187–88. *See also specific states*

Mexican Sugarbeet Workers Union, 46

Michigan: Mexican American communities in, xvii; Mexican labor in, 11; deportation of Mexicans in, 15; repatriation of Mexicans in, 25, 26, 141–42; and U.S. welfare policy, 35; employment of Mexicans born in United States, 41; organizing activities of Mexican Americans in, 46

Michoacán, 19, 51, 169, 170

Migration Advisory Board, 21

Ministry of Agriculture and Development (Secretaría de Agricultura y Fomento): and repatriation policy, 20, 21, 24, 26, 52, 66, 67, 76, 77, 93, 123, 124–25, 137, 140, 141–42; Agrarian Department, 124; and colonization projects, 167, 168–69, 172–73, 178

Ministry of Development, 19–20

Ministry of Finance and Public Credit (Secretaría de Hacienda y Crédito Público, SHCP), 25, 53, 60, 77, 94, 171

Ministry of Foreign Relations (Secretaría de Relaciones Exteriores, SRE): subnational engagement of, xv; on Mexican migration to United States,

Obregón, Álvaro, 20–21, 139
O'Daniel, W. Lee, 113
Oilton, Tex., 113
Ojo de Federico, 125
Oklahoma, 12
Oklahoma City, Okla., 102, 148
Olachea, Agustín, 67
Oliver, Howard T., 164–65
Olson, Culbert L., 161–62, 163
Operation Wetback, 194
Orange County, Calif., 47
Order of Sons of America (La Orden de Hijos de América), 44, 45
Oregon, 37
Ortiz, Estanislao, 48

Pabellón, Aguascalientes, 124–25
Palavicini, Félix F., 64, 131
Pallares, Jesús, 47
Palomas Land & Cattle Company, 125
Parres, José G., 178
Partido de Acción Nacional (National Action Party), 129
Patterson, Ellis, 162
Pecan Shellers Union (Trabajadores de la Nuez), 45
Peralta, Óscar, 63, 80
Perdomo, Elpidio, 126
Perkins, Frances, 40
Peyton, Robert K., 134
Phoenix, Ariz., 102
Piedras Negras, Coahuila, 134
Pinotepa, Oaxaca, 26, 51, 54, 59, 99, 104–5, 113, 158, 166, 170
Pittsburgh, Pa., 120–21
Port Arthur, Tex., 148
Portes Gil, Emilio, 63, 89, 139
Pro-Magaña Committee, 172
Protestant ethic, xx
Public Works Administration (PWA), 31, 33
Puebla, 169

Racism, xii–xiii, 18, 198n7
Railroads: and Mexican repatriation policy, 2, 7, 25, 29, 49, 62, 63, 95–96, 100; and

Mexican labor, 11, 13; and expansion of U.S. economy, 11–12; and land prices, 12; employment of Mexicans born in United States, 41
Railway Workers Administration, 95–96
"Ralph Swing Law," 163
Ramírez, Zeferino, 43
Ramírez Paulin (Mexican Chamber of Deputies), 60–61
Raymondville, Tex., 110, 148, 150, 166
Relief and Rehabilitation Committee of Bexar County, Tex., 35, 37
Remittances, xiv, xix, 107
Repatriated persons (repatriados): resettlement of, xiii, 3, 21, 25; designation of term, 18, 200n4; Mexican reaction to, 130–32; Spanish Civil War refugees compared to, 135–36. See also Mexican returnees
Repatriation: during Great Depression, xiii, 15, 16, 24–29, 36, 51, 53, 188, 200n3; repercussions of, 1; costs of, 17; effect of U.S. deportations on, 18, 19, 20–21, 24–29, 37, 49, 50, 75, 86, 107, 139–40, 194; Mexicans born in United States requesting, 48–49, 102, 103, 104, 159–60, 173, 174, 181; declines in, 49; definition of, 200n1. See also Mexican repatriation policy; Mexican returnees
Reséndez, Moisés, 148
Reynosa, Tamaulipas, 63–64
Richberg, Donald, 108
Richmondville, Tex., 148
Río Bravo, Tamaulipas, 94, 124, 169
Rio Grande, 65
Rio Grande Commission, 136
Río Grande settlement, Oaxaca, 142
Robstown, Tex., 94, 148, 150, 174
Rodríguez, Abelardo, 27, 67, 139
Rodríguez, Luis I., 64–65, 70
Rodriguez, Raymond, 4–5
Rodríguez, Tomasa, 150
Rodríguez Dam, Baja California, 68–69
Rojas, Salvador, 39–40
Romero, Alfonso, 121

Roosevelt, Franklin D., 30–33, 38, 108, 149, 164, 183, 205n9
Rosarito, Baja California, 71
Rouaix, Pastor, 20
Rubio, Pascual Ortiz, 27
Ruiz, Eduardo, 20–21
Rural Population, National Lands, and Colonization Administration, 66, 68

St. Louis, Mo., 102, 120–21
St. Paul, Tex., 80
Saldívar Gallegos, Manuel, 176, 177, 179
Salt Lake City, Utah, 41, 102
San Antonio, Tex.: and U.S. welfare policy, 35; organizing activities of Mexican Americans in, 44, 45; strikes of Mexican Americans in, 47, 202n29; living conditions of Mexicans in, 60; Magaña's speech on repatriation in, 87–88; Mexican community in, 102, 103; Beteta's implementation of repatriation project in, 109, 110, 113, 148, 174, 175; and 18 March agricultural colony, 150–51, 212n17; Beteta's announcement of repatriation project ending in, 159–60
San Benito, Tex., 104, 166, 175
San Bernardino, Calif., 102
Sánchez, George, 4
Sánchez Taboada, Rodolfo, 94, 172
San Cristóbal, Veracruz, 96
San Diego, Calif., 47, 67, 102, 160
San Diego, Tex., 113
San Fernando River area, 123
San Francisco, Calif., 67, 102, 160
San Isidro Ajolojol, Tijuana, 71
San Jose, Calif., 160
San Juan River Valley, 66
San Luis Potosí, 167–68, 169, 170–71, 215n34
San Marcos, Tex., 150, 151
San Sebastian, Tex., 148
Santa Ana, Calif., 172
Santa Barbara, Calif., 160
Santa Clara hacienda, Chihuahua, 125, 169

Santana, Ignacio H., 95
Santa Teresa, Tamaulipas, 140
Santibáñez, Enrique, 24
Santibáñez, Vicente, 178–79
Sarabia, Pedro, 80–81
Sebastian, Tex., 150, 166
Second New Deal, 31–32
Segregation, 18
September 11, 2001, terrorist attacks, xii, xiv, 9, 195
Sepúlveda, Marcelino, 157
Sinaloa: and Mexican migration to United States, 13; and colonization projects, 25, 124, 168; and Mexican returnees, 81
Social Science Research Council, 89
Sociedades Mutalistas Mexicanas (Mexican Mutual Aid Societies), 46
Society of Socialist Agricultural Workers, 179
Sonora: and Mexican migration to United States, xv, 13, 79; and Mexican returnees, 24; and colonization projects, 25, 167, 168; repatriation of Mexicans to, 59
Sóstenez, Feliciano, 176
Southern Pecan Shelling Company, 47
Spanish Civil War refugees: Cárdenas's assistance of, xii, xiii, xxi, 3, 4, 5, 9, 79, 86, 125, 126, 127–36, 191, 210n15; Mexican reaction to, 129–32; reaction of Mexican community in United States to, 132–36, 181
Spindola, Raúl S., 109
Standard Oil, 164
Stockton, Calif., 34
Strikes, 34, 46–48, 202n1
Superba Hosiery and Socks Manufacturing Union, 96
Swing, Ralph, 163

Tabasco, 169–70
Talamantes, Gustavo L., 57, 125–26
Tamaulipas: and Mexican migration to United States, xv, 79; La Sauteña settlement in, 19; repatriation of

CPSIA information can be obtained
at www.ICGtesting.com
Printed in the USA
LVOW11s0428020817
543429LV00008B/436/P